www.wadsworth.com

wadsworth.com is the World Wide Web site for Wadsworth Publishing Company and is your direct source to dozens of online resources.

At *wadsworth.com* you can find out about supplements, demonstration software, and student resources. You can also send e-mail to many of our authors and preview new publications and exciting new technologies.

wadsworth.com
Changing the way the world learns®

The Clubhouse Model

Empowering Applications of Theory to Generalist Practice

ROBERT L. JACKSON, PH.D.
Colorado State University

BROOKS/COLE
™
THOMSON LEARNING

Australia • Canada • Mexico • Singapore • Spain • United Kingdom • United States

BROOKS/COLE

THOMSON LEARNING

Social Work Editor: *Lisa Gebo*
Assistant Editor: *Susan Wilson*
Editorial Assistant: *Sheila Walsh*
Marketing Manager: *Caroline Concilla*
Marketing Assistant: *Jessica McFadden*
Project Editor: *Trudy Brown*
Print Buyer: *Tandra Jorgensen*
Permissions Editor: *Bob Kauser*

Production Service: *Gustafson Graphics*
Copy Editor: *Linda Ireland*
Illustrator: *Amanda Cavalier*
Cover Designer: *Annabelle Ison*
Cover Printer: *Webcom, Ltd.*
Compositor: *Gustafson Graphics*
Printer: *Webcom, Ltd.*

For permission to use material from this text, contact
us by Web: http://www.thomsonrights.com
Fax: 1-800-730-2215 Phone: 1-800-730-2214

International Headquarters
Thomson Learning
International Division
290 Harbor Drive, 2nd Floor
Stamford, CT 06902-7477
USA

UK/Europe/Middle East/South Africa
Thomson Learning
Berkshire House
168-173 High Holborn
London WC1V 7AA
United Kingdom

Asia
Thomson Learning
60 Albert Street #15-01
Albert Complex
Singapore 189969

Canada
Nelson Thomson Learning
1120 Birchmount Road
Toronto, Ontario M1K 5G4
Canada

For more information, contact
Wadsworth/Thomson Learning
10 Davis Drive
Belmont, CA 94002-3098
USA
http://www.wadsworth.com

Library of Congress Cataloging-in-Publication Data

Jackson, Robert L.
    The clubhouse model: empowering applications of theory to generalist practice /
Robert L. Jackson.
        p. cm.
Includes bibliographical references and index.
ISBN 0-534-34940-4
    1. Psychiatric social work.   2. Mentally ill—Services for.   3. Mentally ill—Rehabilitation.
4. Mental illness—Treatment.   5. Fountain House (New York, N.Y.)—History.   I. Title.

HV689 .J3 2000
362.2'0425—dc21

                                                00-031156

Contents

Chapter 4

Roles, Self-Efficacy, and the Work-Ordered Day   56

Chapter 5

Employment and Education   73

Chapter 6

Identity Development through Clubhouse Membership   90

Chapter 7

Socialization into Communities   105

Chapter 8

The Case for Case Management: Food, Housing, and Income Support   121

Chapter 9

Concepts of Culture and the Clubhouse Community   138

Chapter 10

Clubhouse Management and Leadership   151

Chapter 11

Joining Theory and Community-Building Practice   166

Appendices

Foreword

The clubhouse model of psychiatric rehabilitation has proven to be one of the most effective services assisting people with serious mental illness in their recovery and reintegration into the general community. Its success is represented dramatically in its growth from a single organization, Fountain House in New York City, to more than 350 clubhouses worldwide. Today, there are clubhouses in 44 states in the United States and in Albania, Australia, Canada, China, Denmark, Egypt, England, Estonia, Finland, Holland, Iceland, Ireland, Japan, New Zealand, Norway, Pakistan, Poland, Portugal, Russia, Scotland, South Africa, South Korea, Sweden, and Switzerland. Because it is organized around the needs, concerns, strengths, and talents of its participating members, it is adaptable to any community, culture, city, or town.

It is important to know that the first clubhouse formed not as a product of formal theory or an established treatment program, but rather out of the commitment of a few individuals to each other and the belief in the potential for recovery of even the most seriously disabled psychiatric patient. The clubhouse model has developed over time into a complex set of social structures and beliefs that include voluntary membership and participation, a work-ordered day, an evening and weekend social program, a transitional employment program, and a case management and community support function. These components have been based on good sense and developed out of necessity. They address the interrelated, tangible needs and concerns of people with mental illness. They provide the vehicle for recovery and reintegration.

This work offers a new way of looking at the model and the possibilities of community-building. Adding to the primarily intuitive and commonsense views of clubhouse community-builders, Dr. Jackson applies a number of theories and components of theory to give depth and breadth to our understanding of the nature and possibilities of the clubhouse model. Such an understanding of the model will be helpful to academicians as well as those in the larger world of human services. His theoretical exploration underlines the universality of the model and its basis in the human condition.

In the international community of clubhouses we need more trained and committed individuals who have connected their desire to serve others with a clear understanding of what is helpful and not helpful. This book, applying theory to practice, admirably begins to address this issue. Hopefully, Dr. Jackson's work will also inspire others to further develop the theoretical foundations of the clubhouse model.

Joel Corcoran, Executive Director
International Center for Clubhouse Development
Fountain House
New York, NY

Preface

My teaching experience has taught me that students need a variety of ways to understand and transpose abstract theory from text and classroom into the world of practice. If social and psychological theories are to have relevance, then theoretical applications must be brought to life.

The clubhouse model described in this text provides a complex practice approach for bringing theory to life. Replications of this model can be found throughout the world in real clubhouses accessible to students, instructors and other visitors. These clubhouses offer real places for study and understanding. Visitors are welcome to ask questions of staff and members and evaluate what they see and experience. Clubhouses provide learning laboratories, places where theory and multi-level generalist practice can be understood in combination.

Using the clubhouse model and real clubhouses students can explore key questions concerning professional practice. How does one think and plan systematically for generalist practice? How can disciplined, yet flexible approaches be implemented? How can the generalist practitioner's thinking and planning focus on a range of relevant factors, yet exclude extraneous or irrelevant factors? How one develops a personal practice theory, a theoretical toolkit for practice? These and other important questions can be examined both theoretically and practically through the clubhouse model and clubhouse replications.

I hope this book will help students and generalist practitioners understand a variety of useful and creative ways to apply theory—for the most part theory to which they have already been exposed—and to develop their own practice theory. In this enterprise Iíve attempted to bring together major aspects of my earlier world of practice and my more recently entered world of teaching and scholarship. The daily life of the campus is so different from community practice settings, that I find myself needing consistently to relate one to the other in multiple ways to integrate, understand, and explain professional helping. In this endeavor the clubhouse model has provided a unique metaphor and set of approaches for teaching theory and generalist practice.

Although this text describes "community building" practice activities it should not be viewed as primarily macro or community practice oriented. The clubhouse model shows that professional change at all levels is part of the same fabric of generalist practice to enhance adaptiveness, enable and empower clients.

The text assumes that good generalist practice works to create and maintain a variety of supportive social forms and structures and to engage clients at multiple levels: individual, group, family and community. It assumes individuals and groups in society, such as those with serious and persistent mental illnesses, may require time-limited or on-going assistance for finding and maintaining those roles and relationships. They may be candidates for clubhouse community membership.

The text has been organized to demonstrate the way in which theories can be complementary. I have chosen to devote parts of two chapters to systems and ecological perspectives because I view them as especially inclusive of other theoretical elements and most useful for understanding both individual illness and the complex life of the clubhouse as a social system. Their location following discussion of mental illnesses in the text is a reflection of my conviction that an understanding of client issues and concerns should always lead practice theory and action.

I have used complementary and sometimes overlapping theories and components of theory to examine the clubhouse model and illuminate the theoretical complexity of this model and approach. Consequently, certain important aspects of the model—clubhouse values and the defining importance of membership and work—are viewed through different lenses and are reinforced through repetition.

The book is intended to augment and complement primary theory texts for generalist practice in social work, counseling, and human services courses. Inasmuch as it addresses assessment and intervention at multiple levels, the text can be used productively in generalist practice courses in each of the above disciplines. It may also be used as a supplemental text in social work Human Behavior in the Social Environment (HBSE) courses. Instructors and students in community mental health courses may find it useful as either a primary or secondary text. It may serve as a primary text for in-service professional training sessions

All the chapters, and some special topics throughout the text, are preceded by the words of clubhouse members and staff. My own learning in the model has taught me that it is important and empowering to draw out and to listen to the ideas and stories of participants. They are often eloquent, articulate, and revealing. Throughout my career I have been increasingly convinced that healthy communities are drawn together and kept together through the sharing of stories. The statements of clubhouse members and staff included in the text have been collected from clubhouse writings, my own notes and encounters with members at many clubhouses. They introduce lessons and remind students that the voices and collaborations of those directly involved should always precede and guide effective and responsible practice.

Lessons of theory, and their application in community building, can be broadly applied to various populations served by the helping professions. Loss and absence of community can be observed at many levels of society. Major problems of aging, poverty, crime, and racial discrimination are often associated with a loss of community responsibilities, connections and supports. Therefore community building is a natural and needed response for many different individuals and groups excluded and disempowered in our society. Generalist practitioners of the twenty-first century will need to know how to combine and to apply the theoretical tools of social science to help and support a variety of clients in diverse community roles. It is the aim of this text to stimulate student and practitioner imagination to the richness and relevance of theory to practice using a single complex practice example of the clubhouse model.

For their assistance and support in this project I want to thank certain individuals in clubhouse communities, colleagues in academia and those involved in the process of publication. I would especially like to thank these people at Fountain House in New York City who contributed their experiences and ideas to the project in the early stages, especially Steve Anderson, Melaney Mashburn, John Delman, Jacques Englestein, and Donny Lee. Thanks also to Jennifer Euler of Frontier House in Greeley, Colorado for assistance with reviewing the manuscript.

I would also like to give special thanks to Joel Corcoran, Executive Director of the International Center for Clubhouse Development (ICCD) at Fountain House for his advice and assistance and Rudyard Propst, ICCD founder and former Executive Director for his support and contribution of the authoritative history of the clubhouse movement. Their help has been invaluable.

I would like to thank Lisa Gebo and Susan Wilson of Wadsworth/Brooks-Cole for their generous advice and encouragement as well as the following reviewers: John Belcher, University of Maryland, Baltimore; Jean Hyche Jackson, Coppin State College; Sonia Matison, Eastern Washington University (retired); Kathleen May, University of Virginia; Lois Pierce, University of Missouri, St. Louis; and Barbara Shank, University of St. Thomas. Finally, with great gratitude and affection, I want to acknowledge the assistance of my wife, Vicki, who supported my efforts every step of the way.

Robert L. Jackson, Ph.D.
Colorado State University
October 24, 1999

INTRODUCTION: NEW ROLES FOR GENERALIST PRACTITIONERS

MAJOR TOPICS:

BACKGROUND

COMMUNITY AND COMMUNITY-BUILDING

MAJOR CHANGES IN OUR SOCIETY ARE BRINGING ABOUT NEW DEFINITIONS OF COMMUNITY.

GENERALIST PRACTICE

KNOWLEDGE AND SKILLS ARE APPLIED ACROSS A BROAD SPECTRUM OF ROLES, SETTINGS, AND GROUPS.

SYNTHESIS OF KNOWLEDGE

A GENERALIST PRACTITIONER DRAWS UPON DIVERSE SOURCES AND KINDS OF KNOWLEDGE.

APPLYING THEORY TO PRACTICE

THE CLUBHOUSE MODEL OF COMMUNITY SUPPORT FOR ADULTS WITH MENTAL ILLNESS EXEMPLIFIES APPLICATIONS OF THEORY TO PRACTICE.

SUMMARY

This practical approach is helping me cope with reality because I'm expected to use my abilities. I'm finding my abilities because other people need my help.

—A CLUBHOUSE MEMBER'S PERSPECTIVE

I have long believed that self-respect, self-esteem, and self-confidence are phenomena that cannot be given to others. We must earn these things ourselves.

—A STAFF MEMBER'S PERSPECTIVE

BACKGROUND

How does one conceptualize practice? Which theories, concepts, and perspectives are relevant and useful? These questions have followed me from work in juvenile justice and the field of community mental health into the field of professional education. The writing of this book is a natural extension of a career-long interest in the integration and effectiveness of my own professional practice.

One of my first human service jobs was directing a day treatment program that offered ex-mental hospital patients community treatment in lieu of long-term hospital care. The basic program objectives were to provide accessible resources for daily living and an ongoing structure of social activities, therapy, and psychiatric medication. This job helped me become familiar with the sometimes insurmountable but always challenging and complex problems of daily living faced by people with mental illnesses.

Our staff training at the mental health center was intensive and anchored in the medical approach to diagnosis and treatment of mental and emotional problems. We had regular weekly staff meetings to discuss diagnosis and treatment. Occasionally patients—increasingly referred to as "clients"—were interviewed in these sessions. The training approach was similar to "grand rounds" in a teaching hospital where senior medical staff teach students and interns, sometimes through examining and interviewing patients. Through our mental health center training sessions, experienced psychiatrists and psychiatric social workers taught us how to recognize major mental illnesses and understand diagnostic methods. We refined our observational skills and learned to recognize when clients were experiencing "voices" or panic attacks or disabling depression.

In our day treatment program, we applied an array of medical and social treatments to help alleviate symptoms. Although our treatment plans required regular statements of client progress in treatment, we observed that most clients were simply trying to get along despite their psychiatric problems. They also were struggling to understand what was happening to them.

The day treatment program was attractive to many clients. They were lined up outside the door each weekday morning to get inside, sit, smoke, or have a snack, or attend individual or group therapy. Although some drifted away, we were surprised and pleased that they often returned to treatment despite our youth and inexperience as staff workers. However, gradually we became aware of the serious limitations in our vision of these complex illnesses and what should be done about them.

Eventually, we found that the medical model and perspective with its diagnosis and treatment framework was insufficient for understanding the depth and range of daily living problems faced by clients. Problems, needs, and deficits brought clients to the mental health center. They often needed assistance with finances, management of money, social skills, housing, health care, and more. Yet, they also needed to discover and rediscover their own resources and competencies. We had few theoretical alternatives to advise and guide our work.

Although the medical model and perspective addressed the identification and psychiatric treatment of illness (specifically symptoms of mental illness), it could not address the individual needs and aspirations of the whole person. Diagnosis seemed essential for the administration of psychiatric medication; yet diagnosis alone could not direct measures to improve the lives of clients. We concluded that exclusive use of the medical model and perspective might tend to support and direct an unhelpful focus by staff and client upon symptoms and disabilities.

At that time our programming was designed to provide therapy and teach daily living skills. For the most part, it was designed primarily "to maintain" clients rather than to elicit client competencies. Nonetheless through long association, we learned that clients had their own special capabilities and strengths. One client had hitchhiked across the United States, another client was a talented singer, and another client had considerable ability as a cook. Staff often discovered the talents and special abilities of clients by chance, when a situation arose that called for their special skills and abilities, for example, the repair of a staff automobile, accomplished through the assistance of a client skilled in mechanics and willing to help.

Some clients had trouble understanding their own illnesses or even accepting that they had major mental illnesses. A few clients were on parole or probation, most clients were eligible for treatment paid by Medicaid, and almost all clients had been encouraged or directed by their psychiatrists to attend the program. Patterns of poor attendance were frequent subjects of discussion in clinical staff meetings. Attendance was problematic for both agency and clients. Lower attendance meant income loss to the agency that was reimbursed only for face-to-face services provided. In addition, away from the day treatment program, clients would often stop taking their medicine and their symptoms would worsen. Client refusal to attend was often viewed by senior staff as resistance to treatment.

Nonetheless for me and for other young staff members, program conditions of continuous caretaking seemed contradictory to our own values and professional ethics. We felt that our work should first and foremost encourage the discovery of individual strengths, empowerment, and self-determination. After a while, we began to believe that psychosocial day treatment provided continuously and sometimes under conditions of implicit coercion might be unhelpful and unhealthy.

The youthful and energetic staff were able to engage many clients, especially in activities such as fixing food, going on outings, refurbishing furniture, and other useful and enjoyable projects. Although we did not view them this way, the most helpful aspects of these activities were community-building in character. They were integrative and supportive for both members and staff. They naturally built connections based upon shared purposes and activities, created and sustained contributing, complimentary work roles for all, and enabled us to observe and focus on the strengths and competencies of community members. This experience laid the foundation for our discovery and eventual adoption of the clubhouse model.

During my later transition from professional practice to university teaching, the potential of the clubhouse model captured my imagination as a unique tool for teaching the integration of diverse elements of generalist practice education, for bridging university and community, theory and practice. I came to believe that for students, as for staff and clients in the day treatment program, the clubhouse model might similarly stimulate their imagination and aid them in their own integration of theory and generalist practice.

Today, the roles of generalist social workers and human services professionals are well-established in agencies and organizations throughout the country. Most of these workers are trained for the provision of direct services to adults, children, and families. They help staff residential treatment centers and provide individual counseling and case management, group life supervision, and advocacy on many levels. During the next century, as our population grows in numbers, diversity, and complexity, these important traditional helping roles will continue to grow in importance.

New Roles for Generalist Practitioners

At the beginning of the twenty-first century, a new practice role is emerging throughout the world—that of community-builder. This role has relevance for many groups in society but especially for those that are excluded—marginalized or stigmatized groups that are unable to engage in mainstream organizations and institutions. For members of these groups—including the homeless poor, the elderly and infirm, people with addictions and disabilities, and adults with serious mental illness—participation in community-building can be healing, restorative, and rehabilitative.

The concept of community is not new. Human beings are understood to be social creatures. The importance of social affiliation and support to an individual's well-being is well documented and accepted. However, for many becoming part of a community is neither natural nor easy. The creation and re-creation of communities requires initiative and leadership. Trained professionals are needed to provide that leadership.

For this emerging role, new ways to synthesize knowledge and apply theory are needed. The challenge for this new professional is to help build communities that discover, nurture, and make use of the talents, strengths, and abilities of their members. This book is committed to the development of these future professionals and to their understanding of how theoretical knowledge can be applied in this important work.

In order to bring abstract theory to life, this text will examine the complex problems and needs of a marginalized group in our society—adults with serious mental illness. Many of the approximately 2 million people in the United States with serious mental illness struggle to meet their needs from a fragmented and inadequate social welfare system. They often live on the margins of community. Some, however, find support and opportunity in more than 350 clubhouse communities across the world, based upon the clubhouse model first developed at Fountain House in New York City fifty years ago (Anderson, 1998).

Unlike most forms of professional helping, the goal of the clubhouse model, rather than "cure," "maintenance," "discharge," or "graduation," is the long-term engagement of adults with mental illness as members of communities where they can meet their needs, use their abilities, and be regularly "wanted, needed, and expected" (Beard, Propst, & Malamud, 1982). This text, utilizing this single, community-building approach as a practice example, examines how selected theories, perspectives, and other elements of theory can be applied to the complex problems of mental illness and intervention.

It is hoped that the reader will derive new understandings of disabling mental illness and new views of theory, as well as knowledge of community-building methods that can be applied to work with many different populations. The first two chapters lay the groundwork for later theoretical applications to practice. They describe community-building as a method of generalist practice and identify some important components of theoretical knowledge for assessment and intervention. In addition, the problems of mental illness are examined and compared from both medical and ecological perspectives. Thus, our look at theory to practice begins with problems of disabling mental illness and moves to community-building methods of intervention in the clubhouse model.

COMMUNITY AND COMMUNITY-BUILDING

The *Random House Unabridged Dictionary* (Flexner & Hauck, 1993) defines *community* as:

- A *social group* of any size whose members reside in a specific locality, share government, and who often have a common cultural and historical heritage.
- *The locality* (place) occupied by such a group.
- A *social, religious, or occupational group* sharing common characteristics or interests or perceiving itself as distinct from the larger society in which it exists.

The term "community" has come to be used in so many different ways that its meaning has been obscured. The various definitions previously listed suggest the complexity and vulnerability of the concept to new associations and uses. As the social landscape of our society becomes more varied and complicated, the word "community" takes on even more shades of meaning.

For example, "community" means:

- *Commonly held cultural and historical characteristics*
  Our society is comprised of diverse groups based upon nationality, religion, race, culture, and custom. Shared cultural and historical characteristics often de fine these groups as communities. Customs and traditions provide the basis for social identification, social and cultural contributions to personal identity. How community members view themselves is a product of self and social expectations shaped and reinforced by celebrating and continuously affirming the meaning of community membership. Examples of celebrations that affirm shared cultural heritage might be: Cinco de Mayo, in the Mexican American community or the powwows held by Native Americans. Such events are vitally important for the extension and preservation of community customs and culture. They provide a time to renew ties between and among community members and an opportunity for the transfer of rich elements of culture from the old to the young.
- *Shared land or place*
  Cities are commonly defined as communities because their inhabitants share certain locations. These communities have legal and political structures and histories all their own. Most cities in the United States, due to migration within the United States and immigration from abroad, are comprised of a rich mix of ethnic and cultural traditions. A city is also divided geographically, politically, and socially into smaller units—such as districts and neighborhoods. Based upon the preceding definitions, it is quite correct to refer to a city as a community. It is also true that a city contains many communities.
- *Shared interests*
  Now, more than ever, people are coming together in communities of shared interests. The interests that draw them together and define them may be specialized and narrow or may stretch across the globe. For instance, the "educational community" refers to teachers, students, and academics at all levels of the educational system who share common professional interests. The "arts community" describes a group of artists, curators, art buyers, and connoisseurs who share a love of art and seek to extend and protect their interests. The "gay community" identifies a group by sexual orientation. During the celebrations of such groups, "who I am" becomes inextricable from "who we are." Identification with a certain community publicly affirms social and political rights and strongly links self-identity and social identity. Individuals gain strength from their membership in communities large and small.

Commonly held cultural and historical characteristics, shared land or place, and shared interests each show a different aspect of the dictionary definition of community. When these factors are combined in a single community, they can contribute extraordinary strength and resilience.

Major Changes to Community

Social observers and writers find that the nature of community and our relation to it are constantly evolving. In the late nineteenth century, German sociologist Ferdinand Tönnies (1855–1936) identified two basic forms of social life and relationships: *gemeinschaft* and *gesellschaft* (Tönnies, 1957). His typology is still relevant to social structures and relationships today.

According to Tönnies, *gemeinschaft* social forms are found in communities where relationships between people are strong, community will and interests are dominant, customs and moral values are stable, and there is a natural solidarity between people—often supported by belief and religion. This form of social life is still found in many rural areas of our country. *Gesellschaft* social forms, on the other hand, are characterized by relationships based on contract not custom. People act according to their own will and goals, individual interests dominate group interests, and fashion and fad dictate the way that individuals make choices and live their lives.

The historic shift described and predicted by Tönnies has continued. Social, economic, and technological forces have continued to change and, in some cases, weaken traditional *gemeinschaft* family and community structures. The trend toward *gesellschaft* social forms has been influenced by:

- *Increasingly effective and efficient forms of technology.* Jobs can be done faster and more effectively by fewer people than ever before. Employment is less secure, leaving many underemployed or unemployed.
- *Expansion of transportation and communication.* More people relocate more frequently and across greater distances than ever before, thus breaking ties with family and friends.
- *Instantaneous and universal communication.* It is often easier to e-mail or telephone around the world than it is to communicate with a neighbor across a backyard fence. This can have the effect of distancing us from members of our neighborhood community.
- *Economic globalization.* Our economic and social welfare is directly linked to that of other countries. Changes in any major stock market affect economies throughout the world.

Each of these factors can contribute to the isolation of families and individuals by disrupting community ties that provide self-identity and the strength of collaborative support. While most people adapt to the changing environment, some individuals and groups do not.

When Community Breaks Down

It is useful to think of strong communities as social bonding agents in which members are bound to each other by work and shared purpose. Role structures and social connections are strong enough to insure that the needs of most, if not all, members are met. When community purposes, social connections, and functional roles are compromised or destroyed, communities begin to break down. Social values are challenged and cultural features decline.

Typically, the first to experience the effects of such a breakdown are less powerful groups with fewer resources who are already on the margin of community life, such as adults with serious mental illness (Torrey & Bowler, 1990). The natural social and psychological antidote for this isolation is reengagement. This takes a special kind of leadership by people who possess a broad knowledge of human behavior, the energy and skills to awaken dormant abilities, and the desire to draw people back into social life.

John McKnight describes such people as "community guides," people who are able to help communities tap latent processes of caring for their growth and benefit (McKnight, 1995). These people have many of the skills and abilities of competent, helping professionals. What they need is an integrated, theoretical understanding joined to practice values to help them through the inevitable rough spots in the road.

GENERALIST PRACTICE

According to the *Random House Unabridged Dictionary* (Flexner & Hauck, 1993), a *generalist* is "a person whose knowledge, aptitudes and skills are applied to a field as a whole or to a variety of different fields (opposed to specialist)." A skilled generalist can be especially helpful with individuals and groups who have complex, long-term and serious psychosocial problems, whose livelihood, self-concept, functioning, and quality of life are affected by illness, disability, social stigma, and isolation. A *generalist perspective* helps workers in maintaining a focus on the dynamic interplay of the many biological and social systems that affect client behavior and social functioning (Sheafor, Horejsi, & Horejsi, 1997).

Specialists, in contrast, are prepared to help with more defined, time-limited problems or issues which can be addressed and managed with specific approaches and techniques. Specialists have expertise to deal with specific populations and specific problems, while generalists view and work more comprehensively and inclusively in client situations. The term "generalist" suggests a breadth and depth of knowledge for practice, as well as an expertise to intervene at multiple levels. It encompasses the following concepts:

- *Practice roles*—Generalists are prepared to perform direct practice in the formal assessment of individual or family problems, counseling, or leadership of treatment or task groups, or they may be involved in indirect practice, helping with program design and development, political advocacy, or committee work with colleagues. The holistic focus of generalist practitioners means that their educational preparation must be as rich and diverse as the varied roles they may be expected to play.
- *Client groups*—Generalist workers may serve individuals, groups, organizations, and communities. They can expect to work with those on the margin of society— for example, juvenile delinquents, adults with mental illness, and victims of abuse and neglect. The problems of these groups are often defined, categorized, and addressed by social policy and established public and private organizations. Generalists recognize that, regardless of these definitions and categories, all individuals share basic needs.
- *Settings*—Generalist practitioners work in a variety of settings. They often cross organizational and institutional boundaries to help their clients manage complex problems. Divisions of labor that are based upon discipline or problem categories serve to enhance organizational functioning and control. However, these organizational divisions and controls can become obstacles that must be overcome by clients and their advocates. For example, a child welfare worker may need to help clients negotiate the boundaries between school, family, court, and counseling center.
- *Skills and methods*—Many or most of the skills and methods of intervention utilized by generalists have multiple applications. An assessment interview with a teenager accused of some act of delinquency will include many of the elements of an assessment performed with a homebound older citizen. A worker chairing a community task force of adults will employ many of the same skills necessary for activity group leadership in a residential treatment center.

Generalists can combine personal and professional values with skills and knowledge to help build communities in places where individuals have few active or meaningful community affiliations. Community-building is a new professional role for practitioners that will become clearer as we examine theory and the clubhouse model.

SYNTHESIS OF KNOWLEDGE

Common sense and good judgment based on life experience are perhaps the primary sources of understanding human behavior. We each have our own history and experience of solving problems to attain personal objectives. Problems of daily living require us to adapt. Therefore, we learn what works and does not work for us. At times of personal crisis, this may be "the school of hard knocks" about which our parents alerted us. More often, it is the accrued daily experience of becoming a mature social being and managing a broad array of problems that require solutions.

Formal education for generalist practice includes both classroom and field experiences provided through professional education courses in colleges and universities. This foundation for generalist practice includes such disciplines as: sociology, psychology, anthropology, philosophy, speech, and communication. These studies contribute theoretical knowledge and an awareness and appreciation of a range of perspectives for practice application.

Practice knowledge provides a complement to formal education. It is the source of learning gained through doing. It represents knowledge required for the translation of other learning components into practice. The product of practice knowledge is often referred to as *practice wisdom,* a process goal of any mature practitioner. Blending life experience, formal education, and practice knowledge creates the basis for a unique and personal synthesis, a personal "practice theory."

APPLYING THEORY TO PRACTICE

Theory is an inclusive term. It represents a body of knowledge that is comprised of individual theories, the components of which include assumptions, perspectives, concepts, and models. Theories may be abstract or specific and concrete. Nonetheless, they are often viewed as hypothetical and distant from everyday concerns, rather than practical. A major purpose of this text is to change the view of theory as an abstract product of academic thinking and help students and practitioners build their own conceptual bridges between theory and practice. Theories are useful tools to be applied to any situation. They add value by providing alternative ways of understanding.

Theory can help us:

- *Organize our thinking about what should be seen and acted upon and what should be ignored.* In research, theory is used to focus and enhance control over the subjects of study. Theories can help us, as generalist practitioners, to keep our eyes simultaneously on multiple relevant levels of intervention—individuals, groups, institutions, and communities—while selectively intervening at one or two levels. In short, theory helps us to see complex human interactions without blurring our vision in a boundless ocean of data.
- *Verify and validate practice approaches.* Theory helps us ask the right questions. Is there empirical support or practice precedent for a specific form of intervention? Is a specific intervention similar to others? Does it work in terms of its objectives?
- *Develop and organize systematic assessment approaches.* Theory helps us to identify adaptive and maladaptive behaviors and aids us in focusing our change efforts.
- *Construct coherent and effective intervention strategies.* Theory can aid us in the establishment of realistic practice objectives and criteria for outcomes assessment.
- *Discover new avenues of research inquiry.* Theory builds upon prior research and helps to direct our investigations.

The Language of Theory

Social workers and others employ a number of concepts to categorize and bring order to theory that has no universally accepted organization and no conceptual consensus.

- *Theoretical frameworks*—As the term suggests, a theoretical framework is a combination of related concepts that can help to organize one's approach to a given area of research or practice. For example, cognitive theory, as a body of assumptions, concepts, and models, provides a theoretical framework for organizing discussion of assessment and intervention. Although it is comprised of specific concepts and theoretical elements, a theoretical framework is a more general point of reference, a kind of world view. Because of their high level of abstraction, theoretical frameworks tend to resist verification through scientific methods.
- *Assumptions*—An assumption is a supposition; it means taking something for granted. Most often assumptions are accepted although they have not been validated. For instance, it may be assumed that human beings should be treated with respect and dignity. This is a value-based assumption. An assumption of cognitive theory is that "individuals act primarily in response to their cognitive representations of environmental events" (Greene & Ephross, 1984, p 128). As professional helpers, the character of our work is linked to the assumptions we make about clients, ourselves, our work, and the way that change is brought about. Many assumptions are unconscious. Consequently, practitioners have to be ever alert to their own difficulties in observing and understanding.
- *Perspectives*—Perspective is defined as "the faculty of seeing all relevant data in a meaningful relationship" (Flexner & Hauck, 1993). Theory, when used to inform practice, is often described as a perspective or way of looking at things. It may be useful to think of a perspective as a lens through which one understands and explains the object of viewing. Perspectives can be helpful to the process of discovering assumptions, but since perspectives often lack verification, they too can cloud the lens.

    Some perspectives serve to unify and organize the work of practitioners. For instance, an ecosystems perspective focuses on the blend of concepts that describe the degree of person-environment fit, the reciprocal exchange between person and environment, and the forces that support or inhibit that exchange (Germain, 1991). A systems perspective suggests a kind of conceptual organization based upon certain principles concerning social behavior. This perspective is derived from general systems theory (von Bertalanffy, 1968).

    Other less encompassing perspectives may add important components to the practitioner's field of view. For instance, a feminist perspective encourages attention to gender differences and needs particular to women. It is important that generalist practitioners are able to identify and examine multiple perspectives and include them into their own practice theory.
- *Theories*—As a body of research and writing, social science theory is comprised of theories—explanations—some validated, some not. Many theories concerned with specific components of human behavior, like self-efficacy theory, have been thoroughly validated through research. Others are best described as "good hunches," or "collections of good hunches."

    Some theories, such as psychoanalytic theory, are comprehensive, even universal in scope, attempting to explain all human development and behavior. These broad and most inclusive of theories—for example, Freudian or

COMPONENTS OF THEORY

THEORETICAL FRAMEWORKS	INDIVIDUAL THEORIES AND THEIR COMPONENTS	ASSUMPTIONS AND PERSPECTIVES	SYNTHESIS IN PRACTICE THEORY	CONCEPTION OF COMMUNITY-BUILDING AT MULTIPLE LEVELS IN THE CLUBHOUSE MODEL	INTERVENTIONS AT MULTIPLE LEVELS
EXAMPLES Ecological Theory General Systems Theory Symbolic Interaction Theory	EXAMPLES Theories (i.e., self-efficacy theory, exchange theory, labeling theory, role theory, etc.) Concepts Hypotheses Models	EXAMPLES Strengths Perspective Social Constructionist Perspective Ecological Perspective Systems Perspective	EXAMPLES Theoretical Knowledge Life Experience Practice Wisdom and Values	EXAMPLES Elements of the Clubhouse Model at different levels of social organization	EXAMPLES Model Building Community Organization/Institution Group/Family Individual

ABSTRACT ⟶ CONCRETE

FIGURE 1.1

A Continuum of Theory to Practice

Eriksonian theories—may be said to inform practice. Other more precise "theories of the middle range" may show ways in which we see and act to address human problems (Merton, 1968). In these instances, theory may guide and direct practice. Theories, like cars or clothes or anything else that people use, may gain acceptance or even popularity in research or practice for a variety of reasons, not always because they have been scientifically verified.

- *Concepts*—Defined in the dictionary as "ideas," concepts provide a major source for understanding and ordering ourselves and our social environment (Flexner & Hauck, 1993). Concepts, as they are expressed, have everything to do with how we understand and define social problems and what we do in reference to those problems. They are the building materials from which theory and theoretical frameworks, more complex combinations of ideas, are built and changed. In later chapters, we will encounter theory concerning the role of concepts, language, and other powerful symbols in human behavior and development.

  It is important to know that concepts have *denotative* meanings—dictionary, objective, or literal definitions—and *connotative* meanings—collections of inferred or suggested meanings which accrue to concepts through their use. We need to remember that language is inherently symbolic and constantly evolving. This factor sometimes makes language the least reliable medium for communication and understanding between people. But, since we must use language, we need to respect its complexity.

  For example, the denotative meaning of "schizophrenia" is a mental disorder having probable biogenetic origins and involving "emotional blunting, intellectual deterioration, social isolation, and delusions and hallucinations" (Flexner & Hauck, 1993). However, the word "schizophrenia" still carries connotative meanings of pervasive "madness" and "lunacy." It evokes images of peculiar, erratic, and perhaps dangerous, out-of-control individuals. The concept of schizophrenia, formulated by German psychiatrist Emile Kraepelin in the nineteenth century, came to replace other nonmedical terms used at the time such as "lunacy" and "madness," whose meanings were viewed as imprecise and unscientific. Similarly, today, the terms "client," "consumer," or "service consumer" have widely replaced the designation "patient" in the language of mental health service planners and providers. These changes in language have come about in response to concern that the earlier terms were encumbered with negative, stigmatizing, and disempowering meanings. Value judgments such as these contribute to the type of theory selected for practice.

- *Models*—Models serve as plans to give shape and form to many kinds of planned interventions. They are "preliminary representations of something, often based upon analogy, and serving as guides" from which replicas can be constructed (Flexner & Hauck, 1993). Models show or describe in detail how something should look and work. Models most often develop because of a successful experience or deliberate experimentation. Models may be presented or explained as if they were static. However, they are dynamic and open to continuous evaluation and interpretation.

In some situations a worker might directly and consciously "choose" a theory. The most obvious and reliable test for the selection of theory for practice (or inclusion in a textbook) is the extent to which a theory might be *useful* in understanding and intervening. The choice will likely be influenced by many factors: which theories are in most common use, which theories or elements of theories are most compatible with the worker's own beliefs and values, which have been tested and verified, and which appear to be most useful. Utility is the benchmark. Practitioners should have working knowledge of a range of useful theories about individuals and their social environments and be able to consciously select a theoretical approach to help them understand their reasons for engaging in any particular intervention.

To help critically evaluate and select a theory or theoretical perspective, students and practitioners might consider the following set of questions adapted from a list created by Mumm and Kersting (1997).

1. What is this theory attempting to explain?
2. What is the empirical support for the theory?
3. What are the fundamental assumptions underpinning the theory? Which assumptions do I accept and why? Which assumptions do I not accept and why?
4. Are the theory's assumptions ethically and socially consistent with my own values and professional ethics?
5. Can the principles of the theory be practically applied?
6. How applicable is the theory across settings, with different clients and problems?
7. Is the theory clear, easy to understand, and logical?
8. Does the theory address cultural, ethnic, or racial issues? Is the theory culturally sensitive?
9. How does the theory compare and contrast with other theoretical approaches?
10. How does the theory help me compensate for my blind spots, biases, and unconscious assumptions?

This text demonstrates the synthesis of many kinds of theoretical knowledge and its application in practice by using the clubhouse model, an internationally known and respected approach to the problems of adults with mental illness. Subsequent chapters will apply theory to different aspects of the model for clubhouse community-building.

Serious mental illness may be seen as an illness of dislocation from community, as much as a collection of individual, clinical symptoms. Although symptoms are expressed in individual appearance and behavior, mental illness often invades psychological, physical, economic, and social aspects of the lives of those affected. It is a pervasively disabling and often isolating condition that disengages a person from his or her normal community connections. In fact, mental illness, perhaps more than any other complex set of human problems, challenges our understanding and ability to effectively help.

Though help for adults with mental illness has been the focus of the clubhouse model since its origin, generalist practitioners working with other problems and populations can also benefit from understanding the clubhouse model and how theoretical knowledge is used to attain an in-depth understanding of human problems and generalist practice interventions. Any category of human problems, such as serious mental illness, which socially isolates people, minimizes competency and capability, resists "cure" or "fix," and persists in spite of the usual measures, may be helpfully addressed using community-building methods. The need for these approaches is likely to continue to grow in the twenty-first century as populations grow older and social problems remain complex. Lessons derived from the application of theory to community-building in the clubhouse model will have relevance for work with these and other groups.

SUMMARY

Increasingly, complex and diverse social pressures and problems are changing community life in our society. The loss of traditional community supports is most evident among at-risk populations such as adults with mental illness, whose circumstances of personal disability, widespread poverty, and lack of power to influence others, interact to alienate and isolate them.

Generalist practitioners in the fields of social work, human services, and counseling, who are assuming new community-building roles, need to acquire practice competencies based upon the acquisition and synthesis of life experience, formal education, and practice knowledge. Theoretical knowledge including theories and their components such as concepts, assumptions, theoretical frameworks, and models provide a foundation for the development of an individual's "practice theory."

In the next chapter, we will examine alternative perspectives used to assess people and their problems, beginning with a traditional medical perspective. We will examine how the ecological perspective adds to and differs from the medical perspective. We will see how each of these perspectives, based in theory and research, can be applied to understanding major mental illnesses and how they affect individuals and their environments.

APPLYING CONCEPTS

1. Define generalist practice.
2. Describe three primary sources of knowledge for generalist practice.
3. Name and define three major social science traditions. Which do you find most attractive and why?
4. Define and compare denotative and connotative meanings.
5. Name and define the building blocks of theory identified in the chapter.
6. Discuss various ways in which theory can contribute to effective generalist practice.
7. What is perspective and what is its importance to assessment and intervention?

8. Define community and discuss the characteristics of community suggested by McKnight.
9. Name groups in society other than adults with mental illness for whom community-building approaches might be helpful.
10. What characteristics of community have you observed at your student practicum or field placement? Would it be desirable and practical to develop more characteristics of community there? What steps would you take?

Class Projects

Imagine that you are a "community guide," helping community members to mobilize their own strengths and resources. How would you begin to mobilize the positive forces of community-building in any social group? What kinds of helping behaviors would you avoid?

Define and examine a community with which you and your classmates are involved. What are its strengths in terms of meeting individual and group needs and wants and what are some of its weaknesses?

GLOSSARY

Community   a social group which may share governance, a place occupied by such a group, a group sharing common interests or common history and culture.

Community-building   the action of initiating, planning, organizing, developing, and maintaining communities at various levels. Strong communities are based upon a shared sense of purpose held by community members.

Concepts   ideas or thoughts about something. Concepts are the most basic components of theory.

Gemeinschaft social forms   characterized by a common will, the domination of community interests, held together by shared religious beliefs and customs which create a natural solidarity.

Generalist practitioner   a professional helper who draws upon knowledge from many different disciplines and other sources and is prepared to assess problems and intervene at multiple system levels.

Gesellschaft social forms   characterized by the predominance of individuality, private property, and contractual relations. Fashion and fads direct commerce and exchange between community members.

Intervention   action to eliminate, ameliorate, modify, or manage problems, such as those of mental illness. Intervention may occur at multiple levels and may be carried out by individual workers, groups, or organizations.

Model   representation of something, often based upon analogy, and serving as a plan.

Perspective   a way of looking at things, a point of view.

Social problem   a problem or group of problems (may be individual problems or troubles at first) which by their presence, persistence, dimensions, visibility, or impact come to be seen as social problems.

Synthesis of knowledge   the cognitive process of organizing, combining, and transforming components of knowledge so that they can be used to understand complex human environments.

Theory   an explanation about some phenomena (singular) and a group or body of such explanations (plural) which contribute to understanding. Individual theories, perspectives, concepts, models, and conceptual frameworks comprise the building blocks of a body of theory.

REFERENCES

Anderson, S. B. (1998). *We are not alone: Fountain House and the development of clubhouse culture.* New York: Fountain House.

Beard, J., Propst, R. N., & Malamud, T. J. (1982). The Fountain House model of psychiatric rehabilitation. *Psychosocial Rehabilitation Journal, 5*(1), 47–53.

Flexner, S. B., & Hauck, L. C. (Eds.). (1993). *Random House Unabridged Dictionary* (2nd ed.). New York: Random House.

Germain, C. (1991). *Human behavior in the social environment.* New York: Columbia University Press.

Greene, R. R., & Ephross, P. H. (1984). *Human behavior theory and social work practice.* New York: Aldine de Gruyter.

McKnight, J. (1995). *The careless society: Community and its counterfeits.* New York: Basic Books.

Merton, T. (1968). *Social theory and social structure.* New York: Free Press.

Mumm, A. M., & Kersting, R. C. (1997). Teaching critical thinking in social work practice courses. *Journal of Social Work Education, 33*(1), 79.

Sheafor, B. W., Horejsi, C. R., & Horejsi, G. A. (1997). *Techniques and guidelines for social work practice* (4th ed.). Boston: Allyn and Bacon.

Tönnies, F. (Ed.). (1957). *Community and society (gemeinshaft and gesellschaft).* Ann Arbor, MI: Michigan State University Press.

Torrey, E. F., & Bowler, A. (1990). Evidence for an urban factor. *Schizophrenia Bulletin, 16,* 591–604.

von Bertalanffy, L. (1968). *General system theory.* New York: George Braziller.

THEORETICAL PERSPECTIVES ON MENTAL ILLNESS

Despite the fact that I was getting healthier in a clinical sense, I was not "fitting in." Eventually, I became rooted in the work situation. I became a worker. I began to understand that I was real and my fantasies were illusions.

—A CLUBHOUSE MEMBER'S PERSPECTIVE

You cannot befriend a person into wellness.

—A STAFF MEMBER'S PERSPECTIVE

DISABLING MENTAL ILLNESS

This chapter begins an investigation of the problems of serious mental illness with two competing theoretical perspectives—the medical perspective and the ecological perspective. Each is described and evaluated. We will begin to see how the application of theoretical perspectives to the problems of mental illness can be generalized to assessment and intervention with other problems and populations. There are, however, more dominant and less dominant perspectives, more inclusive and less inclusive, more useful or less useful for given situations. Professionals must thoughtfully and consciously include various perspectives on client problems and what should be done about them.

Disabling mental illness has been known throughout history and across all cultures. The great variety of terms still actively used to identify and describe mental illness suggests not only its intractability and complexity, but also the fearfulness and superstition that has historically defined it and individuals affected by it. Today, mental illness is recognized as being many illnesses. In this text, the terminology "serious mental illness," "disabling mental illness," or "mental illness" refers to those illness forms and severity that cause major disruptions and disablement. The most prevalent and problematic categories are described in this chapter.

Recent research into the causes of schizophrenia continues to point to origins in the structure and functioning of the brain (Torrey, 1990, p. 140–174). Scientists employing sophisticated brain imaging devices and other sophisticated research tools are helping to shed light on causes of disabling mental illness. Nonetheless, it is also clear that many variables, including psychosocial factors, influence the course of the illness and the long term adjustment of people in society (Bachrach, 1992).

Applications of Alternative Theories and Perspectives

The lay person or casual observer does not ordinarily give much thought to the matter of how he or she views other people and their problems. Processes of seeing, hearing, understanding, and responding to communications are natural aspects of a person's relationship with others. However, the professional observer/helper is obligated to be aware of and consciously employ various perspectives in understanding human problems. As described in Chapter 1, perspectives drawn from social and psychological theory guide the professional helper to various useful ways to enhance perception and understanding of client problems and situations.

These perspectives permit the professional helper to:

- Focus attention on a field of concern and specific responses within a universe of possibilities.
- Guide practice inquiry as it and other aspects of theory guide research.
- Make values and ethical considerations explicit.
- Broaden the scope of assessment to include new or previously unexamined components.
- Add depth to assessment and intervention.
- Address ethnic and cultural components of the situation and alert the worker to the presence of his or her own biases and prejudices.

Professionals who deal regularly with complex problems strike to become familiar with multiple perspectives concerning human problems and what can be done about them. Strengths perspectives, multicultural perspectives, and feminist perspectives each broaden and strengthen understanding of psychosocial problems.

A TRADITIONAL MEDICAL PERSPECTIVE: DIAGNOSIS AND TREATMENT

The traditional medical perspective continues to be one of the most influential in terms of the treatment of mental illness. Fundamentally, the medical perspective views mental illness as a pathological condition or conditions to be diagnosed and treated as disorders of the mind. This perspective focuses attention on identification of the illness through its external signs or *symptoms*. Although it acknowledges the social impact of mental illness, the medical perspective focuses on diagnostic evaluation of the individual—his or her thoughts, feelings, and behaviors, and whether or not symptoms of "mental disorder" can be identified and classified. Saleebey (1997) describes this perspective as ". . . linear in its logic: causes will bring about effects; diagnosis will lead to treatment that should effect cure; development is sequential, one stage following another and so on." (p. 29)

The traditional medical perspective, although originating in the nineteenth century positivism of medical science, is not restricted to the medical professions. In fact, it has had and continues to have a major influence among psychologists, social workers, counselors, health care planners, and others who work with people who have mental illnesses.

Diagnosis: Labeling and Classification of Symptoms

Much confusion surrounds the matter of psychiatric diagnosis and its meaning. Diagnosis is a process, as well as a label assigned. That process involves systematic comparison of observed and reported symptoms with categories of symptoms in the *Diagnostic and Statistical Manual of Mental Disorders* of the American Psychiatric Association, also called *DSM-IV* (Frances, 1994). It is frequently part of a broader medical assessment of an individual in which a number of background factors may be examined including physical health, family history, employment, education, and community affiliations.

Diagnosis serves four major purposes in the process of helping people with mental illness. First, diagnosis provides shorthand or abbreviated descriptions of groups of symptoms, thoughts and feelings, and observed behaviors. This shorthand aids communication and understanding among individuals and organizations responsible for treatment planning. Second, diagnosis provides a basis for making intake and admissions decisions in hospitals, mental health centers, and residential treatment programs. Third, diagnosis permits qualification of the individual for insurance or other financial support to pay for services. Fourth, diagnosis is the basis for decisions about medications. Diagnosis does not explain the possible causes or origins of the symptoms, nor does it prescribe the best treatment. Inasmuch as its focus is on *psychopathology* or mental disorder, it does not identify or describe a person's "healthy" characteristics, strengths, and attributes.

Professionals have the responsibility to use diagnoses and diagnostic information, as with all treatment information concerning clients, with great care, according to contractual agreements with clients and their own professional ethics. The formal classification and naming of mental illnesses and the assignment of diagnoses are perceived by some people as having great, almost magical significance. It is important that workers remember the symptoms are not the illness nor is the person "the diagnosis," for example, a "chronic schizophrenic" or a "manic-depressive." The diagnosis is simply a shorthand, which is useful if it is based upon adequate and accurate information.

Diagnostic accuracy is important for a number of reasons. Professionals have a responsibility to insure that odd, idiosyncratic, or unpopular behavior is not accidentally or deliberately characterized as mental illness. They also have a responsibility to see that diagnosis is not used arbitrarily to limit personal freedom or to label and control political dissent. In the United States, unless a court of law finds a person diagnosed with a mental illness to be dangerous to self or others or gravely disabled, that person retains the right to be odd or eccentric or mentally ill without interference.

The *Diagnostic and Statistical Manual of Mental Disorders* includes categories of symptoms, named and numbered according to type and severity, and the way they can be differentiated from other, similar disorders. Professionals should have a broad understanding of the manual and the major categories of disorders with which hospitals and community programs for people with mental illness are most concerned. However, no plan for diagnosis or assessment can capture the range, depth, and breadth of an individual's life and experience, especially one which, by design, simply names categories of behavior.

The following sections summarize some of the most common medical diagnoses assigned to people in institutional settings such as hospitals and community mental health centers.

Disorders of Thinking

This category of mental illnesses pertain primarily to disorders of thought and thought processes involving thinking, imagining, dreaming, and so forth. Symptoms of other kinds may be present, but those involving thinking problems are of primary concern.

Schizophrenia   Schizophrenia is a complex condition or conditions, as many researchers believe. Contrary to popular belief, schizophrenia is not a split personality nor multiple personalities but rather a splitting of various aspects of a person's thought processes from everyday reality. Schizophrenia is categorized as a thought disorder because major symptoms often center on problems of thinking and the creation and communication of ideas. Because each person and situation is different, symptoms are expressed individualistically. They often begin in a person's late teens or twenties with changes in routine patterns of behavior. The individual becoming ill may withdraw socially, express strange and uncharacteristic thoughts and ideas, and neglect personal grooming or develop other unusual patterns of behavior.

"Schizophrenia is marked by a number of severe and handicapping symptoms. It would be arbitrary to label any one as the worst, but none has a more pernicious effect than the profound impairment in social functioning that characterizes the disorder. Poor social competence contributes to the impoverished quality of life and social isolation experienced by many patients. It interferes with functioning in the workplace, within the family, and in residential facilities." (Bellack & Mueser, 1993, p. 321)

The first symptoms of schizophrenia are generally observed by family and friends. Social withdrawal and isolation may be the first signs. Affected individuals may have trouble expressing feelings or thoughts. Their thoughts and behavior may seem out of character or strange.

The acute or active phase of the illness often provides the first clear evidence of its disabling nature. The symptoms of schizophrenia are conceptualized as being of two different types: *Positive symptoms* which "appear to reflect an excess or distortion of normal functions" and *negative symptoms* which "appear to reflect a loss or absence of normal functions." During the acute phase of schizophrenia, serious disturbances of thinking and feeling appear. These are called *positive* symptoms because they are present when they should not be. They may include delusions (false ideas that are fixed in the person's mind), auditory hallucinations (hearing voices that are not there), disorganized or illogical patterns of speech, social withdrawal from family and friends, changes in patterns of sleep, changes in personal hygiene and grooming, and inability to concentrate.

The symptoms of schizophrenia interfere with ordinary daily activities such as going to work, having friends, recreating, and relaxing. People with these symptoms often feel great discomfort and distress—they may talk to or shout at voices, laugh, cry, or exhibit emotions apparently unrelated to the social context. For many, the voices are punishing or insulting and are unpleasant or intolerable. Experiencing auditory hallucinations or hearing voices has been compared to having a radio playing intermittently or continuously inside one's head interrupting, confusing, and tormenting. For most people who are affected, these symptoms occur episodically. They tend to diminish with time and can most often be controlled through the use of antipsychotic medicines.

The so-called negative symptoms (Andreason & Olsen, 1982) can last for months or years and may include social isolation or withdrawal, major impairment in daily roles as student, worker, or family member, an apparent lack of feelings or expressiveness, referred to as "flat affect,"peculiar behavior, and strange ideas.

Now medications are available to control and help clients manage both kinds of symptoms. Psychotherapy and psychosocial treatments are primarily used to improve psychosocial functioning.

At this time, we do not have the tools to "cure" schizophrenia, if by "cure" we mean the total elimination of symptoms. Individuals with schizophrenia may experience extended periods of *remission* (absence or reduction and control of disabling symptoms) or they may have the recurring experience of acute psychotic symptoms.

The course of the disease is uneven and episodic. It often strikes at what we consider the essence of the person—the self. Yet, because its manifestations are both personal and social, schizophrenia can elicit fear, misunderstanding, and condemnation from others instead of sympathy and concern. It remains unparalleled as a stigmatizing disease, with all the societal consequences of personal shame, family burden, and inadequate support of treatment, research, and rehabilitation.

Disorders of Affect (Mood)

Disorders of affect (mood) concern the way in which a person's emotions are expressed and what he or she says about feeling (mood), for example, sad, happy, or depressed. Changes in mood are natural and require no special attention unless they are so serious and debilitating that they interfere with the individual's ability to cope with problems.

Bipolar Disorder (also called Manic-Depressive Illness) This group of symptoms is characterized by episodes of mania followed by depression. Symptoms of mania and depression most commonly alternate for varying lengths of time. These cycles, ranging in duration from a few days to months, are usually followed by a return to normal functioning. The most prominent feature of mania is a distinct period of time when the individual's mood is either "high" and excited or extremely irritable, or both. To friends and relatives who know the person well, the "high" mood will seem abnormal, although an uninvolved observer might believe the individual to be just filled with emotional energy.

People affected by mania may get involved in frantic and excessive planning and participation in multiple activities, for example, social, sexual, political, or religious activities, call friends or relatives in the middle of the night, go on buying sprees, make poor business or personal decisions, for example, exhausting personal savings, suddenly changing life plans, and so forth, they may stay up all hours of the day and night, sometimes for several days at a time, appear strange or flamboyant in manner and dress, have loud, rapid speech, experience delusions (false, unconfirmed ideas), and/or experience hallucinations (distortions of perception) that are generally consistent with the elevated mood.

Mania may produce problems with reasoning and cause inflated ideas about one's power and ability to master various tasks. These distorted beliefs range from uncritical self-confidence to delusions, such as the idea that personal communications are being received from outer space or a belief of involvement in a special relationship with some well-known religious or political figure or celebrity. The manic phase of illness is frequently followed by a depressed phase (thus, the term, bipolar) in the cyclical changes that affect thinking and feeling.

Major Depression This is not the kind of depressed state ordinarily meant when we say we are "bummed out" or "depressed." Almost everyone has felt "depressed" at one time or another. We use the term in everyday conversation to describe feeling "blah" or having the "blues." Most of us naturally experience excitement and elation and have times when we are sad or depressed. These are normal and natural shifts in our mental states in response to what is going on in and around us. These experiences are very common in the general population. However, lesser forms of depression or *dysthymia* may be almost universal. Approximately 7 percent of Americans suffer from clinical depression. Symptoms of the depressive phase of bipolar disorder or *major* depression are often disabling, disorganizing, or even life threatening unless treated.

Major depression is a "mood disorder," that is, it is a "pervasive and sustained emotion that colors perception of the world" (Frances, 1994, p. 768). The symptoms of major depression may be seen following or in conjunction with a manic episode or independently of mania. They tend to persist in both time and severity.

Major depression is characterized by a number of related symptoms of considerable duration. They include depressed mood and loss of interest in usual activities, changes in appetite, weight gain or loss, inability to sleep or the inclination to sleep all the time, decreased energy, feelings of guilt and low self-worth, difficulty in thinking or concentration, and with some individuals, persistent thoughts of death or suicide.

The illness causes real pain and misery, as well as impairments in relationships with family and friends. It may have features of psychosis including auditory hallucinations (voices) as well as delusions generally consistent with a depressed mood, for example, the belief that he or she is the devil incarnate or can cause the spread of disease with their thoughts. Some people may be debilitated and even immobilized by major depression.

However, for the most part depression is very treatable with medications and psychotherapy. Not surprisingly patients with depression are often undiagnosed by family doctors, and when diagnosed, accepted treatments are often underprescribed (Katon, Von Korff, Lin, Bush, & Ormel, 1992). For many their symptoms lift when the precipitating circumstances have disappeared. However, for some the origins seem to be internal and the symptoms far more severe. They may be referred to outpatient or day treatment programs because of the psychological and social disruption accompanying their illness. Yet in general, depression is a much less common primary diagnosis among day treatment clients and clubhouse members than the various forms of schizophrenia.

Other Major Mental Disorders

Sometimes psychiatrists or other mental health professionals apply the diagnosis of *schizoaffective disorder* when symptoms of both schizophrenia and bipolar disorder are present. A diagnosis of *psychotic disorder not otherwise specified* may be applied when there is evidence of delusions or hallucinations but little more is known about the individual's problems.

Organic Brain Syndrome (OBS)

Organic brain syndrome is a diagnosis applied to the abnormal psychological or behavioral functioning of a person that is based upon temporary or long-term physical dysfunction of the brain. This dysfunction may have a variety of causes—for example, a brain tumor, extended drug or alcohol abuse, or brain injury from an automobile accident. Any of these factors may have damaged or destroyed brain cells, thereby causing long-term disability.

Treatment Interventions Based upon a Medical Perspective

Because of the complexity of the illnesses described previously, several different kinds of psychosocial treatment responses have been developed. Each has been shown to be effective with some people at some times, however, that effectiveness is often related to combinations of treatment that include psychotropic medication.

- *Psychotropic Medication*—Many major mental disorders can be treated through the use of psychiatric medications. With careful and controlled use, medications are generally effective in dampening or diminishing symptoms of major thought and mood disorders. Most professionals consider medication essential for permitting individuals to manage their mental illness and more fully access their own skills and abilities. Ex-mental patients need to work with a physician or nurse practitioner to have appropriate medication prescribed and effects monitored closely. The use of medication is most often a critical component in recovery from illness.
- *Psychotherapy*—Psychotherapists provide emotional support, guidance, and advice for handling the problems of daily living. Individual, family, and group psychotherapy methods are frequently employed in community-based treatment. Regular sessions of psychotherapy are often supportive. When combined with appropriate medications managements, psychotherapy can be useful in assisting someone experiencing mental illness.
- *Day Treatment and Day Hospital*—During the early years of the deinstitutionalization policy (1970s and early 1980s), community mental health centers and psychiatric centers developed day treatment, partial hospitalization, and day hospital programs. These were based upon program elements that have been important in psychiatric hospitals: medication prescription and management, individual therapy, educational groups, recreational activities, crafts groups, and other activities that might help patients manage disturbing symptoms and teach them skills for greater independence.
- *Sheltered Workshop*—Workshops, designed originally for the rehabilitation of people with major physical disabilities, were intended to help them learn work skills and methods of adaptation despite physical disabilities. They helped people get back to work, earn money at piece rates, and learn skills that might be helpful in regaining jobs in industry or commerce. Although sheltered workshops are still used by some people with mental illnesses, they are not used as widely as some other forms of treatment and rehabilitation. Groups of people with mental illness are often unable to bring the necessary speed and consistency needed to succeed in a piecework environment.
- *Psychiatric Rehabilitation*—Psychiatric rehabilitation came into being in the 1970s and 1980s. It was developed "to improve the competencies of people who have long-term mental illnesses, to help people with mental illness to learn social and vocational skills, to get the education and support they need to succeed in community settings" (Anthony, Cohen, & Farkas, 1990, p. 64). Psychiatric

rehabilitation programs undertook to teach people with mental illness how to live independently: to utilize their strengths and capabilities, to present themselves to prospective employers, to shop for groceries, and to make and keep friends. Although often viewed by mental health professionals as a follow-up or secondary treatment, psychiatric rehabilitation has had a growing impact on the delivery of community mental health services.

Psychiatric rehabilitation is a relatively new development in community work with people who have mental illnesses. In some respects, it is comparable with the clubhouse model. Rehabilitation staff and clubhouse staff share similar objectives. They work to secure housing, assist with vocational training, and in other ways help change the lives of people with mental illnesses. However, psychiatric rehabilitation has grown and evolved methods that are more compatible with the medical model.

This field focuses upon individual change and achievement facilitated and enabled by a range of professional services. Psychiatric rehabilitation counselors train and become individually certified to provide behavioral assessments, help clients set goals, obtain training and prevocational experiences, and eventually gain employment. The principles and practices of psychiatric rehabilitation, like other forms of medical rehabilitation, focus on individual change objectives sought through various professional services rather than the shared work of community-building. The work of counselors is directed by individual rehabilitation plans intended to focus and individualize intervention activities (Glickman, 1993).

THE ECOLOGICAL PERSPECTIVE

The ecological perspective provides a richly descriptive metaphor for the complex, adaptive, reciprocal relationship between the person and environment (Germain, 1991, p. 16). External standards of "normality" and "abnormality" and "sickness" and "wellness" are not meaningful in the application of this perspective. Originating in the field of biology, the ecological perspective is oriented to the study of the relationship between the growing, changing individual and the individual's environment. This perspective sharply departs from the linear, sequential, or stage theories of human development, for example, Freudian or Eriksonian theories. The ecological perspective assumes that people are goal directed and their behavior is purposeful and oriented toward adaptation. It assumes that a variety of environmental variables, as well as personal strengths and limitations such as mental illness, influence the course of adaptation.

The social costs of mental illness are high, and the effects of illness pervasive. Yet public and private social welfare agencies are overwhelmingly funded for and oriented to focusing on the behavior of individuals. Rather than examining the reciprocal influence of individual and environment, professionals must go to special lengths to use and maintain an active ecological perspective for assessment and intervention.

Ecological Concepts

Adaptation and adaptiveness are central concepts of the ecological perspective (Germain, 1991, p. 17). Workers' attention is directed to an assessment of adaptive capacities and nurturing elements in a person's environment. The challenges of growth and development are unique. They are approached with different methods of adaptation.

- *Habitat*—The concept of *habitat* describes the totality of the unique circumstances of the environment in which the individual lives. It includes physical, social, economic, political, and cultural aspects of the lifetime encounter between the individual and environment. It is comprised of physical aspects, such as buildings and open spaces, and social aspects, such as groups and organizations. This ongoing, complex set of relationships between organism and environment can be applied to the understanding of all living things including human beings. The ecological idea of *goodness of fit* refers to the extent to which the organism has successfully adapted to its environment at any given point. Application of this idea can help provide depth and breadth to client assessment.

  One of the most important and often problematic aspects of habitat for people with mental illness is housing. Adequate and appropriate housing is basic to maintaining life. Yet many people have great difficulty finding the resources, organizing, and negotiating safe and stable living situations. Environmental obstacles such as inadequate affordable housing, lack of supervision and support, lack of psychiatric care, inadequate medical programs, and lack of financial resources may interact destructively when combined with symptoms of illness such as confusion or social withdrawal. If individuals with mental illness are to succeed and achieve environmental goodness of fit, these problems must be overcome.

- *Components of Adaptiveness*—The community in which a person finds himself or herself serves as a fundamental source of support, resources, and identification. For people with mental illness the largest and most significant group of helpers are their families.

  Almost as many adults with schizophrenia live with their parents as live independently (Torrey, 1990, p. 10). Families often bear primary responsibility for housing and caring for their children. Their caretaking involves social agencies, hospitals and jails, and public welfare organizations. In many instances, their family homes serve broad functions, as asylums and mental hospitals did at one time. Parents meet the basic needs for food, clothing, and shelter, as well as meeting a whole spectrum of needs related to mental illness. Long after active parenting responsibilities are over for most families, the parents and siblings of adults with mental illness find themselves acting as continuing caretakers.

  Some of these situations are stable. However, many untrained and isolated parents are unable to cope with the needs of their children. Eventually they must return for assistance to the often inadequate and marginally accessible programs and agencies within the mental health care system. This and other individual and environmental factors may interact to create powerful combinations of destructive environmental factors. These must be overcome by families, professionals, or the individuals themselves. A positive place in the environment or niche must be found.

- *Niche*—Within the field of ecology, the term *niche* refers to the position a species occupies in the environment. With regard to humans, niche is used as a metaphor for the status or social position occupied in the structure of the community by particular groups (Germain, 1991, p. 50). The concept can be helpful in understanding problems of adaptation issues that must be considered in regard to individuals who tend to become stigmatized and marginalized.

The terms "mental patient" or "ex-mental patient" or "homeless mentally ill" refer to certain niches or places in the habitat occupied by individuals with mental illness. A satisfactory adaptive niche is attained through continuous reconciliation of the needs of person and environment. The process of gaining a satisfactory niche requires initiative and activity.

- *Stressors*—The ecological perspective directs analysis to factors which block or inhibit adaptiveness. These are called stressors. *Stressors* may be physical disabilities, educational limitations, inadequate housing, or the active symptoms of mental illness. These factors are often given primary attention. Workers see the subject of their assessment and intervention in various ways as they attempt to help clients develop their own adaptiveness. The goal is to help clients identify, manage, or remove stressors in order to shape safe and satisfying niches.

- *Life course*—Using an ecological perspective, human development occurs as a result of complex biological, emotional, environmental, cultural, and historical factors (Germain, 1991, p. 154). It is not viewed as series of invariant age-based steps or stages. It is understood to be a continuing process of interaction and reciprocity between the individual and environment.

  The symptoms of major mental illnesses manifest themselves in the first few decades of a person's life—at important developmental transitions such as school graduation, first employment, or marriage and divorce. Difficulties experienced at these important times may seriously affect later development. However, they do not determine development. The ecological perspective optimistically assumes individual capacity for growth and an ability to claim new opportunities for more successful adaptation, a better fit between the individual and environment.

- *Relatedness*—Relatedness refers to the nature of relationship of individuals to the social elements of the environment such as family and community. Mental illness often jeopardizes relatedness. Individual capacities for relationship may be compromised. The person with mental illness may withdraw from social life, becoming distant and reclusive. In addition, others may stigmatize and pull back from relationships with individuals who behave in a disturbing manner. Neglected relationships become dormant and die. Family members, friends, and professionals can often help to change this destructive pattern, to reestablish a sustaining quality of relatedness.

- *Competence*—Competence is comprised of knowledge, skills, and other individual characteristics required for the individual to adapt. Regardless of disabilities, all people have competencies even though they are not always visible. Competencies are abilities linked to action. They can be discovered and illuminated under conditions in which they are required to complete certain tasks. Latent competencies, unseen and undiscovered skills and aptitudes, have no meaning or relevance to the individual unless called for and expressed in action.

As we will observe in Chapter 4, competency and self-efficacy are complementary concepts. Each contribute to self-esteem, a positive sense of well-being. Ordinarily, people thrive in environments where they are exposed to educational resources and experiences through which they have opportunities to learn and apply their learning.

For people with mental illness, the symptoms of illness often distract and interfere with thought processes and the ability to take advantage of opportunities. It is difficult for an individual to learn when auditory hallucinations (voices) are competing for attention. It is also difficult to achieve and experience competence if one is exceedingly anxious, depressed, or confused. All of these factors tend to turn attention inward causing the individual to withdraw from everyday activities and diminishing the naturally occurring opportunities which, if taken, build competencies.

In addition, the poverty of thought and communication that often accompanies mental illness may be compounded by hospital or residential program conditions where the environment has few stimuli and opportunities. Sometimes an individual's poverty of thought may be worsened by lack of opportunity. It is especially difficult to discover and sustain competencies in institutional conditions where control is a primary objective and patient inactivity and incompetence is understood to be a condition of mental illness. In community settings, the generalist worker can help set the conditions for people to discover and develop competence despite disabling mental illness.

In the previous section, we presented two major perspectives on mental illness. Each directs attention to different features of the problems of illness and what should be done to help. In the next section, we will summarize some of the important similarities and dissimilarities between these perspectives and how they might be understood and synthesized in practice.

A CRITICAL COMPARISON OF TRADITIONAL MEDICAL AND ECOLOGICAL PERSPECTIVES

The medical perspective focuses attention on the identification, classification, and treatment of mental illness symptoms. In order to helpfully intervene, a professional must clearly understand and be able to reliably describe what problems are present in the life of the client. Furthermore, to obtain special assistance and resources, problems must be described and intervention plans must be justified to admissions authorities and funding sources.

Diagnosis provides a legally and socially sanctioned procedure for authorizing involuntary treatment. It names clusters of observable behavior, and it reduces complex descriptions of thought, mood, and behavior to an abbreviated form. Diagnosis is especially important for psychiatrists who need to prescribe with as much precision as possible. The right prescription can successfully lift painful and disturbing symptoms of mental disorders. The wrong prescription or dose can cause harm.

However, that very focus on mental "disorder" means that special care must be taken to include strengths and competencies in the field of view. For people who must adapt to the long-term management of illness, a continuous focus on disability and treatment may result in the gradual adoption of disabling social roles through socialization to institutions and patterns of "patient or client" behavior (Estroff, 1989; Peckoff, 1992). In addition, long-term exposure to institutional hierarchies, schedules, and routines may dampen initiative and self-esteem. In fact, skills and abilities may be ignored or overlooked simply because the institutions and services that comprise the individual's environment may be more oriented to social control.

In contrast, an ecological perspective broadens and deepens a worker's view to include both individual and environment. It draws the worker's attention to competencies and skills of adaptation, as well as problems. It directs the worker to the task of recognizing strengths and giving the client the chance to use and strengthen competencies.

Ecological Change through Community-Building

Eleven years ago, psychiatrist Christian Beels challenged those who care for people with mental illness to adopt what he called "an enabling metaphor for practice," to construct "invisible villages" within which community members could reap the health-inducing benefits of living by the principles of rural, agriculture-based villages. He pointed out that research has shown that people with mental illness who live in agrarian villages tend to live more successfully than their counterparts in urban industrial settings. He suggested that the following principles were key advantages for people with mental illness in these, less complex, environments.

In these villages, people do not have careers that require many role shifts, adjustments, or training. Beels pointed out that first psychotic breaks are observed at times of social change and transition. Villagers are able to identify, visualize, and adopt expected social roles. They are socialized into "very specific and expectable roles" that have ideological integrity. Life is lived in "an atmosphere in which there is agreement among the ways in which work, nature, human relations, and the supernatural are understood" (Beels, 1989, p. 36).

TABLE 2.1	MEDICAL AND ECOLOGICAL PERSPECTIVES COMPARED	
MEDICAL PERSPECTIVE	**ECOLOGICAL PERSPECTIVE**	
Focus on individual	Focus on individual within habitat (family, community, society)	
Identification and management of ecological symptoms of mental disorder	Discovery and improvement of niche	
Attention to elimination, reduction, or management of illness	Attention to adaptiveness (managing one's life and circumstances despite limiting factors)	

Beels cited examples of ways in which these principles can be transformed from invisible village metaphor to community reality. Interestingly, Beels includes the first—and by far the largest—clubhouse, Fountain House, New York, as an example of an "invisible village." Although he incorrectly described Fountain House as a "sheltered employment program," the metaphor and the example (Fountain House) work.

Beels' initial view of the problems of mental illness was an application of a medical perspective—he first examined the symptoms of illness. However, in addition, he considered the context in which those symptoms were experienced and managed. His "invisible village" proposal was an application of the ecological perspective.

In one sense, the idea of village invisibility could suggest the secrecy and separation that accompanies social stigma. However, there is another interpretation. Beels may have been suggesting that, rather than devoting our energies to making society adapt, we should be building active communities (villages) in society, where people with mental illness can be engaged to work and develop their capabilities as community members as long as they choose.

SUMMARY

Two influential, competing perspectives on problems of mental illness have been presented in this chapter. The medical perspective on individual psychiatric disorder, which is rooted in psychiatric tradition, remains the dominant perspective. Because of its historic influence and widespread application, generalist practitioners should be conversant with its uses and those classifications of symptoms that apply to the major disabling mental illnesses. However, because of the limitations of the medical perspective, practitioners should become aware of more inclusive perspectives. Indeed, every model or theory has limitations, which is why the ability to apply many theories is valuable.

The medical perspective has been dominant in the field for most of this century. It directs our attention to the individual and to symptoms or evidence of illness. While it acknowledges social consequences of illness, and the sometimes influential role of environment on individual, the primary concern of a worker employing the medical model is illness—its management, alleviation, and sometimes its cure. Diagnosis is generally viewed as a prerequisite to treatment.

The ecological perspective, drawn from a different scientific tradition in the natural sciences, directs attention simultaneously to individual and environment. Applying an ecological perspective, the key questions for intervention concern the range of physical, psychological, social, economic, and other factors required to create a "goodness of fit."

An ecological perspective sees individual and environment as inseparable. Either or both might be appropriate targets of intervention. This perspective focuses on the ability of the individual to negotiate a place in his or her environment. General systems theory and the systems perspective are attentive to social systems change.

In the next chapter, the ecosystems perspective, a combination of systems and ecological perspectives directs our attention to both individual adaptation and the development and change in clubhouse social environments (Meyer, 1983, p. 1270). The ecosystems perspective guides our choice of the clubhouse model as a holistic, systemic form of intervention.

APPLYING CONCEPTS

1. Define positive and negative symptoms of schizophrenia.
2. Define acute and chronic phases of schizophrenia.
3. What are the symptoms of major depression? How is it distinguished from ordinary depression such as "the blues?"
4. Describe the medical perspective and compare it to an ecological perspective of clients, their problems and situations.
5. Describe examples of the treatment interventions based upon a medical perspective.
6. How does an ecological perspective fit with a community-building approach to clients and their problems?
7. How would you apply an ecological perspective to your student practicum or field placement? What staff and client behavior changes might accompany the application of an ecological perspective to practice in that setting?

Class Projects

Describe the conditions and characteristics of your own ecological niche in words or drawings or both.

Discuss the possible reasons why many people might be uncomfortable, unsettled, or even frightened to be near a person who has a mental illness.

GLOSSARY

Acute or active phase of schizophrenia   characterized by the presence of serious disturbances of thinking and feeling such as hallucinations or delusions, often combined with behavioral changes like social withdrawal.

Assessment   the process and outcome of gathering information relevant to problems or problem situations that may be the object of intervention.

Auditory hallucinations   "voices" that are heard only by the subject.

Delusions   false, unconfirmed ideas.

Diagnostic and Statistical Manual of Mental Disorders (DSM-IV) (American Psychiatric Association)   the diagnostic handbook used throughout the United States.

Goodness of fit   a condition of ecological balance in which the needs of the organism match the available resources of the environment.

Habitat   all the unique conditions of environment in which the organism lives.

Intervention   actions to assist clients and/or conditions that may be problematic.

Medication therapy   use of psychiatric medications to treat the symptoms of mental illness.

Negative symptoms of schizophrenia   characterized by symptoms which reflect a loss or absence of normal functioning; characteristics of mental and behavioral functioning that are absent, but which normally should be present.

Niche   the place in the social terrain occupied by individuals.

Perspective or theoretical perspective   a way of viewing people, situations, or problems that based upon the theory and any research verification of theory that is available.

Positive symptoms of schizophrenia   characterized by symptoms which appear to reflect an excess or distortion of normal functioning; characteristics of mental and behavioral functioning that are present, but which normally should be absent.

Psychopathology   study of diseases of the mind.

Serious mental illness   any primarily mental condition which persists and causes painful symptoms or disability, impairment of functioning, or is associated with significant increased risk of death, pain or disability, or loss of freedom; also known as "persistent and serious mental illness," due to its duration and severity of associated symptoms.

Stigma   a mark by which people with a disease or defect are known, especially with diseases such as AIDS, leprosy, or mental illness.

Symptoms   visible manifestations or signs of illness. In terms of treatment, mental illnesses are known indirectly by their symptoms.

REFERENCES

American Psychiatric Association. (1994). *The diagnostic and statistical manual of mental disorders (4th ed.)*. Washington, DC: Author.

Andreason, N. C., & Olsen, S. (1982). Negative vs positive schizophrenia: Definition and validation. *Archives of General Psychiatry, 39*(July), 789–794.

Anthony, W., Cohen, M., & Farkas, M. (1990). *Psychiatric rehabilitation.* Boston: Center for Psychiatric Rehabilitation.

Bachrach, L. L. (1992). Psychosocial rehabilitation and psychiatry in the care of long-term patients. *American Journal of Psychiatry, 149*(11), 1455–1463.

Beels, C. (Ed.). (1989). *The Invisible Village, 42*(Summer), 27–40.

Bellack, A. S., & Mueser, K. T. (1993). Psychosocial treatment for schizophrenia. *Schizophrenia Bulletin, 19*(2), 317–336.

Estroff, S. E. (1989). Self, identity and subjective experiences of schizophrenia: In search of the subject. *Schizophrenia Bulletin, 15*(2), 189–196.

Germain, C. (1991). *Human behavior in the social environment.* New York: Columbia University Press.

Glickman, M. (1993, August). *A comparison of the Clubhouse and Boston University models.* Paper presented at the Seventh International Seminar on the Clubhouse Model, Worcester, MA.

Katon, W., Von Korff, M., Lin, E., Bush, T., & Ormel, J. (1992). Adequacy and duration of antidepressant treatment in primary care. *Medical Care, 8,* 67–118.

Meyer, C. H. (Ed.). (1983). *Clinical social work in the eco-systems perspective.* New York: Columbia University Press.

Peckoff, J. (1992). Patienthood to personhood. *Psychosocial Rehabilitation Journal, 16*(2), 5–7.

Saleebey, D. (Ed.). (1997). *The strengths perspective in social work practice* (2nd ed.). New York: Longman.

Torrey, E. F. (1990). *Surviving schizophrenia.* New York: Harper and Row.

SYSTEMS PERSPECTIVE AND THE CLUBHOUSE MODEL

MAJOR TOPICS:

SYSTEMS OF LONG-TERM CARE

COMPREHENSIVE PLANNING ILLUMINATES THE FRAMEWORK OF SERVICES NEEDED FOR ADULTS WITH MENTAL ILLNESS

A SYSTEMS PERSPECTIVE ON INTERVENTION

AN ENCOMPASSING PERSPECTIVE AIDS INTERVENTION AT MULTIPLE LEVELS.

THE CLUBHOUSE MODEL: A SOCIAL SYSTEM

SYSTEMS CONCEPTS AND PRINCIPLES ARE EMBODIED IN COMMUNITY-BUILDING ROLES AND INTERACTIONS.

THE CLUBHOUSE MODEL: A SYSTEMS ANALYSIS

POSITIVE SOCIAL SYSTEM FUNCTIONING ENHANCES INDIVIDUAL ADAPTIVENESS.

ENERGY EXCHANGE IN THE CLUBHOUSE MODEL

SOURCES OF ENERGY MUST BE DISCOVERED AND APPLIED IN THE CLUBHOUSE SOCIAL SYSTEM.

CLUBHOUSE RESEARCH

CLUBHOUSE RESEARCH INCLUDES SIMPLE QUANTITATIVE DESCRIPTION AND COMPLEX EXPERIMENTAL COMPARISON.

COMPARATIVE ANALYSIS OF MEDICAL, SYSTEMS, AND ECOLOGICAL PERSPECTIVES

MULTIPLE PERSPECTIVES ENHANCE THE GENERALIST'S FLEXIBILITY AND RESPONSIVENESS.

SUMMARY

I'm proud of my clubhouse and proud of all the work that we do together.

—A CLUBHOUSE MEMBER'S PERSPECTIVE

The clubhouse is a system of people working together to form and maintain a community and to help individual members succeed. Members are free to choose the people and activities with which they'd like to engage, how and when they'd like to become involved.

—A STAFF MEMBER'S PERSPECTIVE

SYSTEMS OF LONG-TERM CARE

As a consequence of deinstitutionalization in the United States during the 1960s, many thousands of mentally ill people were released from state hospitals into communities poorly prepared to meet their needs. New perspectives on community care were required to assist ex-patients in finding their way in the environment beyond the hospital. Some former patients were referred to community mental health centers, where familiar forms of hospital care were available, such as group therapy socialization activities, counseling, and psychiatric care. However, these programs were accessible to a small proportion of those eligible and in need. Most patients were simply discharged with few resources or accommodations for managing in their new environments.

Within the first decade after deinstitutionalization, it became clear to many mental health planners and professionals that services based solely on a medical perspective were inadequate. It also became apparent that mental illness could be treated, but its psychosocial consequences could not be successfully addressed by the use of new psychiatric medications available at the time. In addition to managing their illnesses, people still had to solve problems of daily living, obtaining food, shelter, and other necessities of life outside the institution. Most members of communities outside mental hospitals were not sympathetic, and with few exceptions, mental health centers continued to devote their services primarily to counseling for less disturbed clients. Few referrals of former mental patients were made to mental health centers, and fewer still succeeded in linking them to services.

Community Support Systems for Adults with Mental Illness

The failures of deinstitutionalization were eventually addressed by the National Institute of Mental Health (NIMH) with some innovative staff thinking and planning. The work of this group, the Community Support Project (CSP), eventually succeeded in the development and testing of systems of care. Their planning was not based upon any one model, but drew upon the elements of several different models and approaches in an effort to consider the comprehensive needs of persons with long-term mental illness (Stroul, 1986).

Ten basic components of services were determined to be essential for support networks (Turner & TenHoor, 1978):

- Definition of the population for whom the services are appropriate. (This depends upon an outreach service for those who are isolated and most in need.)
- Assistance in applying for financial, medical, and other resources for which clients are eligible and to which they are entitled.
- Crisis stabilization services in the least restrictive setting. (When outpatient services cannot meet a client's treatment needs, hospitalization should be an available option.)
- Provision of psychosocial rehabilitation services aimed at sustaining functional capacities and slowing the rate of deterioration. These services include but are not limited to the following:
  - Goal-oriented rehabilitation evaluation.
  - Training in community living skills.
  - Opportunities to improve employability.
  - Appropriate housing suited to a patient's condition.
  - Opportunities to develop social skills, interests, and leisure activities that provide a sense of participation and worth.
  - Continuity of care service.
  - Medical and mental health care.
  - Backup support to families, friends, and community members.
- Involvement of community members in the planning of support programs and in selected aspects of service delivery, such as helping to make jobs available.
- Establishment of procedures and mechanisms that protect the legal rights of individuals with mental illness, both in mental hospitals and in the community.
- Provision of case management that can help clients make efficient use of available services.

A SYSTEMS PERSPECTIVE ON INTERVENTION

Planners and service providers developed a holistic way of understanding and acting to address problems and utilize opportunities. While the Community Support Project (CSP) staff and their colleagues did not base their work on a specific theory, their methods and community support approaches exemplified assumptions and principles derived from general systems theory (von Bertalanffy, 1968). That method of holistic viewing, which we refer to as a *systems perspective*, was relevant to their planning in the 1970s and 1980s. It is still relevant to the work of planners and practitioners in mental health, as well as other fields of social service.

The foundation of this perspective is based upon the assumptions that people are complex biological systems and that they live their lives within and in relation to larger social systems, including those comprised of individuals, families, groups, organizations, and communities. This field of psychological and social relations is the social environment where symptoms of mental illness are expressed and identified as problematic. From a systems perspective, this is also the arena where mental illness is treated and managed, where adaptation takes place, and where changes in environment can sustain productive and satisfying lives.

Social System Defined

A social system can be defined as: (1) a group of interrelated individuals, (2) enacting social roles together, (3) for shared purposes, and (4) over an extended period of time. A family that lives and works together is a social system. A business is a social system. A community of any size is also a social system. The parts or units of these social systems are real and interrelated, although they are generally not marked in any obvious way. They are nested inside each other like Russian dolls. For instance, a married couple is a system within a family, within a community.

Social systems are open systems, that is they are interdependent with their larger environment. Their primary elements—social roles and role interactions—are often in conflict and subject to change. Open systems, capable of self-determination through their own processes, can adapt and must adapt continuously to survive. The system that is the focus of attention at any given time is called the focal or subject system. For example, the focal system of this text is the clubhouse model.

The systems perspective assumes that all systems have comparable components and features regardless of the focal system under analysis, from the simplest dyad (two persons) to the most complex (societies). According to systems theory, the structural and interactional features of these small social systems are comparable to those of larger and more complex organizations and communities.

A systems perspective has two characteristic features that enable its application in combination with many different theories. First, it encompasses the whole of complex social entities and all their constituent parts. Its breadth and inclusivity allows application in combination with a variety of other theories and theoretical perspectives. Second, although some would argue that values are expressed in any theory, model, or perspective, the systems perspective is intended to be value neutral. Therefore, in theory, it can be applied with other perspectives and theories that do bear value assumptions. Although a systems perspective does not prescribe interventions, it can help the generalist worker assess appropriate targets for change activities, as well as understand the nature of those changes and the timing and organization of interventions.

Any focal system is encompassed by a suprasystem, that part of the social environment outside the focal system that influences it and has subsystems within it, component systems that are influenced by the focal system. A number of additional system properties add detail to this definition of a social system.

Entropy and Negentropy

Entropy and *negentropy* refer to the physics of systems organization, the presence, movement, and transformation of various forces within the system. All open systems tend to run down over time, to experience what is termed *entropy.* This tendency is opposed by another countertendency called *negentropy.* Change and conflict are assumed to be natural and normal features of social systems life. The student needs to understand how these forces work and their relation to community-building in particular situations.

A systems perspective drawn from theory helps us to frame problems of mental illness and intervention approaches in the broadest, most inclusive terms. Such a perspective applied to the clubhouse model helps us to see the whole of the systemic model as well as individual parts. With such a vision, we are able to understand more completely how people interact in clubhouse community-building.

THE CLUBHOUSE MODEL: A SOCIAL SYSTEM

This widely respected model of community support was developed at Fountain House during the 1950s and 1960s (Lamb, 1994). Based upon its early successes and relevance to problems of people with mental illness living in community settings, Fountain House received a grant from the National Institute of Mental Health in 1976, to begin a national training program. The program goal was to replicate clubhouse philosophy, approach, and methodology elsewhere in the United States. In fact, visitors and trainees came from throughout the world. Now more than 180 clubhouses operate in the United States, and more than 60 clubs have opened in foreign countries. Once called the Fountain House model because of its origins, this place-based intervention approach is now called the clubhouse model.

The heart of the clubhouse model is the belief, shared by members and staff, that even the most disabled members can contribute meaningfully. Ex-patients join a clubhouse to become *members* of a community (not clients or patients). Each clubhouse is intended to offer supportive relationships and opportunities and exert continuing efforts to include members in every aspect of community life and work, to help members assume contributing roles. To attain these objectives, respect and a collaborative spirit are fostered among members and staff with a focus on strengths and competencies, rather than illness. Shared purpose is the cornerstone of clubhouse community-building. This, combined with a variety of opportunities for work, education, and social relationships, addresses the social isolation often associated with long-term mental illness.

A Predictable Schedule Based upon Responsibilities

A clubhouse provides a place for people with mental illness to go. It is not a treatment program or residence. Members initially come to a clubhouse because they are attracted to its opportunities, a daily structure of work and activities, and the possibility of employment in the larger community. Members generally begin their days by assembling in a work unit meeting where the work of the day is discussed. Staff and members outline the tasks of the day, divide responsibilities among those present (see Chapter 4), and make plans to reach out to those who may be absent due to hospitalization or other reasons. Meetings are led by members or staff or both. They bring everyone together, not around the symptoms of illness but around tasks and information to be shared. Levels of community activity predictably vary among the members and staff present. According to clubhouse values and explicit standards (see Appendices), participation is encouraged but never required or enforced. Coercion has no place in the clubhouse model.

Every workday members and staff go to work on a variety of projects until approximately noon, when they break for lunch with others. A noon meal is prepared, served, and shared among members and staff. After lunch, work units resume their activities for the afternoon. Some members may go to employment placements outside the clubhouse or to school. Occasionally, some may have special projects or may simply leave. At the end of the day most depart for home, although some may stay at the clubhouse to attend evening recreational activities and classes.

Opportunities to Match Interests and Capabilities

Many kinds of work are necessary to the operation of a clubhouse. Members and staff participate in work units that prepare and serve meals, produce newspapers, provide maintenance and cleaning for the clubhouse, operate banking services, reach out to isolated members, and perform many other functions. They work together to plan, accomplish, and evaluate each of these activities.

The clubhouse also provides means for overcoming barriers that prevent people with mental illness from taking advantage of opportunities and resources available in society. Transitional employment agreements between clubhouses and local employers enable members to obtain paid jobs with employers in the community outside the clubhouse (described in-depth in Chapter 5). In addition, the clubhouse helps members gain admission to GED programs, colleges, and universities and provides tutoring and other forms of support to help them attain their goals. Clubhouses operate apartments and residential care facilities and help members secure independent housing. Members also receive assistance to obtain income and medical entitlements, as well as legal and psychiatric services. Although members are encouraged and

Not Always a Patient

Marti had worked as a short order cook before her illness, but after five years of going in and out of hospitals and halfway houses, she had lost her self-confidence and interest in returning to work. After her last hospitalization, her hospital social worker suggested that she visit the clubhouse, and if she liked what she saw, she might take an apartment nearby. She might look into becoming a member. She did.

As it happened, she visited the clubhouse at 11:00 A.M. The clubhouse was at a peak of activity as all the members of the food service unit were doing the last of the preparation details: putting out knives and forks, placing a napkin under each place setting, putting flowers into vases at each table, opening the windows for more ventilation, arranging water glasses, and fixing coffee.

She felt very much an "outsider" and very shy. Someone asked if she could get the potatoes ready. Of course she could. Without saying a word, she picked up a peeler from the counter and went to work. The clubhouse was expecting about 30 people for lunch, and the food had to be served very close to noon. Others joined her to help get the job done.

As she watched and listened to everyone working together, Marti began to understand the idea of membership. One older woman offered to show her how to sign up for a medication review at the mental health center. Several people around her were friendly and gave her lots of encouragement. She knew many of the people here from the hospital, but everyone was dressed in their own casual clothes, including staff. The furnishings of the clubhouse were comfortable, colorful, and attractive, quite unlike the institutional surroundings of the hospital. Remarkably, staff and members were working together side-by-side.

helped to manage disruptive symptoms of illness, clubhouse communities work directly to create structures of opportunities that elicit and develop member strengths and competencies and indirectly to help manage symptoms of illness.

A Community-Building Framework

The clubhouse model, once described as a "social invention", embodies the values and the intent of the concept of community support for people with mental illness (Beard, Propst, & Malamud, 1982). Instead of simply providing services, the clubhouse model is committed to engaging members in community-building roles. The model was founded on the assumption that adults disabled by mental illness can live productive and satisfying lives despite disabling symptoms. It provides a framework for the continuous development of new and noncoerced roles for members.

THE CLUBHOUSE MODEL: A SYSTEMS ANALYSIS

From the beginning, clubhouse model development was based on the assumption that mental illness is pervasive and may have a tendency to remit and recur over years, affecting all aspects of an individual's life. Therefore, the clubhouse model includes a wide variety of services and opportunities for members if members wish to continue their affiliation. For purposes of analysis, it is important to be aware of the difference between the clubhouse model and individual clubhouses. The model provides a broad working plan of what is to be embodied in individual clubs or clubhouses.

When we speak of the clubhouse model, we are describing role structures and interactions that are found in most but may be absent in some individual clubhouses. It is assumed that clubhouses that meet or exceed the Standards for Clubhouses provide more consistent opportunities for their members.

Though the clubhouse model developed without the benefit of formal theory, it can be thought of as a fully elaborated expression of the systems model. It encompasses all the systems principles previously described: as well as organization, mutual causality, constancy, spatiality, and boundary. It is a holistic design that addresses the problems of illness/disability as they affect an individual's life and functioning in the social environment. As social systems, clubs exist in relation to larger suprasystems and smaller, component subsystems.

Organization

The clubhouse social system is comprised of and organized by *roles* and *role interactions*. Reporting lines and alignment of responsibilities between units are formalized in that certain aspects of the work are assigned to certain individuals and groups, but assignments are flexible as well, so that peoples' energies and strengths can be utilized effectively. No part of the structure is exclusively owned by either members or staff.

The social system is hierarchical in that the system parts occupy higher or lower positions in relation to the overall community-building mission. The system is subordinate to the suprasystem, and subsystems are subordinate to the system. Each nested component system is subject to what is called the *principle of hierarchical constraints*. That is, each system level is constrained to a considerable extent by material and human resources, the extent of their

44

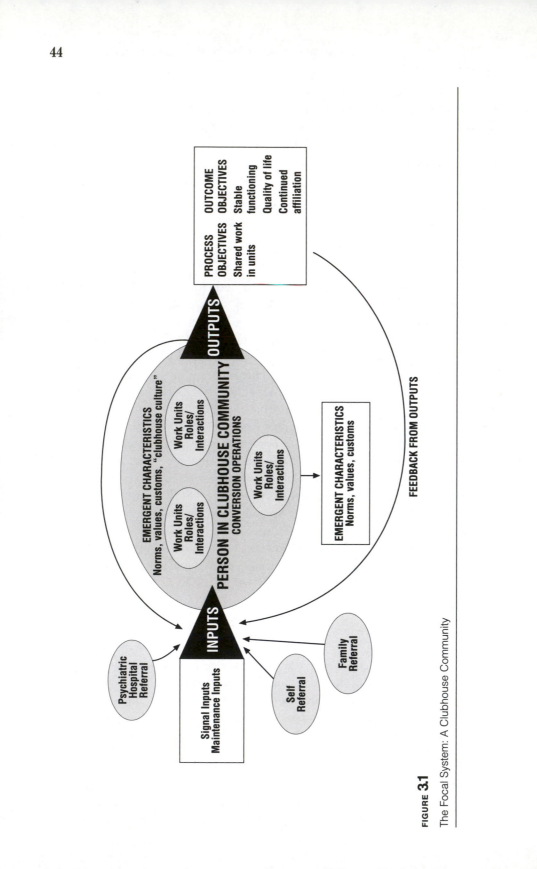

FIGURE 3.1

The Focal System: A Clubhouse Community

operations and activities, and their operating rules by the more inclusive higher system levels. This constraint is not absolute, but it does function to limit the behavioral choices available to participants.

Mutual Causality

Elements of the clubhouse are systemically related to each other in significant ways—staff and members are agents of change which is multidirectional. Each individual and group in a clubhouse must, therefore, work to keep the goals and objectives of serving members at the forefront. The enthusiasm of even one worker for getting the task done is infectious and may be mirrored in the attitudes and behaviors of others.

Constancy

The clubhouse is designed to be a dependable constant in the lives of its members, despite differences and conflict. Although individuals may come and go and relationships begin and end, the social system remains intact as long as requirements for systems maintenance are in effect. In fact, lifetime membership in the clubhouse is guaranteed to its members. They may choose to be involved in and use the clubhouse regardless of their mental status or life situation.

Spatiality

A clubhouse, as social system, is more than an idea, a philosophy, or plan. It is a group of people comprised of individuals who physically occupy space. All the staff, members, and administrators are parts of the system.

Boundaries and Boundary Indicators

The clubhouse social system is a formal organization. It has boundaries which define and separate it from the suprasystem and subsystems. System boundaries are maintained through sanctioned intake procedures, personnel hiring policies, criteria for admission, and other factors that insure the separation of different units of the system. Boundaries are known by *indicators.*

Most clubs have several different kinds of boundary indicators that both indicate the boundaries of the clubhouse as well as provide forms of identification for individual staff and members. Typically clubs are named by the people associated with them. Clubhouse names are posted over outside doors. They are announced when the phones are answered. They are printed on stationery and even on T-shirts. In contrast to hospital, mental health center, or other institutional affiliations, clubhouse affiliation is a source of individual pride and identification for most members and staff.

ENERGY EXCHANGE IN THE CLUBHOUSE MODEL

Social systems, like the human beings who comprise them, have stores of energy that are mobilized and expressed in the shared purpose and work of the system. The continued presence and use of energy is essential to the ongoing functioning of the system. This is an especially useful notion with regard to the clubhouse model. People with mental illness often face extraordinary discouragement, despair, and apathy. For them to reclaim mental health, the inertia of mental illness must be overcome.

Entropy

If a given clubhouse is to survive as a social system, it must find ways to counter the tendency of any social system to experience entropy, to run down or reduce to its constituent parts. Several factors may add to this natural tendency toward entropy:

- *Shortage of staff*—Staff lead the work of the clubhouse, participate themselves, and encourage others to help. If they are not present in adequate numbers, actively leading the work, entropy will become apparent in the slowing of work and the lack of engagement with members. Under this condition, the system has less overall energy.
- *Loss of or diminished sense of ownership*—In the United States, about 70 percent of clubhouses are connected with mental health centers. In this setting, clubs must often compete with other services for facilities and resources. Facilities suited for therapy or educational classes are often not suited to group cooking, composing and publishing newsletters, or the many other work activities of a clubhouse. Factors that might contribute positively to an institutional setting detract from members' sense of ownership and involvement in the shared work and purpose of community-building.
- *Symptoms of serious mental illness*—Schizophrenia and major depression tend to drain energy and motivation. This, in turn, may contribute to inactivity and the winding down of clubhouse work. Indeed, applying a systems perspective the symptoms of mental illness are experienced and may be observed and experienced in the behavior of staff (Luske, 1990).
- *Staff and member initiative and strong leadership* are major factors in overcoming entropy in the clubhouse social system and replacing it with the countertendency, *negentropy*.

Negentropy

Examples of activities that contribute to negentropy in the social system of the clubhouse community include:

- *Implementing the values of wanting, needing, and expecting members,* clarifying the shared purposes of the community regularly in board meetings, community meetings, and unit meetings. Discussing problems and solutions in light of clubhouse philosophy and taking combined action helps insure that the clubhouse remains a value-driven community.

- *Developing an active transitional employment program* where members have real opportunities at competitive jobs. To attain work objectives, members must have adequate placements and other resources, including appropriate space and other tools for the job. They need guidance and support from staff and other members who can help sustain their interest and support their accomplishments.
- *Insuring that there is no institutionalized secrecy within the clubhouse* that (with the exception of medical information and confidential information provided by outside agencies and organizations) nothing within the club is unknown or unavailable to any member. Individual service plans or contracts are completely open for discussion with members. In fact, members are seen as essential for the formulation of their own plans.
- *Making sure that member accomplishments are recognized* however small or large, that occasions are frequently created for the celebration of individual talents and community achievements.
- *Making sure that staff receive appropriate recognition, support, compensation, and consultation* so that they continue to grow in their work.

Inputs

Inputs, which come into the system from outside its boundaries, include:

- *Signal inputs* that initiate or signal the work of the system. They may include people, ideas, and demands for work. Mental health planners provide input to systems for adults with mental illness through performance contracts. Parents provide input for effective programs and positive program activities through public hearings. Ex-patients or clients disabled by mental illness provide input to clubhouse communities when they apply for membership.
- *Maintenance inputs* that are necessary for the conversion of signal inputs into system outputs. In a clubhouse, these include trained staff, other members, and all the resources brought to bear on the conversion of signal inputs into outputs.

Outputs

Outputs are produced by the system and returned to the suprasystem. The clubhouse community is in continuous interaction with its suprasystem. It helps people discover and maximize their own skills and coping abilities. It helps them work competitively in transitional employment placements, find housing to suit their finances, and maintain friendships with those who understand and share the difficulties of mental illness.

Outputs include the following:

- *Task outputs*—signal inputs that have been changed through conversion operations; the products or outcomes of conversion operations in a social system.
- *Maintenance outputs*—maintenance inputs that have been changed through conversion operations. Maintenance outputs include trained and experienced staff, records of activity, clients armed with increased resources, and so forth. Staff and members gain experience and training and are themselves changed by the operation of the clubhouse system.

48

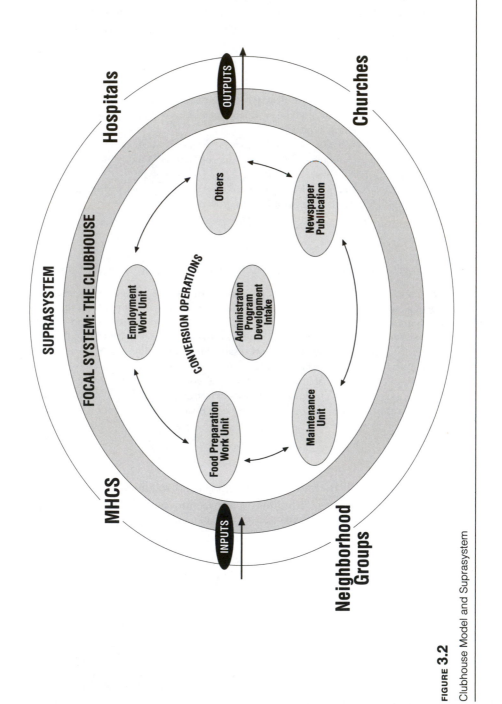

FIGURE **3.2**

Clubhouse Model and Suprasystem

Feedback

Feedback is the result of comparing intended and actual output, returning the information in a feedback loop. Such feedback is often provided to members and staff in community meetings, newsletter articles, and annual reports.

Emergent Characteristics

Emergent characteristics are system characteristics that emerge from the enactment of systems roles around shared objectives. Examples include customs and traditions and culture and social climate, each of which is so important in maintaining the vitality of the community. Some of these emergent characteristics in the clubhouse model include:

- *Times for doing certain activities*—The workday is generally from 9 to 5 or similar full-time hours. During these times, staff and members, who wish and are able to help, work in groups called work units. Play or recreational times are scheduled for evenings and weekends. The structure is intended to be a natural structure and reflect the normal divisions of time among workers elsewhere.
- *Language that is different from mental health or rehabilitation language*— Transitional employment, member, and work-ordered day are all terms associated more or less exclusively with the clubhouse model and the worldwide clubhouse movement. The language of hospital and clinic is avoided.
- *Typical ways of working together*—Staff serve as leaders and organizers, but their leadership is shared with members whenever possible. Naturally the focus of change, the object of the given work task, is the work itself not the member's symptoms or behaviors. Thus, the working objective is outside the workers. This enables both staff and members to share the benefits of working and achieving the work objectives together.
- *Shared views of clubhouse space*—There are no staff only spaces in the clubhouse. Labor is divided for purposes of organization and convenience. Space is divided into work areas for different purposes. Every effort is made to insure that members and staff are part of the working team.
- *Clear, well-defined boundaries*—The clubhouse, as a community system, is intended to provide many of those social supports, opportunities, and forms of assistance that members have often been unable to access or have been simply unavailable to them elsewhere. The clubhouse must necessarily be well-bounded. Therefore, the social system has many clear boundary indicators—clubhouse name, a sign, a separate mailbox, space allocated only to clubhouse activities, and so forth. Clear boundaries are particularly important for members whose illness may contribute to feelings of confusion and isolation.
- *Steady state*—The continuous goal of any social system including a clubhouse community is to achieve a steady state, where the inputs to the system equal the outputs. A steady state is a tentative and temporary condition of dynamic equilibrium that requires regular attention and adjustment to changing conditions.

The systems principle of *isomorphism* tells us that all living systems share similarities of form or structure with all other living systems. Because of these similarities in form and structure, all the previously discussed system principles and concepts applied to understand the structure and functioning of a clubhouse can be applied to other social systems such as families and social agencies.

The clubhouse model is an idealized, conceptualized vision. Changes in funding, mental health policies at multiple levels, and other factors influence the particular goals and objectives of a given clubhouse. These are external, environmental realities within which individual clubhouses and all other social welfare programs and agencies exist and grow. Like other organizations and communities, clubs adapt to their environments through internally directed change, as well as change in their suprasystems.

Clubhouse research was built into the work of Fountain House more than two decades ago (Malamud, 1985). Although research at multiple levels has long been viewed as important to the clubs and the clubhouse movement, the emergence of managed care and the privatized business of mental health services has increased pressures for clubhouse staff and members to demonstrate the efficacy of the model.

CLUBHOUSE RESEARCH

Definition and Description

Most clubhouses have some kind of descriptive research as a part of what members and staff do together. Research work units track the demographic characteristics of members, numbers of active and inactive members, and many other statistics that help describe the clubhouse community and its participants. Many also track statistics on employment outcomes, hospitalizations, and other status changes. Their results are published in annual reports, newsletters, and sometimes in journals (Wilkinson, 1992). Clubhouses have been defined and described through international surveys (Macias et al., 1999).

University Collaboration

Many clubhouses throughout the world have conducted evaluations or collaborated in evaluation. For example, a study done by the Department of Psychology at Curtin University in Australia examined hospitalization frequency and duration, quality of life measures, costs of services, and overall use of mental health services among members at Lorikeet Clubhouse (membership of 206). The study reported that clubhouse member hospital admission rates reportedly dropped by 46 percent and the average length of stay decreased by 31 percent after they joined the club. Regular attendance at the clubhouse meant that rehabilitation services use increased by 32 percent. However, psychiatric consultations were reduced by 21 percent (Bishop & Finney, 1996). Such data, although not offering conclusive evidence that the clubhouse model works, does more fully describe the clubhouse model and contribute to a growing body of shared research.

Program Comparison

Experimental comparison of the clubhouse made with other approaches to psychosocial rehabilitation has been limited. However, an ambitious comparative study sponsored by the Substance Abuse and Mental Health Services Administration is currently being conducted by Fountain House, at Genesis Club in Worcester, Massachusetts. The study is comparing a range of work, hospitalization, and other variables obtained from subjects randomly assigned either to the Program for Assertive Community Treatment (P.A.C.T.) model services or to clubhouse services. More studies of this kind can be expected in the future as clubhouses seek to more fully understand and explain the model.

In 1996, to accelerate and improve clubhouse research, Fountain House developed a list of member and clubhouse variables. These lists provided a basis for the development of a computer software program designed to provide ongoing measurement of factors related to clubhouse members and staff, as well as the clubhouse as a whole. The considerable expense of the software project has slowed its progress; however, the work continues with the help of staff and members at Fountain House and affiliated clubhouses in the ICCD. The software developers have proceeded carefully to limit access and provide adequate information safeguards with which members and staff are comfortable. Once completed, Fountain House has offered to share the software with other clubhouses in the international clubhouse community.

Research has not been universally embraced in clubhouses. There is widespread concern about the violation of members' rights, the possible dissemination and use of personal information concerning mental illness. Some believe that information mishandled by researchers could cause harm to members. For some, research data collection reminds them of onerous hospital recording requirements. Consequently the ethics of research are actively discussed and debated at regional meetings of clubhouse coalitions and worldwide seminars.

COMPARATIVE ANALYSIS OF MEDICAL, SYSTEMS, AND ECOLOGICAL PERSPECTIVES

Our analyses began in Chapter 2 with the application of medical and ecological perspectives to the problems of people with mental illness. In Chapter 3, we have applied a systems perspective to the clubhouse model, a model using a community-building approach.

TABLE 3.1	MULTIPLE PERSPECTIVES		
Perspective	**Medical**	**Ecological**	**Systems**
Focus	Individual mental disorder and symptoms	Individual in relation to environment	Focal system (i.e., clubhouse) and between other social systems
Goal	To minimize pathology	Productive and satisfying niche for individual	Steady state of system
Method	Adequate and appropriate medical management of symptoms	Adaptive individual behavior and environmental change	Openness and feedback as keys to viability of system
Organization	Linear	Circular	Hierarchical

SUMMARY

The deinstitutionalization of adults with mental illness began with little planning or coordination of care. In the 1970s, the Community Support Project of the National Institute of Mental Health began to plan the way that services were conceptualized and provided. Community support networks were proposed to meet the need for services and link the components for the benefit of eligible people with serious mental illness. Although it had few resources, the CSP provoked systems thinking. The clubhouse model was consistent with this thinking and planning.

As we have seen, the clubhouse model has the defining properties of a social system: (1) organization, (2) mutual causality, (3) constancy, (4) spatiality, and (5) boundary. The clubhouse social system is a community; therefore, there is an unusual blending of signal and maintenance inputs. The work (conversion operations) are planned and carried out by staff and members working together. Although staff do not generate signal inputs, they do generate maintenance inputs. Members generate both. Together staff and members work to build and maintain a clubhouse community.

Working together both groups are engaged in shaping the processes and outcomes of the clubhouse social system, and in the process, the system produces some unique emergent characteristics that gives the clubhouse its unique identity and character. A systems perspective permits us to simultaneously account for the whole system and its constituent parts. Each additional perspective adds depth and breadth to understanding the problems of people with mental illness and what can be done to help.

APPLYING CONCEPTS

1. What major federal policy initiative stimulated the development of systems thinking and community support systems for adults with mental illness?
2. Define a social system and its primary properties and elements of organization.
3. What does *value neutral* mean when used to describe systems theory?
4. How does one identify the boundaries of a social system?
5. Describe conversion operations in a clubhouse and give some examples.
6. Compare and contrast a clubhouse and a clubhouse model program for adults with mental illness.
7. How does the clubhouse model demonstrate properties of a social system?
8. How can multiple generalist practice perspectives be combined in the service of people with mental illness?
9. Conduct a systems analysis of your student practicum or field placement by applying the properties of social systems. What evidence of entropy do you find in the system? What can be done to induce negentropy?

Class Projects

Construct an interactive, physical model of a social system at group, organization, or community levels. Point out boundaries and boundary indicators. Describe the roles and interactions of the constituent system elements. Use inexpensive, throwaway materials such as coat hangers, string, wood blocks, plastic cups, and so forth.

Identify factors that contribute to *negentropy* in a selected focal system of which you are a member or have special knowledge, that is, a church or group or sports team. Discuss what you as a generalist worker could do if you were asked to increase or enhance the forces of negentropy in the selected social system.

GLOSSARY

Case management   a method of working with individuals, organizations, and communities to help people with mental illness, as well as other disabilities, meet their basic needs and improve their quality of life.

Community-building   a method of intervention intended to engage the competencies of community members rather than target their symptoms and disabilities. Community-building is the primary approach employed by the clubhouse model.

Conversion operations   those system activities that change inputs into outputs.

Entropy   refers to the tendency of systems to lose energy, run down, and decompose to basic elements.

Feedback   the process whereby output information is returned, enabling system modifications to more efficiently and effectively attain planned outputs.

Focal system   the social system of primary attention or concern.

Inputs   all individual and group elements that enter social systems including people, their competencies and difficulties, and other resources used to create changes, converting inputs into outputs.

Negentropy   the countertendency or force that may be stimulated by adding resources, order, energy, and momentum to the social system.

Outputs   planned objectives and goals as well as actual outcomes of system conversion activities.

Role interactions   related behaviors among members of any social system.

Social system   a group of interrelated individuals enacting social roles together for shared purposes over an extended period of time.

Social system properties   characteristic features of any social system that include organization, mutual causality, constancy, spatiality, and boundary.

Steady state   the ongoing objective of any social system seeking to maintain its viability in spite of conflict and change from within and without the system.

Suprasystem   that part of the social environment that is outside the boundaries of the focal system but influences it.

REFERENCES

Beard, J., Propst, R. N., & Malamud, T. J. (1982). The Fountain House model of psychiatric rehabilitation. *Psychosocial Rehabilitation Journal, 5*(1), 47–53.

Bishop, B., & Finney, H. (1996). *Lorikeet Clubhouse Evaluation* (Program Evaluation). South Australia: South Australia Health Commission and University of South Australia, Psychology Department.

Lamb, H. R. (1994). A century and a half of psychiatric rehabilitation. *Hospital and Community Psychiatry, 45*(10), 1015–1020.

Luske, B. (1990). *Mirrors of madness: Patrolling the psychic border.* New York: Aldine De Gruyter.

Macias, C., Jackson, R., Schroeder, C., & Wang, Q. (1999). What is a clubhouse? Report on the ICCD 1996 survey of USA clubhouses. *Community Mental Health Journal,* 35(2), 181–190.

Malamud. T. J. (1985). Community adjustment: Evaluation of the Clubhouse Model for psychiatric rehabilitation. *Rehab Brief: Bringing Research into Effective Focus,* 9(2), 1–4.

Stroul, B. (1986). *Models of community support services: Approaches to helping persons with long-term mental illness.* Boston: Boston University, Center for Psychiatric Rehabilitation.

Turner, J. C., & TenHoor, W. J. (1978). The NIMH community support program: Pilot approach to a needed social reform. *Schizophrenia Bulletin,* 4(3), 319–341.

von Bertalanffy, L. (1968). *General system theory.* New York: George Braziller.

Wilkinson, W. H. (1992). New Day, Inc., of Spartenberg: Hospitalization Study. *Psychosocial Rehabilitation Journal,* 16(2), 163–168.

ROLES, SELF-EFFICACY, AND THE WORK-ORDERED DAY

MAJOR TOPICS:

VALUING WORK

DAILY WORK PROVIDES FUNDAMENTAL SOURCES OF IDENTITY AND BELIEFS ABOUT AN INDIVIDUAL'S COMPETENCY AND WORTH.

ROLE THEORY AND THE WORK-ORDERED DAY

VIEWED THROUGH THE LENS OF ROLE THEORY, THE WORK-ORDERED DAY IS A STRUCTURE OF INTERLOCKING, CONSTRUCTED SOCIAL ROLES.

SELF-EFFICACY THEORY AND ROLE CHARACTERISTICS

SELF-EFFICACY THEORY ENABLES US TO UNDERSTAND AND ENSURE THE PRESENCE OF EFFICACIOUS ROLE CHARACTERISTICS.

COMMUNITY ROLES

WORK ROLES IN THE CLUBHOUSE COMMUNITY GIVE MEMBERS OPPORTUNITIES TO CONTRIBUTE, LEARN, AND APPLY THEIR ABILITIES.

EMPOWERMENT

EMPOWERMENT RESULTS FROM MEMBERS CONTINUOUS ENGAGEMENT IN ACTIVE CLUBHOUSE COMMUNITY ROLES BASED UPON SHARED PURPOSE AND COLLABORATIVE WORK.

WORK AND RELATIONSHIPS

FRIENDSHIPS DEVELOP NATURALLY AS PEOPLE WORK TOGETHER.

SUSTAINING AND MAINTAINING THE WORK-ORDERED DAY

THE WORK-ORDERED DAY REQUIRES THE CONTINUOUS ATTENTION OF STAFF AND MEMBERS TO KEEP IT STRONG AND EFFECTIVE.

SUMMARY

I cover the phones in my unit and greet visitors. Being needed to help in the unit gives me a reason to get up and get going in the morning.

—A CLUBHOUSE MEMBER'S PERSPECTIVE

Mental illness is no reason for not being productive . . . maybe 95% of a person has nothing to do with mental illness.

—A STAFF MEMBER'S PERSPECTIVE

VALUING WORK

While clinical treatment or therapeutic programs focus on the provision of therapy services, clubhouse model replications focus on work and working together in various ways to build clubhouse communities. Activities of community-building join staff and members in work guided by shared purpose.

Chapter 4 will examine a central theme of the clubhouse model—the work-ordered day. This term, used by members and staff, describes a complex structure of shared, meaningful work roles that provide members with opportunities to build or rebuild positive perceptions of self-efficacy. Elements of role and self-efficacy theories are applied to explain and validate the practice methods of the clubhouse model. In addition, this chapter will explain how staff and member roles are discovered and developed and how these roles and the interactions of these roles create and sustain the conditions for changed self-perception, behavior, and identity.

Work is much more than a way to make a living. It is what we do and how we organize our lives to do it. The enactment of work roles provides a fundamental source of our adult identity. For example, if our work requires us to be at the school, factory, or office by a given hour, we organize our mornings to fit this requirement. We allocate time for the activities of dressing, having breakfast, and getting to work. Even when this schedule might seem a tyranny in our lives, our work organizes and directs our energy into personally and socially valued channels. Regardless of its source or character, our daily work exerts a constant influence on our thoughts, behaviors, and feelings.

Identity, Competency, and Worth

In our society, and in many others, the daily work that people do provides fundamental sources of identity and beliefs about individual competency and worth. According to a poll of laborers conducted in 1964, 80 percent claimed that they would continue working even if they were able to maintain their current standard of living without a job (Williams, 1970). Our self-concept, who we are and what we think about ourselves, is continuously reaffirmed in our work. When people first meet, what sort of work they do and where they work are questions that begin the customary exploration of shared interests and identifications. By stating our work connection, we assert who we are as individuals and as social beings. For example, I am a student, I am a salesperson, I am a truck driver, and so forth.

- *Work produces outcomes for self-evaluation.* It gives us opportunities to set goals, apply our skills, and evaluate our attainments. It provides measures of productivity and self-worth by which we judge ourselves and others judge us. Successful work produces planned results and a sense of satisfaction and accomplishment in the worker. The pride of accomplishment accompanies a job well done.
- *Work structures time and tasks.* Whatever the source or the setting for work, the responsibilities we assume require us to organize ourselves to carry out tasks according to certain expected time frames. Work requires the mobilization of mental and physical energy. No matter what the objective of our work might be, we have to schedule our time according to shifting demands. Each task requires organization of energy and time with reference to other tasks.
- *Work provides socially acceptable channels for the direction of aggression and other forms of energy.* Our work invites us to seize opportunities, grapple with problems, take charge, and tackle difficult situations. Work may be put off, postponed, or avoided, but its existence is joined to expectations. A job requires action, and it requires us to change things. Our interest and enthusiasm for tasks is most powerfully mobilized when the work to be done appears manageable, is shared with others, and is tied to valued outcomes.
- *Work provides roles that contribute to personal identity and social status.* Who we are is affirmed and repeatedly confirmed in the work responsibilities we assume and carry out. Work roles provide a social setting and a script for individuals to express themselves in their own way. Learning and practicing work roles may involve a certain amount of acting, as children do when they dress up and play at being adults. People tend to become what they play at being. Roles change both the action and the actor.
- *Work roles determine a person's social status.* Where people fit into society and how they are expected to relate to others is shaped by the roles they play. Social status is often bound to work roles—student, housekeeper, banker, artist, or truck driver.
- *Work roles build natural social ties.* People routinely make friends and maintain social connections in work settings. They hold meetings, conduct conferences, develop collaborations, and build teams. Work is performed within normative structures of non-intimate, working relationships that are friendly and supportive.

If professionals "are to assume a major responsibility for designing environments and experiences for the prevention of illness and for the maintenance and restoration of health, they need to achieve a more sophisticated understanding of *doing* (Fidler & Fidler, 1978, p. 305). The belief that individuals with mental illness can take action for themselves and others is a pervasive, fundamental assumption of the clubhouse model.

John Beard, director of Fountain House through its formative years, asserted that work, combined with the opportunity to aspire to and achieve gainful employment, is a deeply generative and regenerative force in the life of every human being (Beard, Propst, & Malamud, 1982). Even if work is difficult or unpleasant or even dangerous, it is ours.

Mental Illness and Being Out of Work

To be out of work or unemployed for months or years is far more disabling than being without income. Persistent unemployment erodes self-esteem and self-confidence. When a person is unemployed for extended periods, they are challenged not only to find alternative ways to make a living but to find new meanings, new identifications, and structured ways to spend their days in order to feel that they have social relevance.

Mental illness commonly disrupts daily life and work. It interferes with thinking and feeling and behaving. It tends to strip individuals of their social roles and status and leave them with a sense of emptiness and disinterest in daily activities. For adults with mental illness, the problems of dealing with symptoms and the problems of daily living are compounded by a loss of a normal work role identification.

These individuals may acquire patient or client identifications that can become self-limiting secondary disabilities, learned and confirmed through years of interaction with hospitals, halfway houses, treatment programs, and social services providers (Estroff, 1989; Jimenez, 1988). Repeated enactment of patient behaviors in such settings may grow into a negative social status. Such negative consequences of treatment are referred to as *iatrogenic* effects or treatment or rehabilitation. Social workers and human services professionals are challenged to address both the disabling primary conditions of mental illness and the psychosocial consequences or iatrogenic effects of continuous patienthood or clienthood in treatment.

The work-ordered day of the clubhouse model is designed to address the need to discover abilities and reclaim positive social identifications. The cornerstone of the clubhouse model is the work-ordered day. It is anchored in the value assumption that people discover and rediscover abilities and self-worth through working and contributing. Clubhouse members and staff find the validity of this assumption affirmed daily in the way that clubhouse work provides the motive and medium for change as well as the evidence of accomplishment.

For many members, the work-ordered day of the clubhouse offers the opportunity to be wanted at the clubhouse, needed to carry out the work of the clubhouse, and expected as a participant in the clubhouse community. In the clubhouse, members can volunteer their time in work units or increase their involvement through transitional employment (TE) or independent employment (IE) as an avenue back into the world of competitive work.

Adults with mental illness, like their peers, express interest in gaining all the features of normal living, such as job, marriage, family, and home. Ordinary social roles serve as important symbols of well-being, recovery from mental illness and escape from the social stigma associated with mental illness. Work roles developed in the clubhouse work-ordered day provide members with enabling social role identifications and opportunities to restore their self-efficacy beliefs. The following definitions underline the idea that the work of clubhouse community-building is fundamentally that of role sharing and developing.

ROLE THEORY AND THE WORK-ORDERED DAY

Role theory, more than a simple concept or single hypothesis, is a collection of concepts and perspectives for understanding and explaining the psychological and social components of behavior. Roles are the fundamental structures of social life. Contemporary use of the term *role* reflects at least three different definitions that, when combined, expand and enrich the analysis of the clubhouse model (Deutsch & Krauss, 1965).

- *Prescribed social roles* consist of systems of expectations that exist in the social world surrounding the occupant of certain positions, expectations regarding his or her behavior toward occupants of some other position.
- *Subjective roles* are defined as those specific expectations the occupant of a position perceives as applicable to his or her own behavior as they interact with the occupants of some other position.
- *Enacted roles* consist of the specific overt behaviors of the occupant of a position when he or she interacts with the occupants of some other position.
- *Social roles* are often complex, ill-defined, and demanding. For instance, the prescribed social role of mother or father carries expectations of nurturance, discipline, teaching, entertaining, and more. Even narrowly-defined competitive work roles call for complex mental processing of role performance and other social data. Each role requires the role taker to process multiple social messages and translate them into action.

One's role must be properly understood, often from subtle social cues, and translated into actions the individual feels to be relevant. They require translations of social expectations, as well as decisions about how to behave. Failure to perform according to role expectations may result in the imposition of sanctions. Neighbors may show scorn, the boss may deny a raise, or the community may isolate or punish. This is dangerous and discouraging social terrain for individuals with mental illness. Many of the same social and psychological skills and abilities used to understand and carry out roles are skills and abilities are eroded by mental illness over months and years.

The clubhouse model, on the other hand, is designed to provide a positive experience of learning and carrying out social roles. The clubhouse is a created social microcosm where members can test and carry out various work roles under conditions that allow them to experiment, learn, and experience success without fear of sanctions or failure. The work roles are real, and the benefits are real. Products of the work benefit the community, and during the process of carrying out work roles, members experience the rewards of being on a team and sharing a mission.

Through community and work unit meetings, members and staff address the following questions: What are the existing work roles here? How can they be shared with members? What roles are most important? Why? What objective and subjective factors add to or subtract from the importance of specific work roles? Can specific work roles be expanded or divided to make more work roles? How will members and staff continuously give value and meaning to prescribed work roles? How can member experiences of work roles contribute to their belief in themselves as competent contributors?

For both members and staff, clubhouse work structures their time, focuses energy and skills, provides positive social experiences, and contributes to changed self-perceptions of competency and worth. The clubhouse brings together purpose, meaning, and action in work roles shared between members and staff that give value to the work itself and to the members and staff who do it. Decisions are shared, expertise is shared, and time and energy are shared. These value-based characteristics of clubhouse work unit organization serve to create a network of interdependencies that continuously alter former patient-provider dynamics.

Conditions in the clubhouse are established so that participants must collaborate to get the job done. Staff members, assigned primary or bottom-line responsibility for the satisfactory completion of tasks, genuinely need members to help get the job done. For example, a staff member, in addition to numerous other responsibilities, must get a letter typed, or two staff have responsibility for serving a large noon meal to the entire clubhouse. These situations create a genuine need for member participation. Depending on the size and difficulty of the tasks, work roles may be combined, subdivided, expanded, or contracted to meet the combined needs of members for meaningful roles and the community for services and outcomes. In the clubhouse, it is fundamentally important that people have the experience of being of value to the community.

SELF-EFFICACY THEORY AND ROLE CHARACTERISTICS

The experience of hospitalization for acute psychiatric illness and society's reaction to mental illness tends to reduce the variety, complexity, and importance of a person's roles. However, through engagement in the clubhouse, new and renewed roles are presented. Members are able to choose those roles when they feel they are ready. Their view of themselves as competent and capable or *efficacious* tends to grow with their successful experiences of various work roles.

- *Efficacy* is the capacity for producing a desired result or effect.
- *Self-efficacy theory,* developed by Albert Bandura and other social psychologists, concerns the relationship between knowledge and action, with how individuals

assess their capabilities and how through self-perceptions of efficacy affect motivation and behavior (Bandura, 1982).
- *Perceived self-efficacy* is concerned with peoples' beliefs in their own capabilities to generate the motivations, thought processes, and behaviors necessary to accomplish certain tasks. Affirmative self-beliefs of efficacy can have positive effects upon psychosocial functioning (Bandura, 1989).

Evidence suggests that, like those with mental illness, so-called normal people can also distort reality. They exhibit self-enhancing biases that distort appraisals toward the positive direction. Research into self-efficacy suggests that successful, innovative, sociable, nonanxious, and nondespondent individuals take an optimistic view of their personal efficacy to influence events that affect their lives (Bandura, 1986; Taylor & Brown, 1988).

According to Albert Bandura (1986) peoples' beliefs in their efficacy can be enhanced in four principal ways: (1) mastery experiences, (2) modeling coping strategies, (3) providing exemplification of attainments for comparative self-appraisal, and (4) social persuasion. By applying these theorized sources of self-efficacy, clubhouse staff and members can create conditions for members to perceive and experience their self-efficacy. The following discussion relates these four sources of self-efficacy to the clubhouse task of creating the conditions for positive self-efficacy perceptions.

- *Providing mastery experiences*—The most effective vehicle for developing a resilient sense of efficacy is through mastery experiences. Performance successes build a sense of personal efficacy; failures undermine it (Ozer & Bandura, 1990). A thriving clubhouse is a created community, a repository of opportunities for mastery experiences. Work is created, divided, and apportioned so that members and staff repeatedly share various mastery experiences, whether that is setting the table for lunch, giving a tour to visitors, recording attendance, addressing a state legislative committee, or sweeping the staircase. Each task is a potential mastery experience, an opportunity for staff and members to engage in changing self-perceptions in a positive direction.
  Staff are there to make sure that opportunities and invitation for mastery experiences are always available. They provide leadership and organization. Work is shared, but bottom-line responsibility for making sure that work is prioritized and done satisfactorily rests with staff. Staff resources in the clubhouse are minimal by design, so that the need for members to help with the work remains real. In fact staff job performance is often evaluated on their ability to engage members in real and meaningful work.
- *Modeling coping strategies*—Clubhouse work role learning is experiential and natural not didactic. Staff and member leaders model work and adaptive behavior for others in the clubhouse. Thus, members, who are taking on work roles for the first time, can learn by example how to go about doing a variety of tasks. Clubhouse modeling includes the accomplishment of specific tasks, while at the same time demonstrating personal and social skills and abilities.
- *Providing, by example, attainments for comparative self-appraisal*—Many former mental patients describe a kind of double isolation and loneliness as the most painful and pervasive feature of being acutely ill and separated from family and friends in

hospital or institution. Psychologically isolated by illness that affects thoughts, feelings, and behaviors, they are, in addition, socially isolated from the everyday experiences of work and social connections. Individuals find few opportunities for positive self-appraisals as patients or clients in hospitals or institutions.

However, the clubhouse environment, anchored in work roles and interactions, provides fertile ground for staff and member attainments and comparative self-appraisal. These attainments are identified and evaluated interpersonally in formal and informal groups throughout the clubhouse community, but the basic organizational unit of the clubhouse is the work unit. In work units individual members are able to view their behavior and performance in relation to the behavior and performance of others.

Typical clubhouses serve meals and snacks every day, produce a newsletter or closed-circuit television show, plan recreation and cultural activities, develop and maintain housing for members, develop and provide members with transitional employment and independent employment opportunities, orient new members, keep records, maintain the clubhouse facility, conduct program evaluation and research activities, greet visitors, and more.

- *Social persuasion*—In the clubhouse model, there are multiple formal and informal avenues for social persuasion to influence member self-efficacy. Community meetings are a regular forum for communication and for publicly recognizing the accomplishments of members. When a member gets a first paycheck, a diploma, or performs some special act for the community, that person will receive enthusiastic approval for his or her contribution and encouragement to test new competencies. Such occasions are marked by applause and individual acknowledgment. In clubhouse jargon, these occasions are celebrations in which all participate.

Celebrations take place in work units, too. For example, the work unit might celebrate the successful preparation of a meal, the planting of a garden, the painting of a hallway, or the completion of a large mailing. Indeed, any occasion where members and staff are performing work can provide an occasion for social persuasion of participant members, that they are competent and can effectively accomplish things that other people do. These celebrations have meaning because the work is real and of obvious importance to the life of the clubhouse community.

Members are encouraged to use the clubhouse in the way that best suits their needs and wishes. The clubhouse provides a wide variety of work roles from conducting meetings and assisting with financial operations to interviewing applicants for staff positions, collating publications, or washing dishes. Members can try different kinds of work in different circumstances with different staff and members without risking any penalty.

Work roles, developed and enacted in the social context of the clubhouse, provide structure, organization, and meaning. They become a primary source of social identity and support members to continue to work and grow, try more difficult, more responsible jobs in the clubhouse, and eventually find competitive employment if they choose.

Meaningful Roles Discovered, Created, and Enacted

When I'm working, I don't have time to think about my illness.

—A CLUBHOUSE MEMBER'S PERSPECTIVE

I can't prevent painful or anxious symptoms of mental illness directly, but I can help members discover their strengths. I find my own strengths through helping members discover theirs.

—A STAFF MEMBER'S PERSPECTIVE

COMMUNITY ROLES

The clubhouse model offers its members flexible, comprehensive, and continuous support combined with opportunities for work and friendship. They may choose employment experiences through transitional employment (TE), independent employment (IE), or further formal education (see Chapter 5), or they may choose work roles within the clubhouse.

Members are neither required to be present nor paid for their participation in the clubhouse. A member's reaction to both work and relationships in the clubhouse (and indeed elsewhere) can be and often is ambivalent. Self-doubt and anxiety can cause participation to be tentative and sporadic. Some members come to the clubhouse to eat lunch, socialize, or participate in recreation but have no direct involvement in work. Nonetheless, they are thanked for coming, and when they are able to contribute, they are thanked for their specific contribution. They are never criticized for not doing enough. If members fail to come to the clubhouse, reach-out calls and visits by staff and other members encourage them to return.

The decision to implement the clubhouse model means fundamentally changing and shaping the entire social environment. Change is comprehensive and pervasive. It is driven by individual member and staff choices and by clubhouse community needs. The roles created are quite different from those in traditional programs for individuals with mental illness. Perhaps that is the most significant feature of this way of working—staff and members side-by-side, sharing work.

In the clubhouse the assumptions of intervention are changed. The primary target for change shifts from the patient or client to the work of the clubhouse community. The more enabling designation of "member" is substituted for patient or client and given meaning through voluntary, shared work for the community. The goal is no longer discharge from service, graduation, or termination. Membership, a valued clubhouse community status, offers a sense of ownership and is created to enable and support eligible individuals for as long as they choose to participate. Staff lead and support this change through action and example.

The focus of intervention is shifted from the control of symptoms and the provision of services to the creation of opportunities. Service provision is divided and organized through collaborative staff and member partnerships to meet member needs for help with housing, competitive employment, income support, psychiatric care, recreation, and more. Staff organize and lead the change to establish and support conditions for members and staff to be wanted, needed, and expected for what they can contribute to the clubhouse community.

The field of intervention is changed from the staff office to the clubhouse, where the signs and symbols that separate members and staff are minimized. Work is shared, space is shared, planning and decision-making is shared, and clubhouse roles are shared.

Individual member needs and clubhouse needs are the sources for prescribed roles in the clubhouse. Noon meals are served because members need nutritious, inexpensive meals. Newsletters and closed-circuit television programs are produced because members and staff need to communicate daily activities and information to each other. Maintenance crews are organized for cleaning and repairing the clubhouse facility because everyone has an interest in a clean and smoothly running clubhouse. Each of the work roles created by these units, as well as others, is intended to meet the needs of members at multiple levels. Members cannot be fired because they have not been hired. Therefore, members accustomed to being excluded and devalued are accepted and valued even for many different kinds of contributions.

Each morning a unit meeting is held, work for the day is reviewed, divisions of labor are considered, and work decisions are made. Then staff and members settle down to the work of the day, which varies according to changing priorities and resources. Since the work has value to the clubhouse community, contributing work roles contribute value to those enacting them.

EMPOWERMENT

Mental illness is widely recognized as disempowering. In fact, as a group, people with mental illness are *disempowered,* as that term was defined by Barbara Solomon in her landmark work focusing on the struggles of African-Americans. People with mental illness, like African-Americans, "have been subjected to negative valuations from the larger society to such an extent that powerlessness in the group is pervasive and crippling" (Solomon, 1976, p. 12). For those with mental illness, conditions of daily living have been made worse by poverty, homelessness, and the debilitation of illness itself. They are often unable or feel they are unable to influence or control the social, economic, and political forces that directly affect them.

The clubhouse model in all its various aspects is an inclusive design to empower through community-building work. Work roles are key. The opportunity to do meaningful, contributing work with others is a direct contribution to the sense of control and self-efficacy in one's life. Research into the origins of empowerment suggests that empowerment is linked to self-efficacy (Bandura, 1986). Personal power is regained through the discovery and reclamation of competency, one's capacity to choose, imagine the future, and enact various roles. "Contemplating action reflects a change from seeing the world and one's position in it as permanent and fixed to seeing it as permeable, as capable of being changed; it reflects movement from a position of consumer of an imposed reality to a partial producer of one's reality" (Rose & Black, 1985, p. 97).

It is not possible to simply counsel someone with serious mental illness to feel empowered and act forcefully. Individuals must experience their own ability to change things to make a difference, to make a work contribution, and to be productive. In a clubhouse, or anywhere else, this provides a sound, experiential basis for enhanced self-esteem and competency. Empowerment in the clubhouse model takes place at different levels.

In the clubhouse model power—the ability to control and direct one's life—is not just a goal, but a method. The model joins means and ends in such a way that members are provided a continuously available set of opportunities to gain authority over their daily lives. The focus is on action and doing rather than preparing for action. The focus is on habilitation rather than rehabilitation. Members learn to be advocates for themselves and others.

Some examples of empowering acts that can be initiated by clubhouse staff and others include:

- Giving members the information they need to make their own choices about how to spend their time, where and with whom they would like to work and associate.
- Including members in the decisions about staff hirings.
- Expecting members to help each other with community support problems.
- Expecting members to help insure the permanency of transitional employment positions.
- Encouraging members to apply for positions with the clubhouse. Hiring members as staff, if having been a member is not a major problem and if they have demonstrated their special aptitudes and competencies for doing the work.
- Using member skills and aptitudes in carrying out the work of the clubhouse.
- Not giving authority or responsibility to members just because they are members; never patronizing.
- Giving members keys to vans, buildings, meeting rooms, or any property for which they have responsibility if they have appropriate licensing.
- Expecting that members will decide when to take on additional responsibilities.
- Expecting that tours of the clubhouse and orientation sessions will be done by members.
- Addressing people with mental illness with the same terms of respect used with others.

Empowerment also takes place on group and community levels. Clubhouse staff, other mental health workers, friends, and family can:

- Lobby the legislature for needed reforms in the provision of mental health services.
- Assist in the training of police, hospital staff, professional groups, and other mental health staff.
- Participate in the antistigma efforts of family advocacy groups.

That members are needed to carry out this work is the fundamental basis for both the *subjective feeling of empowerment* as well as the *objective reality of empowerment* (employment goals attained, tasks done, or projects accomplished).

> *I can see members gain self-confidence as they help in the clubhouse community. Even members who are unable or choose not to participate directly, seem to benefit by being in the midst of activities.*
>
> —A STAFF MEMBER'S PERSPECTIVE

> *. . . it gets me to come out, it keeps my mind feeling good, so that I don't get sick again. It keeps my mind alert. I choose to be someplace where something more is expected from you other than just participating in groups or going along on a trip or whatever.*
>
> —A CLUBHOUSE MEMBER'S PERSPECTIVE

WORK AND RELATIONSHIPS

The invitation to work in the clubhouse is an invitation to enter into naturally occurring relationships. Friendships that grow in a clubhouse, like all other aspects of clubhouse life, are uniformly voluntary, never coerced. They grow in the course of working together and caring.

> The work at hand is the source of the relationships. How does this process occur? In a very simplified statement, as follows: there is a task at hand and two or more people are motivated to do it. What happens between the two people is this: as the job gets going, mutual dependence begins—you hold the ladder and I'll wash the window; shared decisions are made—yes, the soup needs more salt; common hopes and anxieties come into being—we hope that the rose bushes will grow and bloom; satisfaction with one another's activity is expressed—we've collated and mailed the newsletter. The completed task visibly before them, they share rewards . . . without having to discuss it, or measure it, or even contemplate it, a relationship is coming into being. Mutual respect, shared history, and future anticipation are being molded, and the work at hand is the medium through which the relationship is growing (Jackson, 1992, p. 64).

Work and relationships that grow together in this way help to manage the symptoms of mental illness. Work helps to focus and structure relationships, providing social support without invasive closeness or intimacy. Relationships

Exporting the Model: Older Adults

Demographic studies show that the population of the United States and many other countries in the world is getting older. Needs for specialized health care services (including mental health services), housing, financial support, social connections, and support for dealing with a variety of daily living problems are increasing and will continue to increase. Older adults are often separated from relatives, excluded, disempowered, and marginalized because of their age and circumstances.

Most of these people in their 60s, 70s, and older are no longer working at jobs or careers. They have many skills but few outlets for contributing work. More than a decade ago, Erik Erikson commented that "we have relegated this growing segment of the population to onlooker bleachers of society, we have classified them as unproductive, inadequate and inferior." He suggested that we need "clear insight into how the elders in our present society can become integral workers in community life" (Erikson, E., Erikson, J., & Kivnick, 1986, p. 294). Certainly many older citizens retain their important connections to family and friends. For others the task is to find or reestablish the conditions for being wanted and needed.

What are the special needs of older people?

Does the clubhouse model suggest approaches and activities to intervening with this group?

How might they meet some of their needs through engaging in community-building?

What could you do to help?

and work combine to rebuild self-worth and a sense of competency, thereby often complementing and reinforcing the intended, symptom-control effects of psychiatric medications.

> *Working side-by-side with members has joined my professional values and my work with members. I have a sense of satisfaction and professional integrity.*

> —A STAFF MEMBER'S PERSPECTIVE

> *I like coming to the clubhouse. I have friends here and work to be done.*

> —A CLUBHOUSE MEMBER'S PERSPECTIVE

SUSTAINING AND MAINTAINING THE WORK-ORDERED DAY

The clubhouse model has been established in more than 350 separate locations in more than 24 countries. Many of these clubhouses are independent organizations with their own boards of directors, budgets, and formal legal standing. In the United States, however, clubhouses have quite often started from day treatment programs, rehabilitation programs, or other units of community mental health centers. This factor has produced two special challenges for both building and sustaining the clubhouse work-ordered day.

First, the change from a mental health program or other program of professional services to a clubhouse entails the creation of a place, building, or separate location within another building, which is suited to the philosophy and methods of the clubhouse. It is a place not simply an activity or service. Because of this, the building or portion of a building that becomes a clubhouse should be physically separated from the mental health center or other parent agency. The separate space permits participants to be members, not patients or clients. It can become a place where the pride of ownership grows among members and staff. The work in *our* place can become *our* work.

Second, the clubhouse belongs to its members and staff. The work of the clubhouse is done not by clients or patients but by staff and members together. This shift is much more than changing the language in a program unit, substituting member for the conventional language of client or patient. There must be a thorough, ongoing commitment to the assessment and redistribution of real work roles to members involving both staff and members. The change is often attained through the feminist methodology of consciousness-raising, group encounters undertaken to bring to light unspoken matters of classism and stigma.

Emotional and ideological change of this magnitude is not easy for anyone, but it can be especially difficult for mental health center staff who have been trained for professional roles where their specialist expertise is highly valued because of their formal training and status. Administrators may also experience the growing staff and member sense of ownership as a loss of central control. These difficult matters of psychological adaptation to clubhouse philosophy and methods are discussed and presented in staff and member narratives in Chapter 7.

SUMMARY

Chapter 4 has shown that work roles are of fundamental importance for defining who we are in relation to others. Some of the psychosocial functions of work have been related to different aspects of daily human functioning including the provision of outcomes for self-evaluation, structuring of time and tasks, finding socially acceptable outlets for aggressive energy, and contributing to personal identity and social status. Individuals with mental illness must often struggle to reclaim these functions of ordinary daily living that others naturally assume to be theirs.

The clubhouse work-ordered day offers opportunities for members to reclaim the identity-building benefits of work and relationships. It substitutes clubhouse membership and community affiliation for patient or client roles. Aspects of role and self-efficacy theory show how sources of self-efficacy can be used to discover and develop empowering clubhouse work roles for members. Chapter 5 will show how mental illness might be analyzed, in part, as a disabling social construction. Transitional employment (TE), independent employment (IE), and supported education are described this chapter as alternatives and antidotes that are part of the clubhouse model.

Applying Concepts

1. How do the roles discovered and developed within the clubhouse work-ordered day differ from the roles typically provided by society for people with mental illness?
2. How does the work-ordered day contribute to the enhancement of member self-esteem and self-efficacy?
3. How are work roles assumed and enacted when member participation is voluntary?
4. Define the various conceptions of role—enacted, prescribed, and perceived.
5. In what ways is the clubhouse like a family? Discuss.
6. Why is individual or group therapy not a part of daily clubhouse life?
7. What is self-efficacy theory? How does it apply to the created community of the clubhouse?
8. In what ways have you experienced work roles as helpful to your mental health?
9. When have you experienced work as unhelpful or destructive?
10. Are clients in your practicum or field placement given opportunities to work and be productive as well as receive services? Explain.
11. What can you do to establish conditions for increased self-efficacy among clients in your agency, student practicum, or field placement?

Class Projects

Visit a clubhouse model program. Take a tour. Interview members and staff. Using the Standards for Clubhouse Programs (see Appendix II), critique and discuss what you have observed.

Together with others in your class, observe the interactions of individuals in selected organizations. How would you characterize the atmosphere or climate? Hopeful? Energetic? Depressed? Anxious? Relaxed?

GLOSSARY

Clubhouse Standards   a set of guidelines or expectations developed and refined continuously at meetings of clubhouse staff and members. The standards describe what values, practices, and behaviors it takes to build or maintain a clubhouse.

Iatrogenic effects   caused by the treatment.

Mastery experiences   those experiences of various kinds in which people experience control and success.

Prescribed social roles   systems of social expectations that inform individuals of certain expectations regarding their own behavior; how they should behave.

Self-efficacy theory   social theory developed by psychologist Albert Bandura concerned with how people assess their own behavior and how these assessments affect motivations and behaviors.

Social persuasion   takes place in formal and informal settings where people receive support for their contributions and accomplishments.

Work-ordered day   the framework of activities in a clubhouse day that is based upon the natural and normalizing structure of work for members, not continuous therapies or activity groups.

REFERENCES

Bandura, A. (1982). Self-efficacy mechanism in human agency. *American Psychologist, 37*(2), 122–147.

Bandura, A. (1986). *Social foundations of thought and action: A social cognitive theory.* Englewood Cliffs, NJ: Prentice-Hall.

Bandura, A. (1989). Human agency in social cognitive theory. *American Psychologist, 44*(9), 1175–1184.

Beard, J., Propst, R. N., & Malamud, T. (1982). The Fountain House model of psychiatric rehabilitation. *Psychosocial Rehabilitation Journal, 5*(1), 47–53.

Erikson, E., Erikson, J., & Kivnick, H. (1986). *Vital involvement in old age.* New York: W. W. Norton.

Estroff, S. E. (1989). Self, identity and subjective experiences of schizophrenia: In search of the subject. *Schizophrenia Bulletin, 15,* 189–196.

Fidler, G. S., & Fidler, J. W. (1978). Doing and becoming: Purposeful action and self-actualization. *American Journal of Occupational Therapy, 32*(5), 305–310.

Jackson, R. (1992). How work works. *Psychosocial Rehabilitation Journal, 16*(2), 63–67.

Jimenez, M. (1988). Chronicity in mental disorders: Evolution of a concept. *Social Casework, 69*(2) (December), 627–633.

Ozer, E. M., & Bandura, A. (1990). Mechanisms governing empowerment effects: A self-efficacy analysis. *Journal of Personality and Social Psychology, 58*(3), 472–486.

Rose, S. M., & Black, B. L. (1985). Advocacy and empowerment: Mental health care in the community. Boston: Routledge & Kegan Paul.

Solomon, B. (1976). *Black empowerment: Social work in oppressed communities.* New York: Columbia University Press.

Taylor, S. E., & Brown, J. D. (1988). Illusion and well-being: A social perspective on mental health. *Psychological Bulletin, 103*(2), 193–210.

Taylor, K. E., & Perkins, R. E. (1991). Identity and coping with mental illness in long-stay psychiatric rehabilitation. *British Journal of Clinical Psychology, 30,* 73–85.

Williams, R. (1970). *American society* (3rd ed.). New York: Knopf.

EMPLOYMENT AND EDUCATION

Working pushes you to come in touch with your very own unique strengths, talents, and abilities. As you discover and rediscover these things in yourself, you gradually begin to define a more consistent representation of who you are to yourself and how you are unique and how you are the same as those around you. This consistent sense of yourself, I think, is the absolute prerequisite to self-esteem and to the real ability to develop relationships with others (Vorspan, 1992).

—A STAFF MEMBER'S PERSPECTIVE

I might never have gone farther if it weren't for Beth. Beth was my staff worker and I really liked her a lot. I took my first TEP, not because I wanted to earn money or work outside the clubhouse, but for a much more basic reason: Beth asked me to try. She said she thought I could do it. And she said that at the end of the week we would go out to dinner if I would stick it out.

—A CLUBHOUSE MEMBER'S PERSPECTIVE

Working competitively or returning to school requires complex adaptations. Social system boundaries must be crossed. New and demanding environments must be managed. People with mental illness often have special difficulties with such transitions. Therefore, a major purpose of clubhouse membership is the provision of opportunities and support for members through these problematic transitional times and events.

This chapter explains how mental illness can be viewed, in part, as *socially constructed*. It also describes some of the primary methods by which the clubhouse model contends with socially constructed views of mental illness. The model implements a *strengths perspective* through transitional employment (TE) programming and supported education. Each of these program components is intended to help members attain employment and education objectives and simultaneously change self and social constructions of disability.

THE SOCIAL CONSTRUCTION OF DISABILITY

Individuals with disabling mental illnesses struggle not only with the realities of illness but with socially constructed views of mental illness in society. Mental illness, from a clinical perspective, is seen to be a disturbance of psychosocial functioning (see Chapter 2). It has certain objective, observable, and classifiable characteristics. To a great extent, these are privately experienced, painful and disturbing realities such as uncontrolled anxiety, auditory hallucinations, or depressed moods. Because these disruptive symptoms often first appear in peoples' lives during their teens, twenties, and thirties—ordinarily developmental periods of great activity and productivity—their work and educational careers are significantly disrupted or stopped altogether. Recovery and the reclamation of jobs and school careers requires confrontation of the *social construction* of disabling mental illness.

According to social constructionists, the problem of mental illness is known not simply through objective characteristics of disorders—for instance, symptoms, their frequency and incidence in the population—but also through *claims* that are made about the nature of disability (Spector & Kitsuse, 1977). From this perspective, language is the essential medium through which mental illness is known subjectively. Individuals recovering from mental illness encounter and incorporate socially constructed knowledge of mental illness from their experience of the world around them. Like illness symptoms, such knowledge may limit or restrict their ability to work and live independently (Harding, Zubin, & Stauss, 1992; Jimenez, 1988). Socially constructed knowledge of mental illness may dampen initiative, limit, and disempower people.

How Social Construction Works

Sociologists studying social problems from a constructionist perspective focus attention on the processes by which people assign meaning to things, on *claims* rather than objective conditions. This is not to say that they dismiss objective conditions. "The reality of everyday life is not only filled with objectivations; it is only possible because of them," (Berger & Luckmann, 1966, p. 35). But constructionists are interested in who is making claims and what is being claimed. Asserting claims, or *claimsmaking,* produces socially constructed meanings of social problems (Best, 1995).

For example,

> The social stock of knowledge includes knowledge of my situation and its limits. For instance, I know that I am poor and that, therefore, I cannot expect to live in a fashionable suburb. This knowledge is, of course, shared by both those who are poor themselves and those who are in a more privileged situation. Participation in the social stock of knowledge thus permits the location of individuals in society and the handling of them in the appropriate manner (Berger & Luckmann, 1966, p. 42).

Claimsmakers and Claimsmaking

Those who help to shape social constructions are referred to as *claimsmakers,* because they are putting forward certain views of social reality in opposition to others. Paradoxically, some of the most powerful claimsmakers can be victims. Others are experts who have been recognized as having special knowledge about certain subjects. Still others are public figures in political life, entertainment, or academia who have authority as well as avenues to the dissemination of their perspectives through books or television, the Internet, or other contemporary forms of media.

Dramatic Examples Often Initiate Claimsmaking

Some—relatively few—people with schizophrenia have hallucinations or delusions, which without medications and therapy, may direct them to harm themselves or others. The incidence of actual harm traceable to these kinds of hallucinations is relatively rare, but occasionally individuals with mental illness take highly visible action. Examples in recent years have included the attempted assassination of President Reagan by David Hinkley on March 30, 1981, and the killing of two Capitol Hill police officers by Russell Weston on July 16, 1998. These individuals were later found to be suffering from schizophrenia and were not being treated. Their violent actions were widely reported in the media. Reporting of incidents of violence such as these contributes to a socially constructed view of mental illness in which the meaning of mental illness is joined with violence. As a consequence, individuals with mental illness come to be characterized as dangerous.

Statistics

Statistics used in conjunction with dramatic examples may powerfully support claims. Several recent studies reported by the American Medical Association tend to support the somewhat greater likelihood of people with mental illness to engage in violent behavior than those without mental illnesses (Lamberg, 1998).

The United States Epidemiologic Catchment Area study sampled more than 10,000 persons in three metropolitan areas in 1990. It found that between 10 and 12 percent of persons with affective or schizophrenic disorders reported having acted violently in the past year, while only 2 percent of persons with no mental disorders did so.

A study in Denmark followed a cohort of 324,000 consecutive newborns from birth to age 43. The study compared the 11,000 women and 10,000 men in this group who had a history of psychiatric hospitalization with all others. Both men and women in all diagnostic groups, except those with organic mental disorders, were more likely to have been convicted of a violent crime than persons with no mental disorder.

These statistics, depending on how and to whom they are reported, may contribute to the social construction of mental illness. In fact, most people with mental illness are not dangerous. Drugs and alcohol make a far more serious contribution to violence in our society. Yet powerful images of mental illness and violence are combined and characterized through claims.

Claimsmakers Act to Implement Their Views

Victims of violence, experts, professionals, professional interest groups, and activists all use various forms of media to put forward their claims about social problems in society. From a reader's or listener's perspective, their stories are engaging, personal, sometimes lurid, and exciting. They are invariably attractive to news media that recognize reader interest in unusual or bizarre stories. Claims of professionals may be especially influential. Professionals make claims and counterclaims through public meetings, forums, lectures, addresses, and presentations to legislatures. They also have access to reports and statistics that are used to support their arguments.

Typification

Through the social process described previously, people with mental illness are often typified as being incompetent, living primarily on the streets, being out-of-control, and even violent. These social constructions of mental illness influence self-esteem, identity, and the sense of self-efficacy of individuals with mental illness, as well as the availability of opportunities for them to work. Employers are not willing to risk hiring individuals whom they view as being part of a class of unpredictable or even dangerous workers.

In his book *Madness in the Streets* (1990), Gerald Grob demonstrated how the social problem of mental illness is combined with the problems of homelessness and "typified" as a major social problem.

> What then is the size of the 'homeless' population, and what proportion are mentally ill? To be sure, the total number is not the two to three million routinely used in press reports. That absurdly high figure came from Mitch Snyder, who told a congressional committee in 1980 of 2.2 million Americans without homes, raising the estimate a year later to three million. In 1984 Snyder admitted, the 'number is meaningless. We have tried to satisfy your gnawing curiosity for a number because we are Americans with western little minds that have to quantify everything in sight, whether we can or not.' (Grob, 1990, p. 3)

Grob's account illustrates the development of a *typification* or social construction. The typification persists not because of its truth of falsity but because of the claimsmaking that creates and sustains it.

A typification provides a kind of working, social definition that evolves and changes depending on the influence of the claimsmakers and what they are claiming. As they gain strength in public consensus, these socially constructed outcomes of claiming contribute to both public policy formulation as well as the individual's self-perception of his or her mental illness.

In order to change these disabling perceptions, socially constructed typifications of mental illness must be confronted and changed at multiple levels.

Implementation of a *strengths perspective* is a prerequisite. The active presence of a strengths perspective in a clubhouse serves to encourage and enable.

A STRENGTHS PERSPECTIVE

A strengths perspective on mental illness serves to counter social constructions and encourages people with mental illness to succeed at school and employment. It is consonant to a great extent with the principles and practices of the clubhouse model. It serves to counter disabling social constructions of mental illness.

In the first chapter of his book, *The Strengths Perspective in Social Work Practice,* Dennis Saleebey (1997) identified a "lexicon of strengths," key concepts and principles in practice based upon a strengths perspective.

Membership

As previously discussed, this is a central feature of the clubhouse model. Membership in the clubhouse community is demonstrated at several levels— the work unit, the community meeting, and special projects. Club membership supports and encourages membership in the wider community in a variety of ways, including transitional employment and supported education.

Resilience

Resilience points to the fact that no matter what their difficulties and limitations, people have real strengths and abilities to encounter and overcome hardships. At one time the chance for recovery from schizophrenia was thought to be uniformly poor. However, major longitudinal research conducted in the 1980s and 1990s has exposed this negative prediction to be to a great extent unfounded (Ciompi, 1980; Harding et al., 1992). Environments such as those suggested by the clubhouse model underline individual and collective resiliency, the tendency of people to "bounce back," to meet their needs and survive.

Healing and Wholeness

These concepts support the notion that the whole person is more than a collection of disabling symptoms or a long record of unemployment or other problem characteristics. His or her life cannot be viewed simply in physical, psychological, or social terms. The person is a whole organism equipped with the capacity, indeed the tendency to change, grow, and adapt. This attitude and assumption leads naturally to alliances between helper and client based on strengths that both can begin to see and experience. In the clubhouse, members tend to view their mental illness as problematic, sometimes painfully real. Every attempt is made to prevent these disabilities from dominating and organizing their lives or those of other members in the clubhouse community.

Dialogue and Collaboration

These concepts underline the importance of relationship based on shared work and experience. They point to the nature of working together, people knowing each other's unique characteristics, strengths and idiosyncrasies. In the clubhouse model, these strengths concepts dramatically alter the nature of professional staff roles (see Chapter 8). Professionals in the clubhouse work with members as colleagues and facilitators. They occupy the same spaces in the club, help with the same projects, and perhaps most importantly, share their own stories. In vibrant examples of the clubhouse model, the presence of dialogue and collaboration is immediately observed and felt.

Suspension of Disbelief

Saleebey (1997) has noted that the traditional clinical practice of suspending belief in client's accounts of their lives may be derived from an older view that counselors and social workers are scientists and should, therefore, adopt a certain dispassion and distance when working with clients. Applying this practice, "objective reality" can only be viewed when all the data are compared and analyzed. Thus, "reality" examined through the professional's assessment may have greater authority than the client's own views.

Alternatively, the strengths perspective encourages a *suspension of disbelief*. This is based upon the assumption that there are multiple "realities" and people are expert in knowledge of their own reality. The client has the tools to understand, interpret, and respond to problems presented in the course of daily living. The clubhouse member is the best judge of his or her readiness for the world of competitive employment.

TRANSITIONAL EMPLOYMENT (TE)

Transitional employment opportunities are major benefits of membership and serve as important connections between the clubhouse and the larger community.

Members managing mental illness symptoms must manage stressful events and conditions in their daily lives. Indeed, competitive work can be a source of stress. However "stress" is experienced differently by different people. It cannot categorically be defined and controlled. Individuals must

Transitional Employment

In the community meeting, Donald held up his last monthly paycheck from his transitional employment placement. A round of applause and cheers came from all of those in the meeting. This was a day that he had worked for all his life, because until recently, he had not been able to hold a job for more than a few days or weeks. With lots of support from others in his work unit and occasional coverage by them, Donald had succeeded in doing the job and holding the placement for six months. He got to work on time and did the job as well or better than anyone else in his department. In addition, his supervisor, who did not give praise casually, told him last week that he had done an excellent job. He arrived at work on time, dressed appropriately for the work, got along with others, and carried out instructions. In short, he had demonstrated the kinds of skills that he wished every employee would have. Donald was justifiably proud of his accomplishments. Now it was time for him to turn the placement over so that others could have the opportunity he had.

He would talk with people in his work unit about getting another placement or perhaps he would have a try at getting his own permanent job. His self-confidence had grown. He began to imagine what else he might do.

encounter or avoid stressful conditions as they are aware and able. Clubhouse members need opportunities to test their abilities despite mental illness symptoms. This clubhouse value is consistent with the values implicit in the strengths perspective. Transitional employment (TE) is designed as a fundamental opportunity for members to experience their strengths and make decisions.

The transitional employment program and TE placements (TEPs) are natural extensions of the work-ordered day of the clubhouse in which members gain prevocational experiences. In a records-based study conducted at Fountain House by Macias, Kinney, and Rodican (1995, p. 151), it was found that "those members who spend more time in Fountain House before beginning a TEP worked more days on their first TEP." This finding tends to underline the natural and logical connection between unpaid, prevocational work in the clubhouse and TE outside.

- *What are transitional employment placements (TEPs) and where are they located?*
  Transitional employment placements are developed as part-time, primarily entry level, competitive employment positions. They are located in service organizations,

manufacturing plants, offices, garages, anywhere an easily learned, straightforward job can be secured, made available to members, and paid at the prevailing wage. Such placements are implemented with the full knowledge and support of administrators, managers, and supervisors.

The duties of the position are not altered to accommodate "a person with mental illness." When employers agree to provide jobs, they are expecting employees who will do the jobs reliably. However, if members encounter difficulties in carrying out the responsibilities of the placement—tardiness, inability to observe schedules, or difficulty communicating with peers or supervisors—the clubhouse unit to which the placement is assigned will provide immediate support to the member/employee as well as backup to the job. Staff and members are prepared to take over, help the member on the job, and protect the position. Members may take several transitional employment jobs before they are able to consistently meet the demands of a TE placement for six months or more. TEPs are understood to be opportunities for learning. Individuals will be replaced at the end of the six-month transition period or if they are unable to handle the responsibilities of the job.

- *Who develops transitional employment placements (TEPs) and how?* Responsibility for developing transitional employment placements is often shared among staff, although the task takes some special skills. The first contacts may be with friends or family members who have businesses or work in the community outside the clubhouse.
- *How does a member obtain a transitional employment position (TEP)?* Transitional employment should be available to anyone who is a member and asks for the opportunity. Consistent with the clubhouse philosophy that opposes coercion, members are neither forced to take placements nor restricted from placements. A member will typically consult with staff and other members in their work unit about their current work performance in the clubhouse. Such issues as timeliness, ability to focus attention, attendance, and other factors may be discussed. Nonetheless, the individual member is viewed as having the ability to make a responsible choice about where and when to take an employment position. The ability of members to make important choices freely is viewed as fundamentally empowering.
- *What skills are needed to succeed in a transitional employment placement?* Often the most important skills that members need are not task or job skills, but rather interpersonal skills, such as the ability to communicate effectively about tasks, to dress and groom appropriately for the job, to report for work on time and regularly, and to carry out instructions of employers.
- *Who manages on-going transitional employment placements?* Management of transitional employment placements is a clubhouse staff responsibility. Work unit staff who have "bottom-line responsibility" for all the work of the unit. also have responsibility for some portion of clubhouse TEPs assigned. All members and staff of the unit share the work of insuring that the job is covered and done satisfactorily.

The member in a placement can learn the tasks and experience success in a short period of time. There are no formal screenings, extended interviews by rehabilitation specialists, or lengthy training periods. These organizational processes, when combined with other systemic disincentives, might tend to discourage people already struggling to mobilize energy and motivation. Instead members receive considerable support from staff and other members for taking paid employment when they feel they are ready to try.

Clubhouse model transitional employment placements are obtained and maintained for the use of all clubhouse members who choose them. At any time some members are beginning placements and some are ending. In a sense, TE placements are held "in trust" by the clubhouse for its members. This design element is intended to insure that placements will remain available. It also insures that everyone has a stake and responsibility in seeing that the work of the placement is done, even if one member on the placement does not arrive or does the job inadequately in some other respect. This increases the importance of outside placements withing the club. It draws employers, members, and staff together in insuring placement success and individual member success. Transitional employment programs are intended to provide a "good deal" for all, a "win, win, win situation."

Job Development: Sources of TE Placements

All clubhouse staff have responsibilities to help promote and develop transitional job placements wherever possibilities arise. However, these responsibilities are sometimes invested with a special job developer who may work directly for all the clubhouse work units or who may staff a TE work unit. Whomever is engaged in job development must have the ability to communicate effectively with clubhouse members and with managers and personnel of community businesses. Developers must select jobs that are real and provide a variety of choices to members.

Research into the effectiveness of transitional employment, although limited, points to an approach that helps members toward independent employment. A study conducted at Fountain House in the 1980s followed 146 members for three and one-half years. At the end of the study, nearly 36 percent were independently employed. Of 104 participants who were members of Fountain House prior to the study, 66 percent obtained independent employment during the course of the research (Malamud, 1985).

Supported employment programming, not part of the original clubhouse model, is now available in many clubs. Developed originally to assist developmentally disabled individuals return to work, supported employment is similar to transitional employment in that clients or members are employed at the prevailing wage rate as regular employees in integrated settings, are in regular contact with nonhandicapped workers, and receive ongoing support (Rehabilitation Act Amendments of 1986, 1987). However, in unmodified form, this rehabilitation approach requires the continuous services of staff rehabilitation specialists. Supported employment use of staff specialists has been viewed by some clubhouse staff and members as disempowering and incompatible with clubhouse values and practices (Bilby, 1992). However, collective opinion of the international clubhouse community is shifting toward acceptance of supported

TABLE 5.1   CLUBHOUSE MODEL TRANSITIONAL EMPLOYMENT (TE) PROGRAM

Beneficiaries	Beneficiaries Are Involved through	Benefits
Members	Choosing a real, competitive job	Members experience competitive work without "failing" the employer or others.
	Learning job skills on the job	Members experience "normal" adult work roles that structure time and require attention and focus, as well as social requirements concerned with the work tasks.
	"Modeling" competitive work behaviors for others	
		Members get wages like other workers.
		Members gain a sense of self-efficacy and self-esteem from working and "a job well done."
Staff and members in the work unit	Providing support and backup for workers in their placements	Unit staff and members are encouraged and motivated by the stories shared about employment successes.
	Insuring that work is valued through effective management of the placement	Unit staff and members discover leaders and leadership qualities and other skills previously unused and undiscovered.
	Learning about the special demands of the transitional employment placement	
All clubhouse staff and members	Valuing the work and the member doing the work	All staff and members see, discuss, and experience member successes.
	Celebrating accomplishments of members	All staff and members become more aware of destructive and enervating socially constructed views of mental illness.
Employers outside the community	Obtaining an employee with a guarantee	Employers are able to meaningfully contribute to members' development, contribute to the clubhouse community and meet their business goals in addition
	Getting the job done reliably and effectively	
	Helping people who are working to help themselves return to work	

employment, as well as transitional employment and independent employment aspects of clubhouse programming.

Many involved in work with adults with mental illness acknowledge that there are too few opportunities of all kinds for employment and many disincentives for competitive employment faced by adults with mental illness (Polak & Warner, 1996). Long-term employment is still problematic, no matter whether the origins are in transitional, supported, or independent employment (Becker et al., 1998).

Now I have a job to go to. It's tough, but it helps me to get out of bed in the morning. It gives me a real purpose.

—A CLUBHOUSE MEMBER'S PERSPECTIVE

CELEBRATING ACCOMPLISHMENTS AND CONSTRUCTING COMPETENCY

Like aspects of disability, competency can also be viewed as socially constructed. The accomplishments of members in their own work rehabilitation are marked in a number of important ways. Every effort is made to repeatedly and publicly underline members' competencies demonstrated in accomplishments. The language of continuous clienthood or patienthood used in most hospitals and other custodial institutions is deliberately replaced in the clubhouse model with such designations as "member," "colleague," and "clubhouse." Such efforts to change perceptions and language are intended to attack and alter disabling social constructions of mental illness.

Employment Dinners

Dinners are a traditional way in which working members are honored. Speeches tell their stories and celebrate their accomplishments. Dinners give support and encouragement to those who have succeeded and to other members who have not yet taken this major step. In addition to these events honoring members, other events and special occasions provide opportunities to thank employers for their continuing support of the clubhouse and its members. Plaques and letters of appreciation are often presented to employers.

Awards and First Paychecks

Many members have not had a competitive employment job or earned a single dollar of taxable income before their first transitional employment position. Their first paycheck is a powerful symbol of their accomplishments. Many clubs display photographs of that first paycheck or of smiling members holding their first paycheck. Such photographs serve to support and encourage everyone involved.

Notice in Newsletters

Headlines and special articles in the newsletter of the clubhouse also make accomplishments visible and highly public. They serve to counter prevailing socially constructed notions about mental illness and disability.

Full-Time Employment Dinners

Some members get and keep jobs for the long term. It is especially important that their accomplishments are honored and that their achievements are known to others who are perhaps struggling with a decision about whether or not to ask for a transitional employment placement. This group of members provides powerful inspiration and motivation to others.

SUPPORTED EDUCATION

Although most clubs support the efforts of members to reclaim their educational careers, some clubs have formal programs to assist members in achieving their educational objectives. Supported education programs assume that members face similar obstacles to those faced in TE or other employment situations—reduced levels of expectation for people having experienced mental illness, lack of self-confidence that members may feel about themselves, lack of self-esteem, and low levels of acceptance by others (Dougherty, Hastie, Bernard, Broadhurst, & Marcus, 1992, p. 93).

Supported education programs perform a variety of tasks on behalf of members. They strive to develop relations, formal and informal, with on-campus admissions offices, financial aid counseling departments, and other campus groups that might be helpful to clubhouse members. They help students master transportation problems, learn bus routes, and arrange for car pools. They help with course selection and the examination of student/teacher compatibility. They also provide individualized assistance with assignments, preparing for tests, and homework. Members needing computers or other clubhouse supplies to complete assignments can often use the office equipment of the clubhouse. Other members and staff are ready to provide encouragement and advice about academic problems.

All of these efforts in support of both transitional employment and supported education challenge disabling social constructions encountered by members, their families, and clubhouse staff. Members demonstrate initiative in choosing to return to work. Their reports of on-the-job experiences, and their struggles to extend their accomplishments are the grist of unit meetings, community meetings, and newsletter accounts. Through communication of their experiences, they share in the creation of a different, more enabling kind of constructed view of people with mental illness.

A 1988 study conducted by Charles Rapp and his colleagues and cited by Dennis Saleebey (1994), demonstrated the ability of adults with mental illness to replace disabling social constructions with enabling new meanings.

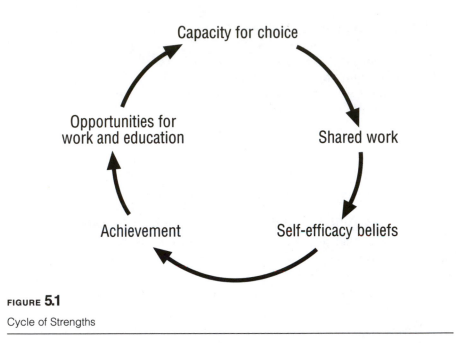

FIGURE **5.1**

Cycle of Strengths

Despite their illness they "began to construct a life—collaboratively—that no one would have predicted . . . their symptoms may have occurred at the same level, but the other parts of them became part of their unfolding story: "me as employee," "me as piano player," "me as driver," "me as spouse and parent." The symptoms move into the background of a much richer symbolic ecology. (p. 357)

The clubhouse model is designed to increase opportunities and create collective and individual changes in socially constructed symbols of disability. Thus, a richer "symbolic ecology" provides the basis for displacing and rewriting disabling social constructions.

SUMMARY

The construction of competency requires the displacement of socially constructed definitions of disabling mental illness with positive, competency-affirming stories and activities. Individual members of the clubhouse often become interested in the world of work beyond the clubhouse through a decision to become involved in transitional employment or education. People taking transitional employment positions or going to school are literally reaching beyond the protective and supportive boundary of the clubhouse social system. Each of these clubhouse model opportunities requires members to contend directly with other people's views of mental illness and people with mental illness. Clubhouse staff and members must have some idea of how people understand mental illness and what can be done to change negative "social constructions" of mental illness.

How can a strengths perspective be continuously implemented?

- Through the creation of continuous opportunities for members to institute choices at multiple levels.
- Through the recognition and reporting of member accomplishments in many ways: newsletter articles, pictures and plaques on the walls, community meeting introductions, and recognition with employers and others in the larger community.
- Through replacing disempowering language and symbols in the environment with empowering language and symbols of strength and hopefulness.
- Through public speeches and presentations about mental illness experiences and stories of accomplishments. These occasions facilitate the rewriting of personal and collective narratives.
- Through dinners celebrating employer contributions and member accomplishments.
- Through public information efforts, including clubhouse tours and talks, that educate the public about the realities of mental illness and disability.

Transitional employment and supported education programs are components of the clubhouse model that provide lively counterclaims to the social construction of disability. They put into operation a strengths perspective. They help members imagine new and more enabling images of themselves in society. Only when people start creating scenarios of possibility do they move in directions more satisfying to them, and the problems become lost or much less influential (Saleebey, 1996, p. 357).

APPLYING CONCEPTS

1. How are aspects of the problem of mental illness socially constructed?
2. What is a strengths perspective? How can it serve as an antidote to disabling constructions of mental illness or other social problems?
3. How does the clubhouse model help members begin to redefine themselves and others with mental illness as capable?
4. How do transitional employment and supported education programs reframe failures on the job and in school?
5. What other marginalized populations in society might benefit from program activities based upon some of the same assumptions and methods?
6. How might you study the impact of socially constructed meanings in your agency or another agency setting?

Class Projects

Examine the signage (the signs) of your school or agency. Are they adequate, clear, and consistent with the assumption that clients or students are competent adults? Are they consistent with a strengths perspective?

Are individuals with certain racial, ethnic, or disability characteristics treated differently than other clients, customers, or students? Document and discuss any "separate-but-equal facilities" you find, such as restrooms, work areas, waiting areas, coffee rooms, or rest areas. How might such facilities continuously construct inequalities?

GLOSSARY

Claims   communications concerning the nature of something. Claims may simultaneously describe and attribute to causes, for example, poverty is linked to a lack of individual motivation.

Claimsmakers   people and groups who make claims through reports, news accounts, television presentations, and so forth.

Competitive employment   remunerative work in the marketplace of competition. Tasks and requirements of the job derive from the employer's needs not the employee's problems or disabilities.

Empowerment   literally the process of "becoming powerful." This process is aided by support and encouragement from others, opportunities for independent choice, and the assumption and exercise of power.

Resilience   The capacity to recover, to "bounce back."

Social construction   a theory of knowledge or perspective concerning the way that we know and understand complex social phenomena in our social environment. Definitions and meanings are understood subjectively through the use of language and other forms of symbolic communication.

Strengths perspective   a way of looking at people that draws attention to strengths and competencies as the fundamental basis for helping.

Transitional employment placement (TEP)   a part-time, entry-level work placement in a competitive employment setting.

Typification   a social construction or characterization enabled by social interchange and the assignment of meaning.

REFERENCES

Becker, D. R., Drake, R. E., Bond, G., Haiyi, X., Dain, B., & Harrrison, K. (1998). Job terminations among persons with severe mental illness participating in supported employment. *Community Mental Health Journal, 34*(1), 71–82.

Berger, P. L., & Luckmann, T. (1966). *The social construction of reality.* New York: Doubleday.

Best, J. (1995). *Images of issues: Typifying contemporary social problems* (2d ed.). New York: Aldine de Gruyter.

Bilby, R. (1992). A response to the criticisms of transitional employment. *Psychosocial Rehabilitation Journal, 16*(2), 69–82.

Ciompi, L. (1980). Catamnestic long-term study on the course of life and aging of schizophrenics. *Schizophrenia Bulletin, 6*(4), 606–618.

Dougherty, S., Hastie, C., Bernard, J., Broadhurst, S., & Marcus, L. (1992). Supported education: A clubhouse experience. *Psychosocial Rehabilitation Journal, 16*(2), 91–104.

Grob, G. (1994). *The mad among us: A history of the care of America's mentally ill.* New York: The Free Press.

Harding, C. M., Zubin, J., & Stauss, J. S. (1992). Chronicity in schizophrenia: Revisited. *British Journal of Psychiatry, 161*(Suppl. 18), 27–37.

Jimenez, M. (1988). Chronicity in mental disorders: Evolution of a concept. *Social Casework, 69*(10) (December), 627–633.

Lamberg, L. (1998). Mental illness and violent acts: Protecting the patient and the public. *Journal of the American Medical Association, 280*(5), 407–408.

Macias, C., Kinney, R., & Rodican, C. (1995). Transitional employment: An evaluative description of Fountain House practice. *Journal of Vocational Rehabilitation, 5*(2), 151–157.

Malamud, T. J. (1985). Community adjustment: Evaluation of the clubhouse model for psychiatric rehabilitation. *Rehab Brief: Bringing Research into Effective Focus, 9*(2), 1–4.

Polak, P., & Warner, R. (1996). The economic life of seriously mentally ill people in the community. *Psychiatric Services, 47*(2), 270–274.

Rehabilitation Act Amendments of 1986: An act to extend and improve the Rehabilitation Act of 1973, 100 Stat. 1807 (1987).

Saleebey, D. (1994). Culture, theory, and narrative: The intersection of meanings in practice. *Social Work, 39*(4), 351–359.

Saleebey, D. (1996). The strengths perspective in social work practice: Extensions and cautions. *Social Work, 41*(3), 296–305.

Saleebey, D. (Ed.). (1997). *The strengths perspective in social work practice* (2nd ed.). New York: Longman.

Spector, M., & Kitsuse, J. I. (1977). *Constructing social problems.* Menlo Park, CA: Cummings.

Vorspan, R. (1992). Why work works. *Psychosocial Rehabilitation Journal, 16*(2), 49–54.

IDENTITY DEVELOPMENT THROUGH CLUBHOUSE MEMBERSHIP

MAJOR TOPICS:

IDENTITY DEVELOPMENT WITHIN FAMILY AND COMMUNITY

THE DEVELOPMENT OF PERSONAL IDENTITY IS A LIFELONG BIOLOGICAL, PSYCHOLOGICAL, AND SOCIAL PROCESS, AFFIRMED AND REAFFIRMED THROUGH OBSERVATION, PRACTICE, AND THE INCORPORATION OF MEANINGS FROM FAMILY, FRIENDS, AND COMMUNITY.

ILLNESS AND IDENTITY

MENTAL ILLNESS OFTEN DISTORTS AND DAMAGES INDIVIDUAL PROCESSES OF IDENTITY DEVELOPMENT.

MEMBERSHIP AS HABILITATION AND REHABILITATION

MEMBERSHIP IN A CLUBHOUSE PROVIDES A PERSONAL AND SOCIAL DESIGNATION INTENDED TO DISPLACE DISABLING DESIGNATIONS AND ACCOMPANY NEW OPPORTUNITIES FOR ADULT IDENTITY DEVELOPMENT.

IMPLICATIONS OF IDENTITY DEVELOPMENT THEORY

PROFESSIONALS INDIRECTLY BUT POWERFULLY ASSIST OTHERS THROUGH FINDING AND CHANGING UNHELPFUL SOCIAL CONTRIBUTIONS TO IDENTITY DEVELOPMENT.

SUMMARY

I wanted to be a professional fisherman for as long as I can remember. I used to work on my dad's boat. I got to know every inch of it, how to run it and repair it. But then I got sick. I lost my energy and interest.

—A CLUBHOUSE MEMBER'S PERSPECTIVE

Who we are is absolutely connected to what we do. The clubhouse offers members an identity alternative to endless patienthood.

—A STAFF MEMBER'S PERSPECTIVE

In this chapter our attention turns to problems of individual identity development. These are matters of critical importance in that identity is concerned with the development of *self,* the accrued social and individual meanings that constitute *who we are.* Identity development can have special risks for adults with schizophrenia because the onset of illness in their lives often coincides with the developmental challenges of adolescence. Researchers believe that symptoms of schizophrenia disrupt and distort patterns of identity development in adolescence and beyond.

Illnesses of all kinds, physical and mental, interfere with development and require individual adaptation. Although bipolar disorder and depression (see Chapter 2) may also interfere with identity development, primary attention in this chapter is given to schizophrenia because of its obvious destructiveness with regard to identity development and its central importance in community mental health practice.

First, we define identity and examine a few prominent theories and concepts concerning identity development. Then, we consider ways in which the clubhouse model can be viewed as an *identity-building intervention* for people with mental illness as well as for other disabled groups in long-term treatment or care in our society.

IDENTITY DEVELOPMENT WITHIN FAMILY AND COMMUNITY

The development of personal identity is a lifelong biological, psychological, and social process, affirmed and reaffirmed through observation, practice, and incorporation of meanings from family, friends, and community.

We can think of the concept of identity as a *sense of self* comprised of the individual's unique collection of personal and social meanings. Although it changes and evolves, due to our own efforts and the circumstances of our environment, identity is *who we are* as social beings. It encompasses biological, psychological, and social determinants. Therefore, identity is variously described as *ego identity, individual identity,* and *social identity,* depending on the perspective of the theorist. However, all agree that the most influential time of life associated with identity development is youth or adolescence.

This fateful time of change has been described by human development theorists in a variety of ways. Stage theorists, including Freud, Erikson, Piaget, and Kohlberg, all view development as a series of relatively fixed, invariant stages through which the organism must grow, building future developmental challenges on the resolution of past developmental stages. Other theorists, for example, Carel Germain (1991), view development as a complex "life course," determined by a wide variety of interacting factors. Regardless of their theoretical orientation, each of these theorists has recognized adolescence to be an especially important period of change and challenge.

Sources of Identification

Family, school, and neighborhood provide opportunities to observe, understand, and incorporate various identities—symbolic, potential components of self. Through much of the period of later childhood, children play at being mother, father, or teacher. As they approach adolescence, they naturally observe and explore the meanings of gender, race, social role, and status in themselves and others. Testing and trial become more serious and relevant to choices of career. Young people look to adults and each other for identifications that "fit." They seek to discover the ways in which they are alike and dissimilar from others. "Taken together—as they can only be—, similarity and difference are the dynamic principles of identity" (Jenkins, 1996, p. 4). Consequently teenagers want to be like others and yet unique, their own persons.

> The study of identity crisis in adolescence, therefore, is strategic because this is the stage of life when the organism is at the height of its vitality and potency; the person must integrate wider perspectives and more intensive experience; and the social order must provide a renewed identity for its new members, in order to reaffirm—or to renew—its collective identity (Erikson, 1975, p. 47).

Identity development is often closely associated with the development of roles. Indeed the key developmental crisis of adolescence Erikson entitles, "identity versus role confusion." Identity theory and role theory (see Chapter 4) share many similarities. What people do is unquestionably bound to who they are. However, identity theory is concerned with a wide variety of sources of meaning. Role theory focuses more narrowly on role expectations and enactments, structures of social behavior. "Identities are stronger sources of meaning than roles, because of the process of self-construction and individuation that they involve. In simple terms, identities organize meanings while roles organize the functions" (Castells, 1997, p. 6).

Contributions to identity development are derived from many sources. Through examining the various dimensions of identity, we can gain a further understanding of what identity is and what some of those contributing influences might be. They have implications for understanding the clubhouse model as an identity constructing intervention.

Social Identity Dimensions

Recently Jackson and Smith (1999) published the findings of a study that produced a framework for examining social identity. They proposed four dimensions that contribute to the development of social identity: *perception of the intergroup context, in-group attraction, interdependency beliefs (common fate),* and *depersonalization.* Their framework suggests the complexity of the concept of identity.

Perception of the Intergroup Context   According to this dimension, social identification is determined in part by the intergroup situation, that is, the history of the in-group in relation to outgroups. What are the special qualities and characteristics of the in-group, which are known in relation to or because of outgroups? Comparison is a key feature of this dimension. Indeed, during the most intense periods of identity exploration, adolescents are constantly comparing themselves, their parents, and their families to others. They are, in effect, trying to determine who they are and who they are not by comparison with others.

In-Group Attraction   Affective ties and the individual's wish to be a part of the group are key components of this dimension. It is similar to the concept of group cohesion, the desire of group members to associate with others in the group and be seen as part of the group. Young people growing through adolescence develop intense feelings for others. Girlfriends and boyfriends occupy places of central significance. Being associated with the "right" individuals becomes paramount.

Interdependency Beliefs (Common Fate)   Self-interest and self-identity bind the members of a group together. This dimension expresses the assumption that a person's fate and future are bound up with the fate and futures of other group members. It is affirmed through regular communications about shared goals and values, attributes, and aspirations. This dimension describes a powerful, binding, and lasting contribution to social identity.

Depersonalization   According to self-categorization theory, social identity requires increasing levels of depersonalization, that is, "a shift towards the perception of self as an interchangeable exemplar of some social category and away from the perception of self as a unique person" (Turner, Hogg, Oakes, Reicher, & Wetherell, 1987, p. 50). In other words, to some extent the individual combines individual meanings and social meanings through association of the individual with important features and characteristics of the group. Each of these dimensions constitutes a resolution or partial resolution of social identity. Therefore, each is applied to the achievement of *identity status.* Each assists understanding how various identity outcomes or statuses are achieved.

Identity Statuses

James Marcia (1980), building on Erikson's work, identified four kinds of adolescent identity status. These are categories of resolution of the continuing encounter between the individual and his or her social environment. They provide images of various outcomes, the consequences of identity struggles.

Identity Achievement   This is achieved through a period of decision-making from which personal values emerge. This is generally thought of as the most positive and helpful resolution of an identity crisis.

Foreclosure   This is the kind of identity resolution that is not the consequence of internal struggles, but rather the outcome of decisions and values of parents or others. This status does not result in the resolution of identity crisis.

Identity Diffusion   This status is found among people who are unable to exercise their own decisions and find their own directions. They have great difficulty making decisions or resolutions and are often uncomfortable with outcomes. Low self-esteem is associated with this continual reliance upon the identities of others to make decisions.

Moratorium   This is a state of crisis characterized by extreme anxiety. Individuals evidencing this status do not run from decision-making, rather they are constantly facing decisions and constantly living with the accompanying anxiety. They are unable to settle and close decisions and take action. The person is "stuck" in a continuous process, unable to arrive at a product or outcome.

Identity statuses grow from the discovery and testing of certain adult roles, symbols, and stories. It is a primary accomplishment and culmination of adolescent development. This complex process is variously referred to as human development, identity development, and individuation. It is at once biological, psychological, and social (Erikson, 1963).

These identity statuses have special relevance to the development of adults with major mental illnesses. They may represent the culmination of struggles to claim or reclaim identity lost or never attained. For them, without new identity-building alternatives the last three statuses may be the most common resolutions of their identity struggles.

ILLNESS AND IDENTITY

It is widely accepted by theorists and researchers that schizophrenia affects the processes of identity development. One individual with schizophrenia describes her experience growing up with schizophrenia as follows:

> When I was 12 years old, the family doctor prescribed medication for my "nerves." In high school, my mother gave me the Phenobarbital that had been prescribed for her. By late adolescence I had learned that I could trust no one with the truth, and after two unsuccessful suicide attempts had decided stoically to see my life through to the bitter end. (Lovejoy, 1982, p. 606)

Tragically, mental illness can become the personal and social identity of the person. It is captured in cruel phrases such as "he's a schizophrenic," a "chronic," or a "CMI." However, the problem of identity development goes deeper. Recent research suggests that information-processing abnormalities connected to persons with schizophrenia may affect identity development (Hemsley, 1998). Identity development is also thwarted by the lack of appropriate social experiences—the inability to observe and to test a variety of roles and responsibilities. Developmental theory suggests that each group of factors—personal illness factors and social factors—can contribute to incomplete identity development processes. Identity diffusion or moratorium may be the limit of identity status achievement.

Psychological Perspectives on Identity and Mental Illness

Schizophrenia negatively impacts identity development in several ways. Auditory hallucinations or voices may compete with real voices. False ideas or delusions may be injected, such as the notion that one might be reincarnated as a saint or in possession of special abilities to communicate with God. When they are present, delusional ideas compete with real world roles and responsibilities. Feelings of depression, anxiety, or generalized anger can block identity development. In addition, negative symptoms such as the inability to experience pleasure, apathy, and low motivation undermine the role testing that is a part of normal identity development.

In addition to the usual symptoms, many people with schizophrenia have trouble establishing and maintaining both psychological boundaries and physical boundaries. They experience an *altered sense of self*. These are major distortions in perception of self in relation to others. The question "who am I" becomes concretized. This plays havoc with the satisfactory resolution of identity crises. Dr. E. Fuller Torrey (1990) explains:

> Closely allied with delusions and hallucinations is another complex of symptoms which is characteristic of many patients with schizophrenia. Normal individuals have a clear sense of self; they know where their bodies stop and where inanimate objects begin. They know that their hand, when they look at it, belongs to them. Even to make a statement like this strikes most normal persons as absurd because they cannot imagine it being otherwise.
>
> But many persons with schizophrenia can imagine it, for alterations in their sense of self are not uncommon in this condition. Such alterations are frequently associated with alterations in bodily sensations. (p. 63–65)

It is easy to see that all of these factors interfere with normal processes of identity development.

Identity formation may be so problematic, so difficult and distorted that *negative identifications* may result. Erikson (1975) asserts that "Every person and every group harbors a *negative identity* as the sum of all those identifications and identity fragments . . . which his group has taught him to perceive as the mark of fatal difference; in sex role or race, in class or religion" (p. 20). Erikson makes the point that some kind of identity, even a negative identity, is better than none. For individuals with mental illness, identity development can be markedly stunted and distorted by both illness and environmental factors.

- *Distorted thought processes.* Individuals experiencing acute symptoms of schizophrenia are distracted and often exclusively attentive to the voices or delusions. They may sit and ruminate, pace endlessly, or walk the streets of their locale trying to get rid of or control the symptoms.
- *Withdrawal from ordinary social life.* Symptoms of schizophrenia, depression, and other major mental illnesses may cause individuals to withdraw from friends and family. They may stay in their rooms, not get out of bed, or avoid other people in other ways.
- *Odd appearance and mannerisms.* People with mental illness, especially those who have had symptoms for months or years, will often look odd or have peculiar mannerisms that might appear "crazy" to others. If they are paying close attention to hallucinations and delusions, they may not be attentive to hygiene and grooming. They may ignore injuries, illnesses, and other health matters.

Sociological Perspectives on Identity and Mental Illness

From another perspective Goffman developed the sociological concept of *stigma*. "Others don't just perceive our identity; they constitute it. And they do so not only in terms of naming or categorizing, but also in terms of how they respond to or treat us" (Jenkins, 1996, p. 74). It is widely assumed that individuals with mental illness suffer from stigma. The National Alliance for the Mentally Ill sponsors a major national program to combat stigma with factual information. Nonetheless, people suffering from mental illness are often shunned and excluded. They tend to be labeled by others and to adopt a long-term or lifelong identity of "mental patient."

> I felt ashamed, helpless, useless and frightened . . . My experiences in the community only confirmed these feelings. At a bus stop once, I struck up a conversation with a woman. The inevitable question arose: "What do you do?" I hesitated, but finally said that I was retired and that I had been in a psychiatric hospital. The woman's reaction was immediate and unforgettable. She gasped, then looked quickly for an approaching bus; seeing none, she flagged down a passing cab. (Lovejoy, 1982, p. 606)

As young people without mental illness are experiencing their abilities, testing various social and vocational roles available to them, people with mental illness are struggling to understand their very different internal and environmental experiences. Young people with mental illness have to struggle with the same developmental tasks as all adolescents, but they encounter special problems. "The very nature of their illnesses and circumstances often means they have to struggle to catch up emotionally, cognitively, socially and vocationally before they are ready to assume adult roles" (Davis & Vander Stoep, 1996, p. 9).

Historically, the schizophrenic patient has been viewed as lacking an adequate sense of self and being a passive participant in treatment. Current concepts of negative symptoms, including anergia and anhedonia, reflect this view. Most patients certainly seem unmotivated and uncooperative at times during their illness. However, both empirical data and clinical experience suggest that it is a critical error to accept withdrawal, passivity, or even active resistance as inflexible characteristics (Bellack & Mueser, 1993, p. 320).

Armed with this body of theory, the helping professional can examine ways to positively influence identity development. Staff can develop the clubhouse or any other kind of constructed community as a kind of "identity development center," one that establishes and sometimes reestablishes conditions for members to resolve many of the challenges of the developmental stage normally associated with adolescence.

MEMBERSHIP AS HABILITATION AND REHABILITATION

Membership in a clubhouse provides a personal and social designation intended to displace disabling designations and accompany new opportunities for adult identity development.

Clubhouse membership is designed to serve both a *rehabilitative* function in that it provides services to overcome symptoms of illness and a *habilitative* function in that the clubhouse is continuously present for members and may remain a central fact in their lives. In addition to providing the opportunity for "lifetime membership," the clubhouse needs to help members find opportunities for identifications within the larger society.

Many members have long-term histories as mental patients in hospitals and clients in halfway houses and mental health centers. Once treatment is terminated, individuals must still solve major problems of meeting expenses, finding and maintaining housing for themselves, obtaining medication, and replacing old friendships and familiar relationships. Paradoxically, "success" in the terms of treatment or institution results in the termination of important and supportive social connections.

The clubhouse model attempts to replace these destructive dislocations of termination with what Castells describes as *identity for resistance* or *exclusion of the excluders by the excluded.* Applying Castells' (1997) definition we can conceptualize clubhouse membership as "the building of a

Members and Friends

At the age of 36, Joe had spent most of his youth in and out of mental hospitals, had lost most of his childhood friends, and had attended, at least briefly, almost all the mental health programs in the area. He had good intentions when he began these programs, but the therapy and socialization groups seemed never to go anywhere. He found himself daydreaming and sometimes listening to voices and "tuning out" the group. Sometimes he was asked questions about his relationships and his feelings in ways that made him anxious and uncomfortable. Therapy always seemed too close. He did not understand. He wanted to be left alone. Often he simply left these situations.

One day a case manager for the mental health center talked him into visiting the clubhouse. Joe came along and was given a tour. When the group walked into the research unit, Joe saw a group of three new computers sitting on long worktables. A staff member explained that the computers had been a gift of a business in the area and that they were to be used for keeping statistics on clubhouse work, attendance, outreach, and other important matters. The only problem was that nobody knew very much about the software applications. They needed some special expertise and training for staff and members. Joe had some computer experience at his dad's small business and had taken a course at the community college a few years ago. He thought he might be able to help.

He turned on a computer and examined the screen. Before long, his few minutes on the tour had turned into two hours. He returned the next day and the next to learn about the clubhouse and tell others how to use the computer. As weeks and months went on, he became an integral part of the work unit. His work and that of his staff and member colleagues in the unit gave the Executive Director all the information needed for annual reports and planning sessions. Without looking for them, he had found others who shared his interest.

---

defensive identity in the terms of the dominant institutions/ideologies, reversing the value judgement while reinforcing the boundary" (p. 9). The clubhouse model provides social support to individual members as they revisit their personal identity struggles and simultaneously help strengthen clubhouse social system boundaries.

The clubhouse invites members to use their membership in a variety of self-fulfilling and socially contributing ways—working in the clubhouse work unit, taking transitional or supported employment positions, obtaining independent employment, or volunteering their skills outside the clubhouse. Regardless of the individual choices of members, productive work of all kinds is the organizing focus of daily life in a clubhouse. The work units often provide what is seen as surrogate family experiences, primary group experiences that once again provide opportunities for members to revisit their own identity development. They can see other members and staff working for the clubhouse.

This focus means that members are surrounded by people involved constantly in activity that benefits others. They are viewing members and staff engaged in tasks that benefit the work unit and the clubhouse as well as individual members. They are offered the opportunity, again and again, to participate in work of their choice. Just as for adolescents, many of these choices do not lead members to continuous employment or career. However, they do expose unengaged members to the adult world of work (unlike hospital or day treatment programs). For the most part, members aspire to be a part of this work world.

The clubhouse provides contributing work roles for any members who choose to accept them. The worth of all kinds of contributing work is upheld through consistently combining attention to "what needs to be done" with the request for assistance from members. No form of work is disparaged. No aspect of work that members do is viewed as small or unimportant. On the contrary, individuals are thanked for their contribution to the group and the community, and members are congratulated for jobs of any size or description that are especially "well done." For example,

- One member continuously maintains clubhouse attendance records. Because he understands computers and statistical software, he is able to regularly load data and provide statistics to members and program administrators. Throughout the year, his work provides "feedback" concerning clubhouse accomplishments and service gaps.
- Another member greets members and staff as they come in the door each day. She makes sure they are greeted with a smile and assisted if they need information or directions. She also takes care of the coat closet and of checking coats and jackets.
- Another member helps prepare food in the kitchen, but after lunch she goes to her regular transitional employment placement on the bus. Working in the clubhouse keeps her in touch with friends in the clubhouse, but the employment placement gives her competitive work experience.

Not everyone works consistently. One member smokes silently on the porch, apparently concentrating on something but not sharing his thoughts.

Nonetheless, he arrives on time in the morning and is welcomed and encouraged to stay and participate in whatever way he would like. Members who come to the clubhouse and keep to themselves for long periods of time are often able to participate more actively later. They receive encouragement but not pressure or coercion. For other members, daily attendance at the clubhouse would not be feasible. Some are employed full-time or are in school. They just participate on special occasions such as the Thanksgiving dinner or clubhouse camping trips.

Through its ongoing development, the clubhouse provides a set of psychological and social conditions or influences that are very different from those of the hospital, mental health center, halfway house, and therapist. The clubhouse socially constructs the environment, including enabling symbols of all kinds such as the language used to describe members and their roles, the name of the facility, and the customs of sharing space, resources, and governance of the clubhouse. It replaces formal legal statements of "patient rights" with clubhouse standards, and it opens meetings of all kinds to both members and staff. Confidentiality, a cornerstone principle of hospital and mental health center treatment is eliminated from all except a limited number of records and transactions. In short, the clubhouse supports the provision of needed psychiatric treatment and medication. At the same time, it eliminates or attempts to eliminate any vestige of the norms, customs, and practices of psychiatric treatment in the clubhouse. It establishes expectations of growth and change throughout the clubhouse community using combinations of relationships and shared work.

Relationships between members and between members and staff are characterized by naturalness and normality. A simple schedule of planning, work, and social experiences provides environmental structure. No effort is made to develop a therapeutic transference in relationships between staff and members. In fact, the psychological distance ordinarily expected and required in psychiatric treatment settings is specifically avoided and excluded. Friendships are encouraged, yet bounded and structured by shared work roles. Staff help members incorporate the structure and maintain their own boundaries through work in the clubhouse and other activities. The collective focus on a variety of kinds of shared work and play structures relationships and reduces the potential of a destructive blurring of social and psychological boundaries.

Daily experience within the clubhouse is structured to provide opportunities that can be evaluated and "seized" by members. Members actively shape their daily experiences as well as their long-term goals. They have opportunities to experience success and failure. They are not protected from the consequences of their behavior and choices. Therefore, they are able to experience their own power to shape their lives despite mental illness.

Regardless of members' state of mind and behavior, the clubhouse attempts to provide the social context for a more successful resolution of "identity crises." Sometimes members (or others with mental illnesses) are confronted with an unusual career choice: Shall I become a professional patient or a contributor and worker despite my mental illness? This choice is not necessarily conscious nor explicit, but many internal and external incentives support the choice to stay within the same protective and defining frameworks of hospital, halfway house, or mental health center. The clubhouse model seeks to offer alternatives and counterincentives.

The development of meaningful work activities involves the identification and elaboration of a structure of member roles. The complex roles of helping professionals include establishing and maintaining the conditions for the development of individual and social identity. The development of a social *identity for resistance* means being an active participant in the construction of clubhouse symbols and meanings and encouraging others. Typically, staff and members co-lead this activity in group gatherings: unit meetings, community meetings, transitional employment meetings, and so forth. Members contribute to this process through sharing their experiences, ideas, knowledge, and skills.

The member who speaks up in a community meeting to explain that he or she is working at a competitive job after being hospitalized more than six times in one year is helping the group and its members distinguish and value their own unique identities. Through the sharing of stories like this, meanings and symbols of "mental patient" and "hospital" are transformed into badges of honor and symbols of identity for resistance.

IMPLICATIONS OF IDENTITY DEVELOPMENT THEORY

As suggested in the previous chapter, the clubhouse in its entirety is a social construction intended to shape personal and social identity. Other disabling conditions, illnesses, and statuses can be examined and altered in a similar way by the thoughtful involvement of clients and professional helpers. Professionals establish and maintain the social conditions that raise the consciousness of all concerning negative identity factors. Helping environments involving long-term care and change, including activities and day programs, schools, and other institutions, can be regularly examined by all who influence and are influenced by the factors that contribute to the development of social identity. The following are some of the steps that can be taken to positively affect the identity development in strengths focused environments:

- Identify targets for change in the structure of socially constructed identity factors. These include all those factors that might contribute to a negative identity development. There may be separate staff and client entrances, separate

bathrooms, exclusion of clients from decision-making in the agency or endeavor, subtle messages of marginalization from staff, and so forth.
- Eliminate disabling or destructive contributions to identity development.
- Implement changes that construct a more enabling, more positive set of factors for identity development.
- Maintain processes, procedures, and customs that sensitize everyone to these factors and permit ongoing evaluation of them.

SUMMARY

Identity is an accrual of personal and social meanings which comprise the continuous sense of self. Identity may be disturbed or destroyed by schizophrenia or other major mental illnesses.

Adolescence is the defining stage and event in identity development according to Erikson's theory. The epigenetic crisis of "identity vs. role confusion" is its hallmark. These developmental challenges have both psychological and sociological aspects. Alternative perspectives contribute depth and richness to our understanding of identity development. Each perspective also contributes to our understanding of helpful identity development interventions.

Clubhouse models serve as contributing, powerful, yet indirect, identity-building features organized to elicit skills and competencies from members with mental illnesses. These community-building, identity-building approaches are relevent to other social welfare populations that exist outside or on the margins of community.

APPLYING CONCEPTS

1. Describe the similarities and differences between concepts of *role* and *identity*.
2. What are some of the reasons why identity development is problematic for people with schizophrenia?
3. Identify and discuss different applications of the concept of *identity for resistance*.
4. Identify major components of your personal and social identity. Discuss your ideas about their sources.

GLOSSARY

Adolescence   the developmental stage between childhood and adulthood; youth.

Epigenetic crisis   a period of developmental risk and opportunity that results in resolution of one of a series of developmental stages.

Class Projects

Implement a "consciousness-raising" group in your organization or agency. Identify and work to reduce stigmatizing behaviors and other organizational customs, symbols, and practices that might contribute to the negative identity development of some members.

With others in your class, visit a clubhouse in your area and ask members to explain what kinds of people and experiences help them feel better and more in control of their lives.

Habilitation   to equip or make capable.

Identity   sameness and continuity of biological, psychological, and social aspects of the personality that comprise a sense of self.

Identity for resistance   personal and social identity comprised of exclusion of the excluders by the excluded.

Identity status   the culmination or resolution of identity struggles.

Identity-building intervention   all of those socially constructed, deliberately planned patterns of behavior that contribute to the development of individual and social identity.

Negative identity   the "sum" of irreconcilable or undesirable identifications and identity fragments.

Rehabilitation   to make capable again, following a period of disability or deprivation, for example, those caused by acute illness, hospitalization, and so forth.

Stigma   a socially assigned, negative characterization of a person or group of people such as those with mental illness.

REFERENCES

Bellack, A., & Mueser, L. (1993). Psychosocial treatment for schizophrenia. *Schizophrenia Bulletin, 19*(2), 317–336.

Castells, M. (1997). *The power of identity.* Malden, MA: Blackwell.

Davis, M., & Vander Stoep, A. (1996). *The transition to adulthood among adolescents who have serious emotional disturbance.* New York: Policy Research Associates, Inc.

Erikson, E. (1963). *Childhood and society* (2nd ed.). New York: Norton.

Erikson, E. (1975). *Life history and historical moment.* New York: Norton.

Germain, C. (1991). *Human behavior in the social environment.* New York: Columbia University Press.

Hemsley, D. R. (1998). The disruption of sense of self in schizophrenia: Potential links with disturbances of information processing. *British Journal of Medical Psychology, 71*(2), 115–124.

Jackson, J. W. & Smith, E. R. (1999). Conceptualizing social identity: A new framework and evidence for the impact of different dimensions. *Personality and Social Psychology Bulletin, 25*(1), 120–135.

Jenkins, R. (1996). *Social identity.* New York: Routledge.

Lovejoy, M. (1982). Expectations and the recovery process. *Schizophrenia Bulletin, 8*(4), 605–609.

Marcia, J. (Ed.). (1980). *Identity in adolescence.* New York: Wiley.

Peckoff, J. (1992). Patienthood to personhood. *Psychosocial Rehabilitation Journal, 16*(2), 5–7.

Torrey, E. F. (1990). *Surviving schizophrenia.* New York: Harper and Row.

Turner, J. C., Hogg, M. A., Oakes, P. J., Reicher, S. D., & Wetherell, M. (1987). *Rediscovering the social group: A self-categorization theory.* Oxford, England. Blackwell.

SOCIALIZATION INTO COMMUNITIES

MAJOR TOPICS:

SOCIALIZATION THEORY AND CLUBHOUSE LEARNING

MEMBERS AND STAFF LEARN THROUGH OBSERVATION, EXPERIENCE, REPETITION, AND INCORPORATION OF THE ATTITUDES, VALUES, AND BEHAVIORS NEEDED.

SOCIAL EXCHANGE: THE MARKETPLACE ANALOGY

MEMBERS AND STAFF ARE ATTRACTED TO OTHERS FOR THE POSSIBILITY OF REWARDING EXCHANGE RELATIONS.

INTEGRATION AND DIFFERENTIATION OF SOCIAL ROLES

THE DISTINCTIVE NATURE OF THE CLUBHOUSE EMERGES FROM EXCHANGE RELATIONS.

SOCIALIZATION, SOCIAL EXCHANGE, AND ADAPTATION

AN INCREASE IN EXPLICIT AND IMPLICIT SOCIAL CURRENCY IS A CONSEQUENCE OF SOCIAL INTERACTIONS CONSTRUCTED ON MULTIPLE LEVELS.

SUMMARY

My spirits pick up when I get to the clubhouse and someone meets me at the door with "good morning" and calls me by name. My friends are here.

—A CLUBHOUSE MEMBER'S PERSPECTIVE

Members' social skills improve in the reality of the clubhouse. They're not practicing or taking lessons on how to get along in a community. They're doing it.

—A STAFF MEMBER'S PERSPECTIVE

This chapter reviews and applies two related bodies of sociological theory. First, socialization theory directs our attention to a range of factors that contribute to the acquisition of knowledge and skills for adaptation. In exploring socialization theory, we discover new ways to view the clubhouse social construction as a complex of learning experiences.

Another complementary theory focuses on social exchange relations. This theory provides a way of understanding how attraction and reciprocity function in relationships. Social exchange theory focuses our attention on the benefits of social relationships: what the benefits are, who gets them, who gives them, and under what conditions. Understanding social exchange helps us to understand the uniqueness of relationships within the clubhouse and how the model establishes and maintains conditions for these relationships. Together these two bodies of theory help illuminate complex social relations in the clubhouse model.

SOCIALIZATION THEORY AND CLUBHOUSE LEARNING

Socialization refers to the aggregate of social experiences in which we participate to become valued members of our culture. It can also be thought of as a spontaneous educational process involving the acquisition of the values, knowledge, attitudes, and skills needed to function effectively in society (Johnson, 1995, p. 267). Clubhouse members and staff learn through observation, experience, repetition, and incorporation of the attitudes, values, and expected behaviors.

Unlike schooling, this education occurs as a result of spontaneous interaction without any explicit attempt to train or educate. It involves the acquisition of roles and a lot more. Role theory primarily focuses on roles and role behavior. Socialization involves all the conditions of social education: observation, experience, development of self-control and adoption of the social values and behaviors needed to get along with others, and management of one's own behavior in a manner that furthers personal development (Gecas, 1981, p. 166). It is closely associated with identity development. In fact, the anticipated outcome of both identity development and socialization is the emergence of a social self. Crucial aspects of these processes first occur in childhood. However, socialization is a lifelong process that continues to shape the social self.

Implementation of the clubhouse model involves creating socially-constructing conditions that can enhance the competency and life satisfaction of adults with mental illness. These conditions of planned and deliberate socialization set the stage for people to learn new and more adaptive patterns of relationship. The processes of socialization are cumulative (Goslin, 1969, p. 11). They contribute to the individual's development of aspirations and ambitions and skills and discipline, as well as enabling the further acquisition of social roles.

Positive Conditions for Clubhouse Model Socialization

Socialization is a somewhat awkward subject of study. We are not used to thinking about the way in which we are socialized or the processes involved. Yet they occur and recur throughout our lives. In the clubhouse model, social-ization takes place within the framework of the culture of a given clubhouse. Socialization succeeds where there are effective member and staff role mod-els, established customs and traditions, and a community that addresses mem-ber needs.

The conditions for clubhouse socialization include all those elements that comprise the clubhouse standards. In summary, these conditions include the development of a place whose ongoing life is driven by staff and member col-laboration, where individuals with mental illness have work that needs doing. Clubhouse model socialization has a strong component of values that gives the model its uniqueness and vitality. Members and staff often discuss, review, and critique clubhouse standards and their own values. Such discus-sions and the planning that follows them generally lead to a high level of involvement and consensus.

Supportive relationships of all kinds are encouraged. Staff may invite a member or a group of members to a ball game, a movie, or a concert after work in the clubhouse. A member might invite members and staff to a birth-day party or other personal celebration. The shared purpose of all clubhouse activity guides staff and members into natural, collegial relations. It is critical that the socialization experiences available to members within and through association with the clubhouse instill knowledge, skills, and values compatible with those in the world outside the clubhouse.

Members are not recipients but active participants in socialization processes. First, they seek out others for guidance in their efforts to "do the right thing." Although new members may be ambivalent about their new asso-ciation, in general they want to conform to the expectations of staff and mem-bers who have greater experience in the clubhouse.

Negative Socialization Conditions. These are unhelpful or destructive conditions of socialization. Because clubhouses are socially constructed, these conditions are occasionally found in clubhouses despite their incompatibility with clubhouse standards and their inherent destructiveness. They include the following:

- *Explicit or implicit coercion.* Coercion builds resistance and resentment. It does not work. It makes something else the focus of concern. It leads to misunderstanding and confusion on all sides. The clubhouse model adheres firmly to the idea that real learning takes place in situations where the learning can be tested, consequences experienced, and behavior changed according to the assessment and decision of the member.
- *Individual as object of work.* The clubhouse model assumes that when individuals become the primary target of change their defenses are activated. They often resist the control implicit in being the object of another's work. They may experience such helping efforts, however well-intentioned, as hostile and invasive. This is especially true when some people do not know or do not believe that they have mental illness. They develop alternative understandings about what the problem is and what to do about it.

  Another product of a continuing focus on individual change is that a social stratification tends to develop that is unhelpful to individuals, groups, and the community-building enterprise as a whole. The clubhouse tends to divide into staff workers and member nonworkers. Then the tendency is toward resumption of patient or client roles and statuses.

  Although the clubhouse model is a design to assist people with mental illnesses, that assistance is derived from the shared purpose of community-building. People may want and use various forms of mental health treatment while they are members of the clubhouse, but it is critically important that the clubhouse is not viewed as a treatment.
- *Imitation or pseudowork for members.* Many members have hospital or institutional experience where the activities are intended to be therapeutic but not necessarily tied to real life responsibilities. Members sometimes speak of institutional experiences producing ceramics that are simply shelved and forgotten or participating in group outings and activities that simply fill and structure time (Jackson et al., 1996). They contrast these experiences with their work in the clubhouse.

  The various work roles taken by members in a clubhouse must be genuine. They must have outcomes or products. They must be seen to contribute positively to the community in some way. The genuineness of the tasks will contribute to staff and self-appraisal of work accomplishments.
- *No permanent discharge or graduation.* Members come and go from clubhouses often for all kinds of reasons: they want to move, they are bored or excited about something else, or they develop another circle of friends who offer support and friendship. But they are not discharged by staff. The socialization objectives of a clubhouse are to develop and, if desired, sustain a network of friends and others who can be present in the person's life to assist the process of continuous adaptation. Discharge would only make sense if the service offered was treatment and the members had a short-term illness or set of disabling conditions known to be temporary. Under such conditions, it would

make sense for the "clients or patients" to use the service and then separate
and leave.

- *No mandated "therapeutic distance."* Clubhouse model processes of socialization
  operate in conditions where social distance is determined naturally, by the nature
  of the relationship. Behaviors that construct role divisions are explicitly avoided.
  Staff do not wear uniforms, do not have offices for their exclusive use, nor do
  they put their academic credentials on the walls or do other things to
  symbolically or actually differentiate themselves from members. Clubhouse
  members and staff who like each other and share interests often socialize outside
  of the clubhouse.

Socialization theory deals with all of those aspects of clubhouse model life
that affect the behavior of members. Therefore, it overlaps other theories and
theoretical perspectives such as identity theory, role theory, and social
exchange theory. Each of these explains aspects of socialization.

First, people naturally see how people behave to get what they want and
need from others. Observation is fundamental. They need to see people interacting in normal and normalizing circumstances. New clubhouse members
look to older and more experienced members as well as staff to understand the
ways that people are expected to behave. This helps them understand how
others greet people, how they assume work responsibilities, how they deal
with anxiety, and so forth.

Second, experience is a powerful way to learn. People seem to learn most
effectively when they concretely apply their learning in doing. Learning how
to work with others is complex. It is enhanced and affirmed through practice
in situations where demands are real and where successful communication
and behavior activities are necessary for everyday life.

Third, repetition helps consolidate learning. Unfamiliar behaviors become
customs through practice. The daily life of the clubhouse is filled with routine
patterns. These routine or customary ways of behaving provide a repetitive
structure of time and activities. Doors of the clubhouse open and close at certain times of the day. Work units begin their business with meetings at routine
hours. Community meetings are regularly scheduled. Each of these routines is
understood and applied to all participants, in the same way that the routines
of a business or school organize the time of all employees or students. The reg-
ularity and predictability of schedules helps social and personal organization.
It diminishes chaos and the associated anxiety.

Finally, the social milieu of the clubhouse invites, but does not compel,
natural communication between individuals within work groups on projects
and community support of isolated members or members with special needs.
The invitation to participate or help out carries opportunities as well as social
obligations that must be met. If the task needed to be addressed requires that
members put on their best clothes, then their best clothes are worn. The character of the work to be done determines the social, psychological, and other

resources that must be brought to bear on the task. This single factor changes the nature of the request for help. It is an opportunity for members to try out skills and take on responsibilities.

Clubhouse values and culture are often regular subjects of discussion in work units and community meetings. Discussion of values pervades formal and informal discussions. Such discussions help to confirm the shared purposes of the clubhouse. They help to draw members and staff together in what is approvingly referred to by members and staff as "strong" clubhouses, that is, clubhouses guided by clubhouse standards and driven by shared values.

> Value consensus is of crucial significance for social processes that pervade complex social structures, because standards commonly agreed upon serve as mediating links for social transactions between individuals and groups without any direct contact. (Blau, 1964, p. 253)

Although common in day treatment and partial hospitalization programs, the posting of rules for appropriate behavior is not the standard for clubhouse communities. Such external requirements for adherence to rules would be viewed as paternalistic and inappropriate for adults. Nonetheless, as in a strong family, vocal and lively discussions concerning values and goals of the group go on continuously. Since the development of clubhouse standards, such discussions focus on proposed changes in clubhouse practice and procedure that will better reflect shared values embedded in the clubhouse standards.

This kind of experiential education for living is inherently egalitarian and accessible in the clubhouse model. Socialization experiences seem natural and "normal" in the context because the clubhouse creates community-building conditions that are similar to those found elsewhere in the larger society.

SOCIAL EXCHANGE: THE MARKETPLACE ANALOGY

The clubhouse model can be thought of as a context or stage for social exchanges. Exchanges continuously make it and reshape it. As a social construction, many aspects of the clubhouse model can be and are modified to fit local circumstances and changing conditions.

The marketplace analogy helps us understand social exchange processes. This theory is sometimes described as applying an economic model to social relations. Social exchange processes are examined as transactions in the economic marketplace (Blau, 1964, p. 253). According to this theory, people individually and in groups are attracted to others for what benefits they can accrue from their exchange of social "currency."

To understand social exchange theory, we need to understand some of the basic assumptions that provide its foundation. The following are theoretical assumptions underpinning social exchange theory (Martin & O'Connor, 1989, p. 107):

- *Unspecified obligations.* Unlike the obligations of economic exchange, social exchanges remain at an implicit level. They are unstated, not codified or institutionalized. They exist because "that's the way things are," or "it's the expected thing."
- *Trust.* This is a necessary condition of social exchange. Exchange relations grow in an environment of trustworthiness. Therefore, although it is impossible to guarantee that people and programs will be reliable and available to members, clubhouse administrators, funding bodies, and staff work to assure a high level of responsiveness, program stability, and accessibility. These factors contribute to a foundation of trust and feelings of trustworthiness.
- *Attraction.* People are socially attracted to each other because of the possibility of rewarding exchange relations. Based on behaviorist psychology, exchange theory asserts that people work to obtain rewards and avoid punishments. If rewarded, they will repeat their behaviors. If punished, behaviors will tend to diminish. In this way exchange behaviors help to shape social life at the individual and group levels. Social exchange theorists assume that people are attracted to others for what rewards they can gain from their association. Processes of social exchange are based upon the possession of desirable benefits and the capacity to engage in exchange.
- *Rewards.* The rewards of social exchange are both intrinsic and extrinsic. Intrinsic rewards include approval, status, experiences, support, love, and power. Extrinsic rewards include jobs, money, housing, and material goods. Any clubhouse can analyze and roughly estimate the extent to which these rewards are available to members. Adequate and appropriate social rewards strengthen social ties. They reinforce the connections between people and increase the likelihood that exchanges will occur again and with greater frequency. Inadequate rewards lead to the opposite.

Possibilities of social exchanges diminish as an exchange equilibrium is approached.

These assumptions constitute hypotheses that have been tested in the study of group life. Social exchange can be seen as driven by wants and needs for the accrual of social currency. Social exchange is based on norms of reciprocity without which social life would be impossible. It grows from unspecified obligations between people. These mutual obligations include the expectation that people should help people who help them and they should not injure people who help them. This principle can be thought of as a sociological equivalent of the biblical injunction, "Do unto others as you would have them do unto you." Social imbalances that hold promises of reward promote the initiation of relationships.

"Processes of social attraction create integrative bonds between associates, and integrative processes also unite various groups in a community. Exchange processes between individuals contribute to differentiation and intergroup

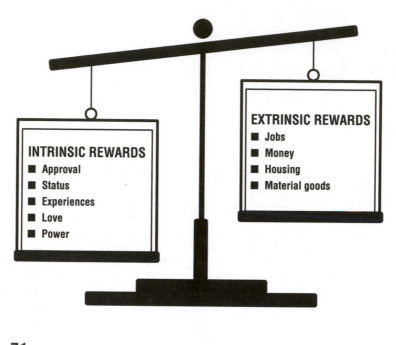

FIGURE **7.1**

Exchange Rewards Scale

exchanges further differentiation" (Blau, 1964, p. 255). These processes form the basis for the unique characteristics of social groups, organizations, and communities including clubhouses. They also give rise to the differentiation of power among individuals and groups.

In earlier chapters, the symptoms and environmental challenges of people with mental illness were described. It was noted that the disabling characteristics of mental illness were often pervasive and debilitating, affecting psychological and social life. It was argued that illness factors tend to disempower and create ongoing reliance on others for meeting basic needs. Social exchange can be drastically affected by mental illness factors.

An individual without resources but in need must either force someone to give assistance, go to another source, or figure out how to get along without help. The only other alternative is for the individual to subordinate himself or herself as an inducement for obtaining the needed help (Blau, 1964). This principle of social exchange helps us understand the subordination often found in long-term care facilities.

Subordination is characteristic of institutional life for many adults with mental illness. Control and efficiency objectives may displace other patient care objectives in hospitals and other institutions. To receive help patients must subordinate themselves to service providers in the ward or living situation. Their social exchange currency is low or nonexistent, therefore, their need for help (initiation of professional assistance) confirms their subordinate status. This contributes to feelings of incompetence and low self-worth often reported by adults with mental illness. Understanding this paradox of helping is difficult. Institutions and institutional resources have been established presumably to help not harm.

Care in the hospital or long-term care facility is intended to create conditions of safety, support, reduced responsibilities (other than to cooperate with treatment), and reduced social stimuli so that, for the most part, patients can be cared for, treated, and released with improved capacity to cope with problems of daily living. However, attitudinal expressions of subordination from staff, such as condescension and patronization can and do enter relationships in the mental ward or hospital. Social experiences characterized by these conscious and unconscious expressions of institutional staff often contribute to feelings of low self-worth and disability among patients. Regardless of the intentions of professional staff, such communications may be experienced as disempowering.

From a social exchange perspective, the clubhouse model provides an alternative to the institutional pattern of social exchange. It does this in a number of ways. A basic goal is to insure that members have and can acquire more social currency.

Rather than reduce or eliminate responsibilities, the clubhouse model creates a network of responsibilities, intended not to be burdensome or anxiety-producing but rather to help individuals join the provision of services. The clubhouse model establishes the conditions for them to meet the needs of others and their own needs, to have value and to be valued. Inasmuch as their participation is by invitation and is not compulsory, they are free to join the clubhouse work force as they see themselves able. However, the clubhouse model destabilizes status positions. People earn the approval and appreciation of others for their work, not for continuously occupying a job. Staff or members who gain rewards primarily by occupying certain positions may tend to grasp and hold onto them, thereby denying the opportunity of work to someone else.

The focus of work in the clubhouse model is designed to exclude the conventional provision of services by providers and receipt of services by recipients. The focus of staff and member energy in a clubhouse is on the mutually beneficial work, rather than the symptoms or problems of the member or ex-patient. Therefore, tasks can be defined, planned, and carried out as regular and repeated exchanges between staff and members. The collaborations are based on the work to be done.

From a social exchange perspective, this shift in focus to shared work tasks has a number of other transformative features. It offers the possibility of coming to know the member as a contributor, a person with resources. Community involvement draws the individual into community life without insisting that he or she take a specific job. The work is explicit, concrete, time-limited, and above all, real. Therefore, member contributions are genuine and discussions about the work are real.

This genuineness increases the significance of staff opinions about the member as a contributor. Simple reassurance that someone is a "good" person or "everything will be all right" does not have the same significance and power as "a job well done." Of course, members must manage their illness with medications and therapy. However, he or she is no longer the continuing focus of change.

Work and Exchange

It is a gray, drizzly morning. Carrie runs from her bus to the door of her employer. She has a half-time transitional employment job at the Gables Manufacturing plant. Her job is to see that mail is distributed and collected throughout the large plant. She shakes her jacket and hangs it in the employees' lounge, then walks with her supervisor to the mailroom. She trades greetings with three people sitting at the table. They know about the TE program through which Carrie got her job, and they know Carrie to be likable and conscientious about her work responsibilities.

The company has recently made a major sales pitch. The mailroom is flooded with responses. Carrie and her colleagues have to work overtime. She's proud of her work and pleased that her colleagues treat her as an equal because she works hard and gets the job done.

This vignette illustrates that members of the clubhouse are assumed by staff and members to have exchange currency that others want. They have skills, knowledge, and abilities to do work, help others, and benefit themselves. The exercise of these in the clubhouse, the community, or on transitional employment placements builds their store of intrinsic and extrinsic value or social currency. They acquire status as workers and colleagues. They gain approval and recognition from other members and staff. They become exemplars of clubhouse membership. They gain power as contributing members of the clubhouse. For competitive employment in the community (TE or regular employment), they gain money, which has both extrinsic value and intrinsic or symbolic value. As the behavior continues, the rewards multiply. In these ways the clubhouse model works to remediate destructive, institutionalized conditions of social exchange established by treatment in many institutions of long-term care.

INTEGRATION AND DIFFERENTIATION OF SOCIAL ROLES

As in any social system, the forces of equilibrium and disequilibrium are in constant contention in any clubhouse. They are identified and managed through formal and informal social processes of group meetings, discussions between individuals, and committees. It is the continuous interplay of all these social forces at multiple levels within clubhouse communities that gives them what Blau (1964) would call their "distinctive nature and dynamics."

Individual Level

On first contact with the clubhouse new members may feel overwhelmed or shy or frightened. In any case they have many questions. For instance, where is the community meeting? What is the schedule? Where are the supplies? How do I get transportation to this or that activity? Like a newcomer anywhere, he or she must take steps to understand the community and find a role and niche. Before long, the new member has accumulated much knowledge about the clubhouse and how it works. This is now added to the knowledge and special talents that he or she brings and can be demonstrated in work and activities. In this environment, knowledge of people, customs, and procedures is not solely the realm of staff. Members know and are encouraged to know as much as they can about the clubhouse, others, and themselves. Clubhouse "expertise" is accessible and obtainable. Staff and members in the clubhouse model work to share the expertise and all other aspects of daily life. The focus is on the clubhouse and its work, not mental health or recovery of the individual per se. Because of this shift in focus, patterns of exchange imbalances, institutionalized in hospitals and long-term care facilities, can be changed.

Group Level

By design every task is planned and carried out in groups. Group relationships provide a number of social exchange benefits. They provide a sense of belonging based on real work contributions. They provide a stage for cooperation and collaboration, for observing, testing, and adopting alternative social behaviors. They enable members to experience being "the expert" in different ways, depending on the task or group of tasks. Genuine pride and self-esteem are gained genuinely through work accomplishments.

Clubhouse Community Level

To the extent that a clubhouse is seen by the larger community as a productive and beneficial place, staff and members can share and experience this positive appraisal. Community accomplishments can be claimed by the individual contributors. Clubhouses are places designed to enable access to all the intrinsic and extrinsic rewards of social exchange. Paradoxically, the more the clubhouse members gain the rewards of social exchange and are recognized for their competencies, the more the larger community tends to see them as not needing clubhouse benefits.

SOCIALIZATION, SOCIAL EXCHANGE, AND ADAPTATION

Although social exchange theory had its beginnings in the examination of dyadic relationships (Simmel, 1950), it has also been applied to social relations within and between larger groups and organizations (Blau, 1964). In the clubhouse model it can be applied to member-member relations, staff-member relations, and organization-environment relations.

Because social exchange theory focuses upon social balances and imbalances, it may have special relevance to understanding the relations of staff and members in the clubhouse model. Applying the marketplace analogy of social exchange theory, clients or members with mental illness may have less to exchange: fewer material resources, less power, less social influence, and less attractiveness. As a consequence, they have less social "currency" to use in the social marketplace and are less able to have their wants and needs addressed. The social exchange equation changes and becomes one-sided due to mental illness factors. However, in addition, the institutional environments of hospital and residential treatment facilities may reinforce the social exchange imbalance. "Exchange processes then give rise to differentiation of power." (Blau, 1964, p. 253).

The institutional experience of many patients and ex-patients is that therapists, social workers, nurses and doctors have extraordinary influence and power. These professionals regularly have responsibility and authority for clients or patient care and treatment. They have access to client or patient records. They have special areas of the institution in which to do their work—offices, group activities rooms, and so forth. They have control over daily schedules and the management of supplies and human resources, as well as the primary production outputs of the institution. Important jobs, indeed careers, are held by counselors, social workers, nurses and doctors, but not clients or patients. The difference often underlines a "we" and "they" kind of division characteristic of life in institutions. By design the clubhouse model avoids this dichotomy.

Socialization and social exchange are fundamental processes of adaptation to social relations. They point to a primary objective of the clubhouse model. Members should be enabled to become more capable and adaptive through their association and involvement with the clubhouse. It is a staff

Exporting the Model: People with Developmental Disabilities

At one time they spent their lives isolated in institutions. Today most individuals with problems of intellectual development often live in their home communities. Depending on the extent and nature of their disabilities, they may live with their parents or siblings in supervised or independent living situations. They have special problems with building enduring social connections and ways to discover work opportunities. Many individuals and groups in society also stigmatize them.

Although the nature of the disability is quite different from mental illness, people with developmental disabilities (DD) and those with mental illness share some characteristics in common. This disability often requires lifetime adaptation and adjustment for skill deficits. Without special family supports, the disability often precludes ordinary social connections and opportunities.

Do you see ways that the quality of lives of people with DD might be enhanced through participation in clubhouse model community building?

How would you adapt the clubhouse model and its activities to the special needs of this group while preserving the shared values that undergird this approach?

How would you begin to explore the need or applicability of a clubhouse model in your area?

responsibility to be aware of social relations in the clubhouse and to construct and manage clubhouse social roles in the service of adaptation. The role structure of the clubhouse provides the medium. Socialization theory directs our attention to the remedial learning experiences that occur in the social environment of the clubhouse model. Members (and staff) are socialized through observation, experience, repetition, and incorporation of learning into ongoing behaviors.

SUMMARY

Socialization theory directs our attention to primary, enabling and empowering aspects of the model. Staff must be vigilant to identify and eliminate negative socialization factors such as the presence of explicit or implicit coercion, "treating" or otherwise making members the object of work, or the creation of imitation work. They should look to strengthen community-building positive socialization factors, all those aspects of the clubhouse day oriented to shared work.

Social exchange theory, based upon the marketplace analogy, provides another perspective on relations between individuals and individuals and between individuals and groups. It underlines the responsibility of staff to include members in all aspects of clubhouse life. Clubhouse staff should continuously examine ways to increase the social "currency" of members in and outside the clubhouse.

These two components of theory undergird the central clubhouse mission of increasing members' abilities to adapt, to find a niches that are stable and satisfying despite mental illness. They don't provide explicit instructions but these theory components can help staff make sound community-building decisions.

APPLYING CONCEPTS

1. How does socialization function to increase social control inside and outside the clubhouse?
2. What can be done in a clubhouse or other social program to increase the social currency of members or clients?
3. Why would clubhouse leaders and planners support members' use of psychiatric medication but insist that a medication clinic operate outside the clubhouse?

4. Why does the clubhouse model focus daily work of the clubhouse on services and activities that benefit the clubhouse and its members rather than on the members themselves?
5. What are the applications of socialization and social exchange theories to other populations and settings? Discuss.

Class Projects

Examine social exchange in your family. What are the primary forms of "currency?" Who possesses the most? How did they gain it?

How does socialization occur in your school? Identify explicit, manifest contributions of socialization and implicit or indirect and unstated ways of socializing students to "appropriate" behavior. Discuss with other students and record your observations.

GLOSSARY

Implicit coercion   a sensed but unseen and unknown force or pressure to act in a certain way.

Reciprocity   a condition of mutual give and take that underpins exchange theory.

Remedial socialization   a planned, deliberate process that aids individuals and groups in evolving more adaptive and satisfying social selves.

Social exchange theory   a body of theory concerned with implicit obligations and the exchange of valued resources among people.

Socialization   a process through which people are prepared to participate socially, generally the result of spontaneous interactions. Socialization instills social values, knowledge, attitudes, and skills for living in society.

REFERENCES

Blau, P. (1964). The structure of social associations. In J. Farganis (Ed.), *Readings in social theory* (pp. 247–261). New York: McGraw-Hill.

Gecas, V. (1981). Contexts of socialization. In M. Rosenberg & R. H. Turner (Eds.), *Social psychology: Sociological perspectives.* New Brunswick, CT: Transaction Publishers.

Goslin, D. A. (Ed.). (1969). *Handbook of socialization theory and research.* Chicago: Rand McNally.

Jackson, R. L., Purnell, D., Anderson, S., & Sheafor, B. W. (1996). The Clubhouse Model of community support for adults with mental illness: An emerging opportunity for social work education. *Journal of Social Work Education, 32*(2), 173–180.

Johnson, A. G. (Ed.). (1995). *The Blackwell dictionary of sociology.* Malden, MA: Blackwell Publishers, Inc.

Martin, P. Y., & O'Connor, G. G. (1989). *The social environment: Open systems applications.* White Plains, NY: Longman.

Simmel, G. (1950). *The sociology of Georg Simmel.* Glencoe, NY: Free Press.

THE CASE FOR CASE MANAGEMENT: FOOD, HOUSING, AND INCOME SUPPORT

MAJOR TOPICS:

CASE MANAGEMENT: A RESPONSE TO INADEQUATE AND UNRELATED SERVICES

CASE MANAGEMENT ASSISTANCE MUST BE PLANNED ACCORDING TO THE SPECIFIC CHARACTER OF UNMET NEEDS AND THE NATURE AND LIMITATIONS OF RESOURCES TO MEET THOSE NEEDS.

STRIVING FOR SELF-ACTUALIZATION: MASLOW'S HIERARCHY OF HUMAN NEEDS

CASE MANAGERS SHOULD HAVE AN UNDERSTANDING AND APPRECIATION OF THE RANGE AND NATURE OF HUMAN NEEDS TO BE ADDRESSED THROUGH THEIR WORK.

COMMUNITY SUPPORT CATEGORIES OF NEEDS AND SERVICES

A VARIETY OF STYLES AND APPROACHES HAVE CHARACTERIZED THE DEVELOPMENT OF COMMUNITY SUPPORT AND CASE MANAGEMENT.

CASE MANAGER: TRAVEL AGENT OR TRAVEL COMPANION?

VARIOUS STYLES OF CASE MANAGEMENT REFLECT A DIVERSITY OF CASE MANAGEMENT PHILOSOPHIES.

COMMUNITY SUPPORT THROUGH THE CLUBHOUSE

CASE MANAGEMENT RESPONSIBILITIES ARE SHARED IN THE CLUBHOUSE COMMUNITY.

OUTREACH TO DISENGAGED MEMBERS AND POTENTIAL MEMBERS

ASSERTIVE OUTREACH PROVIDES ASSISTANCE TO PEOPLE UNABLE TO USE THE CLUBHOUSE DUE TO ILLNESS FACTORS.

SUMMARY

After years of being sick myself, I know a lot about what other members need and want. Lots of times when people are absent from the clubhouse they're having problems. I call to tell them that we need them, that we miss them, and that we need their help. Sometimes they'll come in and sometimes they won't, but in any case they know that someone cares enough to check up on them.

—A CLUBHOUSE MEMBER'S PERSPECTIVE

Sometimes members don't want to come in or stay in touch when they're having trouble. They withdraw. Then it's our job to reach out.

—A STAFF MEMBER'S PERSPECTIVE

CASE MANAGEMENT: A RESPONSE TO INADEQUATE AND UNRELATED SERVICES

Primary responsibility for the care of most people with mental illness passed from state hospitals to community providers in the 1970s and 1980s, but before that time hospitals and other long-term care facilities provided for basic needs. Individuals might spend their lifetimes in the same hospital. Their housing, food, medical and psychiatric care (including emergency assistance), dental care, socialization activities, work rehabilitation, and employment were all provided in or around the same place. Since then, the provision for these needs have been a concern of professional case managers. Basic human needs, once addressed in long-term care hospitals, are now met continuously in communities.

It should be mentioned that case management is provided to many different groups of people in our society who have difficulty obtaining assistance and meeting their needs due to system inadequacies, administrative red tape, and limitations imposed by their disabilities. This chapter focuses on needs of adults with mental illness, but the objectives and methods of case management described are relevant to other populations and problems.

Case management for adults with mental illness is provided today through community mental health centers, residential care facilities, day treatment centers, clubhouses, and emergency clinics. However, regardless of the source of support, resources are limited and rationed by legislation and the policies of managed care companies. Case managers must continuously evaluate needs and prioritize their interventions according to available resources.

This chapter begins with an examination of Maslow's theory concerning universal human needs. His hierarchy of human needs serves as a tool for prioritizing the type and extent of case management interventions. Next, the origins of case management approaches in community support are highlighted and current styles of case management are presented. Following this, case management services delivered within the clubhouse model are described, together with special efforts to reach out and engage other adults with mental illness.

STRIVING FOR SELF-ACTUALIZATION: MASLOW'S HIERARCHY OF HUMAN NEEDS

In the 1950s, Maslow developed a framework for examining the range of biological, social, and psychological needs. He called it a *hierarchy of human needs* (Maslow, 1950).

His framework was both optimistic and humanistic. It was based on the following assumptions about human beings:

- Humans naturally strive to learn about themselves and develop their capacities. They are naturally curious. They seek to understand and explain, and they are drawn to the unknown. They are everyday theorizers. They are driven to test their capacities and test theories about problems of everyday living.
- Their needs are both unconscious and conscious. However, in the average person they are often experienced unconsciously. As needs emerge in consciousness and grow in urgency, the individual becomes more engaged in behaviors to meet them.
- The most strongly experienced of all needs are physiological. Hunger, thirst, pain, and other physiological issues will be addressed before any others. Accordingly, it is not possible to focus attention on any "higher" level needs before meeting these fundamental "lower level" needs.
- At any time gratification or deprivation of needs determines behavior. Maslow's theory assumes that we are striving animals. We seek increasingly higher levels of gratification until needs are met.

FIGURE 8.1

Hierarchy of Human Needs

- Chronic gratification of needs renders them unimportant as determinants of behavior. Chronic deprivation makes them the focus of thought and behavior. People who are starving will search for food until their need is satisfied. If it is regularly satisfied, they will no longer pursue this need but may instead seek to meet higher level needs.

> *Self-actualization*—According to the theory, few people are able to rise to meet this level of need. Presumably the self-actualizing individual is able to access a combination of individual and environmental resources that permit the pursuit of knowledge, artistic interests, relationships, and spiritual concerns. The self-actualizer is able to take for granted the continuing presence and adequacy of lower level, need-meeting resources.

> *Self-esteem needs*—"Satisfaction of the self-esteem need leads to feelings of self-confidence, worth, strength, capability, and adequacy, of being useful and necessary in the world. But thwarting these needs produces feelings of inferiority, of weakness, and of helplessness" (Maslow, 1954, p. 91). In other words, people need contributing roles in relation to others, which contribute to self-worth and a satisfying sense of social identity.

> *Belongingness and love needs*—The person becomes aware of these needs as lower level needs are satisfied. Maslow makes the point that these needs are not to be confused with sexual intimacy. He suggests that needs at this level are met through various kinds of relationships.

> *Safety needs*—These organize and mobilize behavior in a manner similar to physiological needs. They may also dominate and exclude higher level needs. People who must be continuously prepared to defend themselves against threats, internal or external, are not able to pay attention to higher level needs. Related to physiological needs, these needs can be as consuming and exclusive as any physiological needs. In essence, safety needs compel the individual to pay continuous attention to threats until they begin to diminish. People with mental illness may have difficulty distinguishing delusional or imagined threats from real threats to safety. Whether real or not, safety needs are fundamental.

> *Physiological needs*—Homeostasis, a balance of internal and external factors, is the goal of the organism trying to meet physiological needs. Adequate food, clothing, and shelter are paramount. They must be met from some source if the organism is to survive. Other needs are biologically subordinated to meeting physiological needs.

Practice Implications for Professional Helpers

Case management assistance must be planned according to the specific character of unmet individual needs and the nature and limitations of resources to meet those needs. Maslow's hierarchy of human needs reminds us that the most fundamental needs must be met before higher level needs can be met.

For instance, a man with mental illness who is living in a city under a cardboard shelter has to contend with real and perhaps hallucinated threats to safety before other needs can be met. Case managers must try to assess and understand the nature of the threats and what can be done to control them. Are outside temperatures dangerously high or low? Is the individual in danger of starving or being exploited in some way? Will he or she accept assistance?

Help cannot be provided without the individual's consent unless there is a threat to life or property.

Belongingness and love are just above the most fundamental needs in Maslow's hierarchy of human needs. He theorizes that human beings are social. They need to be affiliated and connected with others. As we have indicated before, individuals with mental illness may withdraw into their own thoughts and become estranged from family and other social connections. Case managers and program planners need to develop ways of either reintegrating such individuals into their natural social connections of family and friends or insure that these needs are met through relations built in clubhouses, churches, places of employment, or other social groups. The clubhouse model is fundamentally a design for meeting belongingness needs. People with mental illness find belongingness needs met in hospitals, informal drop-in centers, public libraries, or cafeterias of a college. There it is possible to have relationships with others. However, it is not possible for anyone to feel useful and necessary in the world without being able to contribute. Being in community with others is the beginning of meeting belongingness needs. These needs must be satisfied in order to meet the higher level self-esteem needs.

In Maslow's hierarchy just above belongingness is self-esteem. There are many different contributions to self-esteem, but of central importance are feelings of being useful and necessary to others. This is one of the key assumptions that underpins the clubhouse model. It is captured in the clubhouse emphasis on shared work and the expectation that members will be "wanted, needed, and expected" at the clubhouse. The hierarchy of human needs helps practitioners think about the type and level of intervention.

The method of intervention is important. To paraphrase the Hippocratic oath of physicians, helping should not harm. Since the earliest days of professional helping in the nineteenth century, there has been concern about making sure that professional help, whenever provided, does not contribute to the same or other problems. In particular, there has been great concern about introducing professional initiative and action in a manner that displaces and replaces naturally occurring desirable traits such as independent problem-solving ability, initiative, and reliance on family and friends.

Today the concern is often expressed that case managers and programs might "promote dependency," through professional helping. Many believe the elimination of dependency should be a primary goal. Exclusive attention to this goal of independence presents special problems. How independent is someone who has been hospitalized 10 times due to psychiatric reasons? The frequency and duration of hospitalizations suggest that they may need ongoing assistance, but a kind that can change with changing needs and conditions. Effective case management is flexible. It is prepared to increase the intensity of work when necessary and maintain relationships but diminish contacts if that serves client goals and interests.

In that regard, the golden rule for helping professionals may be reframed as follows:

> Do unto others only to the extent that they are unable to do for themselves and in a manner likely to enhance their own competency and sense of self-efficacy.

This can be followed by what we might call the silver rule:

> Whenever possible, do *with* others, so they may gain the benefits of meeting their own needs, being valued by others, and building their innate capacities as the work to be done is shared.

These "rules" can be applied to meeting needs at any level of Maslow's hierarchy of human needs. They certainly apply to the Clubhouse Model, but they can be applied to a variety of other service populations and settings. Clients should have key and continuing roles in determining exactly what form assistance should take. Any categorical program or agency goal to make clients with mental illness permanently independent may be seriously flawed.

COMMUNITY SUPPORT CATEGORIES OF NEEDS AND SERVICES

The defining characteristics of community support were developed through the use of focus groups involving professionals, family members, and other stakeholders throughout the country (Turner & TenHoor, 1978). Their recommendations were published as a listing of community support system components. These were as follows:

1. The identification of the population for whom the services are appropriate. This depends on an aggressive outreach program for those who are most in need of services.
2. Assistance in applying for financial, medical, and other resources for which clients are eligible and to which they are entitled.
3. Crisis stabilization services in the least restrictive setting. When outreach services cannot meet a client's treatment needs, hospitalization should be an available option.

4. The provision of psychosocial rehabilitation services aimed at sustaining functional capacities and slowing the rate of deterioration of the chronic mentally ill. These services should include, but are not limited to, the following:
   - Goal-oriented rehabilitation evaluation
   - Training in community living skills
   - Opportunities to improve employability
   - Appropriate housing suited to a patient's condition
   - Opportunities to develop social skills, interests, and leisure activities that provide a sense of participation and worth
5. Continuity of care service.
6. Medical and mental health care.
7. Backup support for family, friends, and community members.
8. Involvement of community members in the planning of support programs and in selected aspects of service delivery, such as helping to make jobs and housing available for the population at risk.
9. Establishment of procedures and mechanisms that protect the legal rights of the mentally ill, both in hospitals and the community.
10. Provision of case management that will help clients make efficient use of available services (Turner & TenHoor, 1978).

Twenty years later, this list of community support components remains primarily a partially realized goal rather than reality in many areas of the United States. Over the intervening years, a great deal of the responsibility for making community support a reality has been transferred to case managers and other mental health workers, whose day-to-day work with clients is now expected to compensate for divided, isolated, and inadequately funded resources.

CASE MANAGER: TRAVEL AGENT OR TRAVEL COMPANION?

Several descriptions and models of case management have appeared in the literature in the last 20 years (Intagliata, 1982; Bond et al., 1988; Rapp, 1998). They have been variously titled: clinical case management (Kanter, 1989), assertive case management (Stein and Test, 1979; Olfson, 1990), and strengths-based case management (Macias, Farley, Fraser, Vos, & Jackson, 1992; Saleebey, 1997). A range of service philosophies and activities that might be considered legitimate components of case management roles are represented across the country.

Any definition of case management is necessarily broad and inclusive. Put simply, *case management* can be defined as the task of helping people with mental illness obtain what they need to live as fully and satisfactorily as possible despite mental illness.

A recent descriptive study of case management styles practiced in three different states ($n = 362$) asked case managers to rank five different functions associated with case management (Hromco, Lyons, & Nikkel, 1997):

- *Supportive intervention*—counseling to reassure clients, help them mobilize their own abilities, and provide assistance.

- *Advocacy*—helping clients get specific services as well as advocating for the enhancement of additional needed services.
- *Monitoring and crisis intervention*—observing the behavior of clients, being available to help, and providing assistance in emergencies.
- *Linking to services*—connecting clients to what they need in the community.
- *Formal psychotherapeutic intervention*—helping clients work through psychological difficulties in office-based therapy sessions.

Using *cluster analysis,* the results identified four "styles" of case management: supportive social worker, individual therapist, therapist broker, and community advocate. Each of these styles suggested different perspectives on the role of the case manager. Certain functions were ranked higher than others in importance by surveyed case managers.

The *supportive social worker* cluster, comprised of 60 percent of case managers sampled, was the most prevalent in the study. This group of case managers shared a belief in the importance of supportive interventions and listening more than in formal therapy or advocacy.

The *individual therapist* cluster, 17 percent of the sample, tended to place a high value on therapeutic interventions and little emphasis on advocacy. The case management approach suggested was office-based, with consumers attending sessions for the purpose of therapy, support, and monitoring.

The *therapist broker* cluster, like the individual therapist cluster, tended to see therapy as useful but placed far less importance on supportive interventions. This group of case managers, representing 10 percent of the sample, emphasized the importance of linking clients to services and brokering or helping them negotiate the terms of service affiliations.

The *community advocate,* comprised of 13 percent of the sample, devalued treatment-oriented relationships, whether through formal psychotherapy or supportive interventions. These were the only case managers in the study who rated advocacy as relatively important. They also emphasized linking and monitoring functions.

A majority of case managers in this study placed high value on the professional-consumer relationship and viewed formal psychotherapy as a relatively unimportant task in case management for people with severe mental illness. Teaching and listening functions were emphasized.

In another recent study, Charles Rapp (1998) described a number of different case management "active ingredients." Most can be found or should be found in clubhouse model programs.

Structure

1. Teams should be structured for the purpose of creative case planning, problem-solving, sharing knowledge of resources, and support to team members.
2. Team leaders/supervisors should be experienced, professionally trained mental health professionals.

3. Case managers can be paraprofessional (for example, B.A. level) but need access to specialists. Involvement of nurses seems particularly important.
4. Case load sizes can vary based on client severity, geography, and so forth but should never exceed a ratio of 20:1. The average across program clients should probably be a ratio of from 12:1 to 15:1.
5. Efforts should be made to enhance the continuity of relationship between the client and case manager.
6. Clients need 24 hour, 7 days per week access to crisis and emergency services. That service should require access to staff who have familiarity and a relationship with the client (can be and perhaps should be the case manager).
7. Preservice, in-service, and technical service should be available.
8. Length of case management services should be indeterminate and expected to be ongoing, although intensity at any point in time would vary.

Service

1. Case management contact with clients should be in vivo (limit office-based contacts).
2. Frequency of in vivo client contact will vary based on the client but across clients should average a minimum of six in-person contacts per month. This should be supplemented by telephone and collateral contacts.
3. Case managers should deliver directly as much of the "help" (for example, modeling, resource acquisition, skill training, or advice) as possible.
4. Referrals to traditional mental health programs (for example, partial hospitalization, day treatment, in-office counseling, sheltered and many transitional employment programs, congregate housing, and so forth) should be avoided.
5. The use of naturally occurring community resources (landlords, employers, coaches, neighbors, churches, friends, clubs, junior colleges, and so forth) should be encouraged.
6. Case managers should have ultimate responsibility for client services with the exception of medication. They retain authority even in referral situations.
7. Clients should be given equal or greater authority than case managers or other professionals in treatment and life decisions with the exception of hospitalization decisions.

Case management relationships and the variety of informal approaches to helping are often philosophically consonant with the clubhouse model. However, many clubhouses are challenged to insure that case management needs of individual members effectively compete with the range of other clubhouse work responsibilities. To connect with the most unengaged members and others with mental illness, clubhouses also collaborate to provide nonmember services or provide them directly as an adjunct to the clubhouse.

COMMUNITY SUPPORT THROUGH THE CLUBHOUSE

Because of connotations of control, many clubhouse staff and members dislike the terms "case management" and "case manager." There is a preference in many clubhouses for describing the functions of case management under the nonauthoritative term "community support." In fact, "community support" has been substituted in the clubhouse standards in lieu of "case management." Regardless of the naming, these functions are assigned considerable importance, but clubhouses try to blend them into the fabric of the community in such a fashion that they become part of the ongoing work of the club. Like all other jobs to be done in a clubhouse, staff have basic or "bottom line" responsibility for community support forms of assistance needed by members, but these tasks are shared between members and staff.

Community support activities are centered in the work unit structure of the clubhouse and include helping with entitlements, housing, and advocacy, as well as providing assistance in finding quality medical, psychological, pharmacological, and substance abuse services in the community (Propst, 1993, p. 3).

The Work Unit

This is the first line of responsibility for helping members with the problems described previously. The work unit staff have primary community support responsibility for members in their unit. This makes sense in the clubhouse community. Members and staff, who work together regularly, become especially attuned to each other's moods and patterns of behavior. They are aware of the idiosyncratic signs that someone is beginning to experience an increase or change in symptoms. Because of the relationships developed in the work unit, help can be supportive rather than controlling or authoritative. If someone demonstrates through behavior that hospitalization is necessary, work unit staff and members of their own group are often in the best position to help. They are also in the best position to provide assurance that hospitalization does not mean faliure or exclusion from the clubhouse. Members and staff will predictably express their concern and connectedness as well as wishes for a quick return.

Routine daily living problems are the most common sort of community support issues handled in the work unit. A member may need assistance applying for Social Security benefits, shopping for groceries, obtaining an apartment, or scheduling a review of medication with a psychiatrist. The assistance may be provided by members or staff or both, depending on the situation. However, it is well understood that the needs of members can be the basis for meaningful work contributed by other members. Everyone in the clubhouse community gains from this kind of neighborly helping.

Community support services routinely appear on the agendas of morning work unit meetings. Members who are absent are identified and the nature of their absence is established. Perhaps, they simply have a dental or medical appointment, are physically ill, or have decided to meet a relative or friend. Members are absent from clubhouses for any of the reasons that people may be absent from work, school, or social group. If the absence seems to be unusual or prolonged, a plan will be developed to make contact, to "reach out" to the absent member. That might mean a telephone call or a visit, depending on the situation. If members or staff have reason to believe that an individual may be experiencing an acute episode of mental illness or may be in some kind of trouble, extra care will be taken to insure a speedy follow-up.

Community Support

Jan comes early to the clubhouse. She enjoys a cup of coffee with other work unit members at the snack bar before she goes to the work unit. Sometimes they tell stories. Sometimes they just sit together quietly. Today, they gossip about who is going to enter in the up-coming talent show. Jan glances at her watch. It is 8:45 a.m., time to go to the clerical unit meeting.

They walk up the hallway to the clerical unit, pausing briefly to hang up coats. When they arrive, they find that the chairs, ordinarily positioned at computers and work tables, have already been turned into a circle for the morning meeting. Jill and Ron, the staff members, are just finishing a conversation with one of the members and getting notes together concerning the work of the day. Members gradually arrive and take spots at the unit meeting.

Jill calls the meeting to order and asks how everyone is doing. There are a few reports. Jan points out that Keith, another member, has not been to the unit in several days. He used to attend regularly and is known by almost everyone present. This new pattern arouses concern. Ron asks if anyone has seen Keith or knows about him. Hearing no responses, Ron says that he wants to do an outreach to Keith's apartment to find out if he is OK. He asks if a couple of other members will help. He has two volunteers. They arrange to meet at the end of the day for the outreach visit.

The Clubhouse Community

Some case management functions, notably group advocacy, are handled through meetings of the entire clubhouse. Clubhouse staff and members recognize that the allocation of mental health monies and other resources is an intensely political activity. Like other citizens, clubhouse members work to express their views through voting, contacting legislators, and otherwise taking active roles in helping people with mental illness as a group.

Clubhouses hold community forums to educate others about the realities of mental illness and encourage support for clubhouse activities such as transitional employment programs, housing, and income support. Many clubs hold open houses to explain their work to their neighborhoods and communities.

OUTREACH TO DISENGAGED MEMBERS AND POTENTIAL MEMBERS

"Freedom of choice is in direct contrast to hospital programs. I have been hospitalized at least 14 times over much of my adult life. Freedom helps root me in reality by allowing me to shape my immediate reality."

—A CLUBHOUSE MEMBER'S PERSPECTIVE

Choice and a lack of coercion are hallmarks of the clubhouse model. Nobody is forced to come to a club or stay at a club. Relationships thrive and connections grow in conditions of freedom and choice.

Nonetheless, there are some times when helping someone negotiate a crisis requires arranging for a brief hospitalization for evaluation and/or treatment. Familiar staff and friends can help. Certain kinds of symptoms such as command hallucinations or suicidal depression can—at certain times—pose a condition of danger to the individual or to others. A hospital or hospital alternative may be used to help people through those times, helping them stabilize and reclaim self-control. However, members and staff should see that any institutional controls imposed are adequate, respectful, clear, and extremely limited. A quick return to ordinary routines with family, clubhouse friends, and others should be the declared objective.

Reaching out to clubhouse members and other eligible individuals is a natural and neighborly extension of the clubhouse. In any group of adults with mental illness, there are some who choose not to attend or engage in the clubhouse. Although individuals may be invited to come to the club from time to time, the right of choice to not engage is respected. It is understood that some individuals with mental illness live and work quite satisfactorily without being regularly connected to social or educational programming of any kind.

Nonetheless, because mental illness impairs reasoning and judgment, people are sometimes too ill and disabled to choose the help that they need. They may be so disorganized and disturbing to others that they are not able to be present in the clubhouse. For these people, an outreach program or clinic adjacent to the clubhouse that offers psychiatric evaluation, medication, and case management can meet these specialized needs, using the necessary conventional and authoritative mental health methods. If involuntary hospitalization appears to be required, they can initiate the necessary legal procedures to insure that individual rights are protected and individual safety is insured. They can encourage involvement or a resumption of involvement in the clubhouse whenever possible. Such a program activity may be under the auspices of the clubhouse or mental health center, but it remains separate so that the clubhouse remains free from coercive policies and roles.

> *Several years ago a member of the club became very sick, to the point that he lost his housing. He was wandering the streets in bare feet. I intervened by calling the outreach team. They had their psychiatrist interview him. They called the police. As a result, he was involuntarily hospitalized. Later, when I visited him in the hospital, he thanked me for this. Before long, he returned to the clubhouse, and we maintained a much closer, trusting relationship than ever before.*

—A STAFF MEMBER'S PERSPECTIVE

Prioritizing Case Management Tasks

Maslow's hierarchy of needs has clear implications for case management or community support work with members. Faced with daily tasks including responsibilities for case management, unit staff must prioritize. First, members must have food, housing, and the basic necessities to support life. Physiological and safety needs must take precedence over others. Individual members of clubhouse work units must be safe and also feel safe if belongingness, self-esteem, and self-actualization needs are to be addressed.

The clubhouse brings members and staff together in the shared purpose of community building. It is critical that respect and trust remain primary characteristics of these relationships. Strong relationships enable the potential healing or rehabilitative power of shared work roles to be released. They permit the affirmation of competency and self-worth.

Exporting the Model: Youth Separated from Their Families

For young people who do not have stable, supportive families, the passage between childhood and adulthood is often a lonely, frightening, and stormy time. A large number of youth between the ages of 14 and 22 are living on the streets of American cities, often making their way by selling drugs and engaging in prostitution. Many are without job skills and have very low opinions of their abilities. Some of them have serious mental illnesses. They have few places to go.

These "transitional youth" are characterized by their family and social dislocation, their retreat to living on the streets (Davis, M., & Vander Stoep, A., 1996). School authorities or law officers often first discover them when their mental and emotional difficulties are expressed in truancy, running away from home, substance abuse, and criminal behavior. Due to the combination of problems and a lack of effective parental advocacy, many are unable or unwilling to access conventional social agency services. They sometimes join gangs or "hang out" in asocial or antisocial groups in the larger community.

Does the clubhouse model have anything to offer?

Could these youthful street people discover their competencies through community-building?

Could transitional employment opportunities help them develop the basic work skills and habits necessary to get and keep legitimate work?

Within their clubhouse community, could they provide each other with the educational support to return to school and find success?

SUMMARY

Maslow's hierarchy of human needs provides an assessment tool for considering the range and ranking of human needs. It directs attention to the level and kind of help that might be most appropriate and useful. It underlines the importance of meeting lower level physiological and safety needs before others are addressed.

The meeting of needs of adults with mental illness has changed sharply over the last three decades. The era of large state hospitals has been followed by community mental health programs and services. Variously described case management services now provide direct and indirect assistance to clients with mental illness living in the community.

How case management services are delivered is almost as important as that they are delivered. Again, some of the needs represented on Maslow's hierarchy of human needs can serve to guide the nature of helping, the "how" of service delivery.

Case management services, referred to under the term "community support" in the clubhouse model, are provided as aspects of the shared work responsibilities of clubhouses. They are part of the planned effort to construct the principles of "wanted, needed, and expected" into the experience of members. Reaching out to absent members is a regular part of the work of units in the clubhouse. However, for some especially withdrawn and isolated members and potential members, extra effort must be exerted to actively connect, to go where they are despite obstacles that might be presented by factors of the illness.

Cost cutting, limiting, and prioritizing services remain paramount in the era of managed care. Case management services, insuring that eligible clients are able to meet a range of basic needs, is likely to remain a central method of community mental health services as long as our system of public and private supports remains under-funded and divided and people are disabled by mental illness.

Community Support Internet Sites

Many excellent resources are available on the Internet to assist case managers and others working with people with mental illness. Here are a few:

http://www.pprainc.com The National Resource Center on Homelessness and Mental Illness

http://www.mentalhealth.com Internet Mental Health

http://www.nimh.nih.gov National Institute of Mental Health

http://www.nami.com National Alliance for the Mentally Ill

http://cmrg.com Case Management Resource Guide

APPLYING CONCEPTS

1. What does Maslow's hierarchy of human needs provide to professional helpers and their organizations? How can it be applied in other settings and with other populations?
2. What is "case management?" How can the role of a case manager be distinguished from other helping roles in the field of mental health such as therapist, residential counselor, or day treatment worker?
3. Why might clubhouse members and staff and some other mental health providers and users object to the terminology "case management?" Is this a trivial or important matter? Why?
4. Describe several of the "core requirements" of community support as developed by the National Institute of Mental Health.
5. Describe the four styles of case management discussed in this chapter. Which of these styles suits you? Why?

Class Projects

Discuss with other students how you, as clubhouse staff, might act to help a member who was experiencing many severe symptoms and disrupting the group due to unusually high anxiety and the presence of auditory hallucinations (voices).

Find out where the major community support services are in your area. Are they available and accessible to people with mental illness? What are the requirements to obtain their services?

GLOSSARY

Case manager   a professional whose job it is to provide direct or indirect assistance for people to manage problems of daily living in the community.

Community support   the overall caption for a plan developed by the National Institute of Mental Health and others to provide assistance to people with mental illness living in communities; the term preferred by clubhouse model service providers in lieu of "case management."

Outreach   a variety of special activities to identify people in need and work to address them.

Self-actualization   the peak of Maslow's hierarchy of human needs; it represents a category of needs met through seeking knowledge, finding artistic expression, exploring relationships, and spirituality.

REFERENCES

Bond, G., Miller, L. D., Krumwied, R. D., & Ward, R. S. (1988). Assertive case management in three mental health centers: A controlled study. *Hospital and Community Psychiatry, 39,* 411–418.

Davis, M., & Vander Stoep, A. (1996). *The transition to adulthood among adolescents who have serious emotional disturbance.* New York: Policy Research Associates, Inc.

Hromco, J. G., Lyons, J. S., & Nikkel, R. E. (1997). Styles of case management: The philosophy and practice of case managers. *Community Mental Health Journal, 33*(5), 415–428.

Intagliata, J. (1982). Improving the quality of community care for the chronically mentally disabled: The role of case management. *Schizophrenia Bulletin, 8,* 655–674.

Kanter, J. (1989). Clinical case management: Definition, principles, components. *Hospital and Community Psychiatry, 40*(4), 361–367.

Macias, C., Farley, O. W., Fraser, M., Vos, B., & Jackson, R. (1992). Assessment of the Strengths Case Management Program in Utah: Adapting the model to fit rural needs. *Outlook, 2*(3), 9–11.

Maslow, A. (1954). *Motivation and personality.* New York: Harper and Row.

Olfson, M. (1990). Assertive community treatment: An evaluation of the experimental evidence. *Hospital and Community Psychiatry, 4*(6), 634–641.

Propst, R. (1992). *Standards for clubhouse programs: Why and how they were developed. Psychosocial Rehabilitation Journal, 16*(2), 25–30.

Rapp, C. A. (1998). The active ingredients of effective case management. *Community Mental Health Journal, 34*(4), 363–380.

Saleebey, D. (Ed.). (1997). *The strengths perspective in social work practice* (2nd ed.). New York: Longman.

Stein, L., & Test, M. (1979). The community as the treatment arena in caring for the chronic psychiatric patient. *New Directions for Mental Health Services, 2,* 431–451.

Turner, J. C., & TenHoor, W. J. (1978). The NIMH community support program: Pilot approach to a needed social reform. *Schizophrenia Bulletin, 4*(3), 319–341.

CONCEPTS OF CULTURE AND THE CLUBHOUSE COMMUNITY

MAJOR TOPICS:

CULTURE DEFINED

CULTURE IS COMPRISED OF IDEALS, VALUES, AND ASSUMPTIONS THAT GUIDE BEHAVIOR.

ALTERNATIVE PERSPECTIVES ON CULTURE

ALTERNATIVE PERSPECTIVES SERVE AS AIDS TO UNDERSTANDING THE CLUBHOUSE CULTURE.

THE DEVELOPMENT AND MAINTENANCE OF CLUBHOUSE CULTURE

NEW ASPECTS OF CULTURE DISPLACE THE OLD.

ARTIFACTS OF CLUBHOUSE CULTURE

SYMBOLS, LANGUAGE, MYTHS (EXTENDED METAPHORS), STORIES, IDEOLOGIES, HEROES, CEREMONIES, AND CELEBRATIONS ARE BOTH TANGIBLE AND INVISIBLE COMPONENTS OF CULTURE.

SUMMARY

We get together in Community Meeting on Wednesday afternoons to share news, make announcements and organnize activities.

—A CLUBHOUSE MEMBER'S PERSPECTIVE

One important part of my job is to help see that the clubhouse culture grows and develops to support the life of the clubhouse.

—A STAFF MEMBER'S PERSPECTIVE

The study of culture has been associated historically with the disciplines of sociology and anthropology. However, in the last 15 years a considerable research literature concerning organizational culture has developed in the fields of management and organization. Management books are available in every airport bookstore, bringing the lessons of corporate culture, organizational climate, and value-driven organizations to everyone who works in social settings. Indeed, there is a pervasive, widespread interest in how best to solve the people problems found in organizations and communities. The explicit use of culture for organization and community management now has precedents throughout the corporate world. "Culture building activities" are deliberately employed in the service of creating and carrying on strong organizational cultures (Reichers & Schneider, 1990).

The applied aspects of this expanding literature suggest its relevance to the study of how community-building works in the formal organization of the clubhouse. Clubhouse directors, staff, and members have a deep interest in this area. A recent book on Fountain House by longtime staff member, Steve Anderson, is subtitled, "The development of clubhouse culture"(Anderson, 1998). At Fountain House and in other clubhouses, there is a firm belief that "strong culture" provides some of the key ingredients that contribute to individual and group identity development.

Each of the primary topics of the last few chapters—the social construction of meaning, personal and social identity, and now culture—are inseparable in practice. However, in this text they are handled separately to bring them sharply into focus as different but complementary aspects of clubhouse community building. Culture is appropriately the last of these. It is a richly layered concept that encompasses many socially constructed meanings relevant to understanding the development, maintenance, and dissemination of organization and community forms.

CULTURE DEFINED

Culture is experienced subjectively. It is generally not discussed in the course of daily activities. Culture is transmitted from generation to generation with primary responsibility for its care in the hands of parents, teachers, leaders, and respected elders. Culture makes it possible for people to "fill in the blanks" of understanding and behavior. It carries rules and expectations. This makes the posting of explicit rules for behavior unnecessary and even demeaning.

For example, in Asian cultures it is generally considered rude for people to maintain continuous eye contact. The Inuit culture of North America is very group oriented. Individual planning and action is generally frowned upon. Violation of these cultural expectations may alienate people or even end communication. Cultural values must be understood and observed.

Culture is a configuration of *assumptions or understandings,* implicit and explicit, commonly held by a group of people. These assumptions serve as guides to acceptable and unacceptable perceptions, thoughts, feelings, and behaviors that are learned and passed on to new members of the group through social interaction. Culture is dynamic. It changes over time, although the tacit assumptions at the core of culture are the most resistant to change (Sackman, 1997, p. 25).

ALTERNATIVE PERSPECTIVES ON CULTURE

Of necessity clubhouse leaders are amateur *ethnographers,* students of culture. They give special attention to the language of the clubhouse, the communications of members, staff, and others, and the nuances of usage so that they can understand and help shape the shared definitions and interpretations that constitute clubhouse culture. There may be paradoxes and contradictions in the culture of a clubhouse, but it is generally integrative and shared. It tends to strengthen interpersonal bonds.

The preceding definitions and descriptions illustrate the complexity of the concept of culture. The following chart illustrates three perspectives on culture. These charted perspectives show us some characteristics of culture relevant to the clubhouse model in contrast with others.

TABLE 9.1   THREE PERSPECTIVES ON CULTURE IN ORGANIZATIONS (MARTIN, 1992, P. 13)

Perspective	Integration	Differentiation	Fragmentation
Orientation to consensus	Organization-wide consensus	Subcultural consensus	Multiplicity of views (no consensus)
Relation among manifestations	Consistency	Inconsistency	Complexity (not clearly consistent or inconsistent)
Orientation to ambiguity	Exclude it	Channel it outside	Focus on it
Metaphors	Clearing in the jungle, monolith, hologram	Islands of clarity in sea of ambiguity	Web, jungle

The preceding perspectives illustrate the dynamic characteristics of culture. Individual clubhouse model replications might be described at certain times as having cultures of differentiation or fragmentation. However, the model primarily reflects an integrationist perspective of culture. The following paragraphs explain why the integrationist perspective is most prevalent in the clubhouse model.

As a psychosocial response to the disruption of mental illness, the clubhouse goal is to establish and maintain a structure that is orderly, "normalizing," and naturally built around shared work. Culture becomes both process and product of shared work.

- *Orientation to consensus*—A variety of decision-making approaches are applied. However, the most prominent and visible approach is consensus of the group. Consensus is sought through unit meetings, community meetings, ad hoc work meetings, and social gatherings of all kinds. When applied consistently, consensus methods tend to strengthen the social structure, the integration of all the social elements of the clubhouse. Consensus is one of the important sources of an inclusive sense of ownership among members.

  Of course, care must be taken that consensus methods are applied even-handedly and that decisions emerging from groups do not exclude or "roll over" minority opinions. The group leader must be very sensitive to subtle, nonverbal communications.

- *Relation among manifestations*—Explicit and implicit features of the model tend to reinforce consistency. The strength of the culture is often evaluated through examining the degree of consistency and congruence in all its visible cultural aspects. Cultural empowerment ideals are actualized in real opportunities for members, real opportunities to produce genuine accomplishments and thereby demonstrate competency. Clubhouse Standards provide descriptions of shared values and clubhouse behavioral expectations that are applied in peer consultations and ICCD certification site visits.

  Sometimes, mental health planners choose to develop certain components of the clubhouse and ignore others. Their action may be based on their judgment of the inadequacy of resources or their wish to improve the model with a hybrid that "fits" their local environment. They may develop just a prevocational program or just a transitional employment program. This piecemeal approach tends to undercut the building of community and the integrated culture that must accompany it. It is often based exclusively upon the judgments of service providers and planners. Consequently, it risks substituting program or service technology in place of community. It also risks reinstatement of the authority relations of conventional mental health service providers in place of the community.

- *Orientation to ambiguity*—Through its standards and practices, the clubhouse model attempts to explain and account for and, to a certain extent, prescribe staff and members' behavior. Through its processes of social construction, it tends to be neutral or intolerant of alternative perspectives and features of culture. Inasmuch as mental illness can be thought of as a condition of personal ambiguity, the clubhouse offers a clarifying substitution of structure and forms.

- *Metaphors*—Clubhouse membership is described in terms similar to those of other important affiliations. The model is often illustrated through the use of "family" and "community" metaphors and other expressions of belonging.

- It is the nature of metaphor to aid understanding through linking present and past meanings and associations. Since the model can be adequately described and understood using familiar metaphors, it can be made understandable to members of the outside community, including potential employers, agency staff, financial donors, and others in positions to help the clubhouse and its members. The model is sensible, understandable, and made vital through metaphor.

". . . The integration paradigm emphasizes harmony. Consistency and consensus (and sometimes leader-centeredness) are the defining characteristics of this paradigm" (Martin & Myerson, 1988, p. 104). The predominance of an integrationist perspective in the model may at times artificially collapse the complexities and contradictions of culture and homogenize and prematurely resolve conflicting viewpoints. Therefore, skilled clubhouse leaders must work to create a supportive integrationist culture while acknowledging and encouraging the inclusion of other perspectives.

Ethnic and Racial Diversity in the Clubhouse

As might be expected in this community-building approach, there appears to be a high degree of tolerance in clubhouses for differences of all kinds. Perhaps everyone's experience with the stigma of mental illness helps to promote this. Perhaps the focus of the model on individual choice, equality, and working together contributes to this positive climate of inclusion and acceptance. In any case, a significant number of clubhouse members are ethnically or racially diverse. In the 1996 ICCD survey of clubhouses in the United States, 25 percent of members from 152 respondent clubhouses were reportedly ethnic minorities. The range of ethnic minorities reported from individual clubs was from 0 percent to 94 percent (Macias, Jackson, Schroeder, & Wang, 1999). Regardless of the ethnic composition of communities outside clubhouses, it is understood that members and staff share responsibility to insure diversity in the clubhouse and see that all potential members feel equally "wanted, needed, and expected."

THE DEVELOPMENT AND MAINTENANCE OF CLUBHOUSE CULTURE

The original clubhouse, Fountain House, located in New York City, has served as a working model for developing clubhouses throughout the world. Today, it continues to have a central role in carrying forward the culture of clubhouses, although there are now six other clubs that serve as training bases for dissemination of the model.

Cultural Conflict

Cultural conflict is inevitable and sometimes intense during the early stages of clubhouse development. Organizational research has identified different kinds of cultural change. *Cultural drift* is gradual change involving a few members of a given culture. This takes place all the time when there are deviations from cultural norms and understandings. Changes originating on a small scale as drift may combine with other factors and change into *incremental change*. This change includes a majority of members in several important domains of organizational functioning. *Cultural transformation* is described as change in several significant domains for a majority of members. This is often the extensive kind of change that takes place when the clubhouse develops under the auspices of community mental health authorities.

In the United States, most clubhouses have been developed within or by community mental health centers. In these settings their development has been often greeted with ambivalence and misunderstanding or outright hostility. In such situations, the clubhouse culture has been brought into sharp focus. The cultural themes, practices, and forms have often developed in conflict with those of the clinic or mental health center. Cultural change in these settings has occurred through a variety of actively directed processes. Sometimes this kind of change has resulted in a "cultural collision," in which one culture must ultimately dominate. This is not surprising inasmuch as all the components of culture—language, symbols, customs, and traditions—are very different.

In mental health centers names are program/organization names, for example, "the outpatient department." Personnel are generally referred to by their affiliation with a discipline (social work, occupational therapy, or psychiatry) or rank (Chief of Outpatient, Intake Supervisor, or Social Worker II). The subjects of service (clients or patients) have no special designation because the role is not a work role. Their only jobs as patients or clients are to get better. In fact, institutional work roles are generally unavailable to them. Clients or patients are separated and distanced from the workers in such settings because they are recognized for their needs, not for skills or competencies they might have. Culture wars are often waged through memoranda, staff meetings, supervisory sessions, and all other points where there is interface between the conflicting systems and cultures. One of these is the intake and orientation of new members.

A new member begins learning the culture the moment the door is opened. The clubhouse director, staff, and member "elders" are some of the most influential carriers of culture. They show newcomers the ropes, how things are done, and what is important to the group. When asked "what do you do," members and staff are likely to respond by naming the work unit of the clubhouse in which they work. Affiliation is stated. Rank or status is not. This avoidance of rank and status is intentional. Clubhouse members and staff believe that hierarchies destructively assign and fix rank and status. Often in such social arrangements, people with mental illness, having no power and few resources, go to the bottom. For many the hierarchy presents a ladder down for the affirmation of failure.

Humans have an inborn tendency to want to affiliate with others. Ordinary people evolve informal meetings at restaurants, bus stops, someone's house, a city park, or some other place. Many adults with mental illness also want to be with friends to hear the latest news or simply be with people who know and understand them. These factors have brought and continue to bring people together in the same way that the legendary, original group of Fountain House members began meeting on the steps of the New York Public Library in the 1940s. It seems true that if clubs are not created and made attractive to people with mental illness, that people make their own places to meet and socialize. These may be in restaurants, on street corners, or on the steps of a mental health center.

ARTIFACTS OF CLUBHOUSE CULTURE

Symbols, language, myths (extended metaphors), stories, ideologies, heroes, ceremonies, and celebrations are both tangible and invisible components of culture. Together they contribute to strong and enduring community life.

Symbols

Examples of clubhouse symbols could include the logo that is on walls, signs, and stationery. The name of the clubhouse is a very important symbol of clubhouse values and ideology. According to Standard 11 in the Clubhouse Standards, a clubhouse must have "its own identity including its own name, mailing address, and telephone number." These not only contribute to organization and community identity, but they also define the clubhouse as different from other organizations and communities. Individual clubs have a number of important symbols of accomplishment. Photographs and artwork of members decorate active clubs. Fountain House refers to a real fountain that symbolizes the aspirations of members and the shared meeting of needs.

Some clubhouses have pets as mascots. The house cat or dog is fed and looked after by members as if the animal were part of a family.

Language

The language of the clubhouse is more than a shorthand method of communication. Its repeated use affirms the culture and includes the user as a participant, a member of that clubhouse culture. It also serves to define boundaries, to identify nonmembers who are not a part of the culture.

The way in which people are described is most important. Of course, ex-mental patients are called "members." The term connotes connection and inclusion. Staff members are called simply "staff," a neutral term that does not define authority, and/or "colleague," which suggests egalitarianism and professional affiliation. Trainees at clubhouse training centers are called "visiting colleagues." The terminology is intended to reinforce connections, minimize differences, connote importance, and underline the intentionally constructed "flatness" of community structure. Interestingly, the term "consumer" that is widely used in other mental health settings to describe the clients or potential clients is not favored in clubhouses. Clubhouses create and use their own special language.

Clubhouse names and naming processes are both important to the development of culture. Despite having characteristics of a formal organization, program, or group of programs, the clubhouse is generally referred to by its given name such as Horizon House, Chinook Club, and so forth or "the club" or "the house." The name of the clubhouse is a product of staff and member discussions and decision-making.

Stories

The central importance of individual stories and group narratives has grown during the last two decades in diverse disciplines including sociology, psychology, philosophy, and English literature. Narrative theory has grown to underline the importance of the act of storytelling as well as the content of individual and group stories. Consequently, narrative theorists employ ethnographic methods to study individuals and groups: tape recording, observation, and content analysis. The narratives obtained illuminate qualities that give color and meaning to individuals and groups. They are fundamental components of culture.

> There are many ways to construe and construct a world of meaning, and we will benefit as practitioners if we come to understand more clearly how people and cultures create a world of meaning and what implications such meanings have for our work. (Saleebey, 1994, p. 351)

In applied human behavior fields such as social work and educational counseling, narrative therapy has developed from these theoretical roots. Narrative therapy has as its purpose to help individuals and groups "rewrite" disempowering, disabling stories.

Many clubhouse members arrive at clubhouses from hospital offices, day treatment programs, and therapists' offices where their relations have focused exclusively on illness and management of illness. Often their communication has been guided by the purposes of formal clinical assessment. They have not had opportunities to share the stories of everyday experiences—what happened on a trip downtown, how good or bad the movie was, what family members are doing, or what plans are developing for the weekend.

In a clubhouse, storytelling is encouraged. In the ordinary structure of a week, numerous forums and opportunities for storytelling are provided—morning unit meetings, community meetings, visits with members at lunch or over snacks, special dinners, and newsletters or special publications. Now in many clubs it is possible for members and staff to chat on-line with others around the world using computers and connections to the Internet. (See Internet sites listed at the end of this chapter.) With continuous retelling some stories may become sagas or even legends. These kinds of stories tend to fuse individual and collective identity. They are the social constructions that build and sustain the important aspects of the clubhouse. They help create, maintain, and transmit shared meanings.

Ideology

Since the development of the clubhouse standards, the values and ideological foundations of the clubhouse model are codified and made real in a single document. Now the standards are read and interpreted. Their inclusion in regional training centers is mandated. Members and staff evaluate their implementation when they conduct certification site visits. They are periodically reviewed and revised. Their very existence, use, discussion, and revision all serve the social construction and maintenance of the clubhouse model.

Heroes

Clubhouse heroes are recognized, and their accomplishments are publicly lauded in the clubhouse community. A hero might be anyone, staff or member, whose accomplishments embody the highest cultural ideals and values. At Fountain House, the group of members who first came together to form We Are Not Alone (WANA) are heroes, and their story is mythic in the life of the clubhouse (Anderson, 1998). An important staff hero of the clubhouse movement is the former director of Fountain House, John Beard, who died in 1983. Under his guidance, Fountain House and the clubhouse model first became known and replicated throughout the world.

Heroes of the clubhouse are of many different kinds and descriptions. Members who have served the club for many years, who have overcome extraordinary personal adversity, or who have contributed to the movement in significant ways may be heroes. The book, *Fountain House: Portraits of Lives Reclaimed from Mental Illness,"* is comprised of heroic stories, told by various members of the clubhouse and the movement. Conscientious community builders work to make it possible for many members to become heroes in contribution to the clubhouse and heroes in recovery from mental illness.

Ceremonies and Celebrations

Groundbreaking ceremonies, employment dinners, and holiday traditions are examples of ceremonies and celebrations that carry clubhouse culture. They are important times at which participants dress up, make speeches, applaud accomplishments, and enjoy being together. A graduation from high school or college, first paycheck on a job, new home or apartment for a member, or acquisition of new facilities to serve the membership are all occasions for ceremony and celebration. These are individual and group *rites of passage,* occasions of public recognition of major steps in growth and development. They reinforce growing notions of individual and collective self-efficacy.

Informal greetings and good-byes have special importance in the clubhouse model. Everyone greets each other with "good morning" when they first meet. The function of reception, greeting people, is given great importance in the Clubhouse Model. It is the first place to communicate to members that they are "wanted, needed, and expected" at the clubhouse. Regardless of what individual members are able to contribute on any given day, they are made to feel that their arrival is noticed and their presence is valued.

Individual and Community Adaptation

A common criticism of this community building approach to individual rehabilitation is that it may subordinate individual treatment needs to the needs of the group. It is true that by focusing on shared work and group activity, individual needs may be set aside at times or even ignored. However, most clubhouse staff and members see clubhouse work and treatment or therapy as complementary but different. Clubhouse staff cooperate with treatment providers so that members are provided effective treatment in addition to the opportunities that the clubhouse can provide. This distinction permits members with long-term illness to have a life apart from treatment where other institutions and programs do not enter.

Sometimes mental health providers attempt to create clubhouse-type activities in their ongoing day treatment or rehabilitation programs. However the attempted inclusion of or merger of the clubhouse with a clinical treatment or conventional rehabilitation culture is often confusing and destructive. For example, psychiatric medications have tremendous power as pharmaceuticals and special meaning as change agents. However, to include them and their dispensation as part of the work detracts from the normal work of the club. Medications and the provision of medications should remain separate. Like medication management the addition of other psychological and social treatments is also confusing. Explicit member treatment roles and statuses based on diagnosis or prognosis or behaviorally based systems of treatment such as token economies may seem at first to be positive additions to clubhouse culture. However, like the introductions of medications management, they can erode cultural norms and reduce the beneficial influence of the clubhouse culture.

Exporting the Model: Social and cultural "outsiders"

Within the United States, there are thousands of migrants, as well as immigrants from other countries. These people may have few ties to others and serious problems of employment and underemployment. Their lives may be complicated by the lack of education, English language skills, and job training. Perhaps the clubhouse model, like its distant relative the settlement house of the late nineteenth and early twentieth centuries, might help such citizens maintain their cultural traditions, support each other, and increase their skills.

How could a clubhouse be developed that would simultaneously aid individual adaptiveness to the larger society and preserve important cultural traditions of the group?

How could a work-ordered day be constructed to provide support and encourage risk taking to obtain education, training, and jobs?

How could stories and narratives contribute rich meanings to the task of community-building?

SUMMARY

Culture is comprised of ideals, values, and assumptions that guide behavior. In the clubhouse model culture is both a product of community-building and an integral part of that process. The integrationist perspective describes several important features of the clubhouse model.

A variety of artifacts express and manifest the culture. These artifacts include symbols, language, stories, ceremonies, and celebrations. All of these comprise the clubhouse culture that is valued and protected by members and staff. Creative community builders work to enable members to become heroes to the community, their families, and themselves.

APPLYING CONCEPTS

1. What is clubhouse culture? How is it manifested?
2. As a staff person, what might you do to introduce new elements of culture or strengthen existing elements?
3. Attempts to combine the clubhouse model culture and the very different cultures of day treatment or rehabilitation programs have been viewed as difficult and sometimes quite destructive. Explain.
4. What do you think would be a good clubhouse name? Why?
5. If psychiatric medications are very useful in helping people to manage symptoms, why not make them directly available in the clubhouse?

Class Projects

Visit a clubhouse or clubhouse regional seminar and investigate the presence of *heroes* and *heroines*. If possible, search for them and interview them. Why have others given them their special status in their clubhouse or groups of clubhouse staff and members?

Walk around your building or campus. Look for artifacts of culture. What are their special meanings in the lives of community members?

GLOSSARY

Artifacts of culture   the symbols, language, myths, stories, heroes, sagas and legends, ceremonies, celebrations, and ideologies that are the tangible and invisible components of culture.

Cultural drift   gradual change involving a few members of a given culture.

Cultural transformation   cultural change in several significant domains for a majority of members of that culture, for example, the imposition of a Clubhouse Model on clinical programming and practice.

Culture   implicit and explicit ideals, values, and assumptions held by a group of people that serve as guides to acceptable and unacceptable perceptions, thoughts, feelings, and behaviors.

Ethnographers   students of culture.

Rites of passage   occasions of public recognition of major steps in growth and development.

REFERENCES

Anderson, S. B. (1998). *We are not alone: Fountain House and the development of clubhouse culture.* New York: Fountain House.

Macias, C., Jackson, R., Schroeder, C., & Wang, Q. (1999). What is a Clubhouse? Report on the ICCD 1996 survey of USA clubhouses. *Community Mental Health Journal, 35*(2), 181–190.

Martin, J. (1992). *Culture in organizations: Three perspectives.* New York: Oxford University Press.

Martin, J., & Meyerson, D. (1988). Organizational culture and the denial, channeling and acknowledgment of ambiguity. In L. Pondy, R. J. Boland, & H. Thomas (Eds.), *Managing ambiguity and change* (pp. 93–125). New York: Wiley.

Reichers, A. E., & Schneider, B. (1990). Climate and culture: An evolution of constructs. In B. Schneider (Ed.), *Organizational climate and culture.* San Francisco: Jossey-Bass.

Sackman, S. A. (Ed.). (1997). *Cultural complexity in organizations: Inherent contrasts and contradictions.* Thousand Oaks, CA: Sage Publications.

Saleebey, D. (1994). Culture, theory, and narrative: The intersection of meanings in practice. *Social Work, 39*(4), 351–359.

CLUBHOUSE MANAGEMENT AND LEADERSHIP

> *The director asks what I think and she takes my ideas seriously. I serve on the Board of Directors.*
>
> —A CLUBHOUSE MEMBER'S PERSPECTIVE

> *During my education we certainly used the metaphor of the toolkit, but it was always the worker's toolkit. The idea of actually giving members a toolkit or showing them how to make their own was not taught.*
>
> —A STAFF MEMBER'S PERSPECTIVE

Clubhouse social systems must be constructed and maintained thoughtfully, carefully, and continuously. The director has the primary responsibility of safeguarding the clubhouse mission. He or she must be both watchful and involved. Staff and member leaders share the responsibilities of implementing clubhouse values and engaging members in the life of the clubhouse.

Staff and members often work side-by-side with the director to help establish clubhouse norms, activities, and characteristics of culture, because clubhouses are usually small and have relatively flat organizational structures and clubhouse values require shared purpose and shared work. Their leadership roles and responsibilities are parallel to those of the director. They lead in their own work units or special programs of the clubhouse.

CLUBHOUSE MANAGEMENT: A SYSTEMS VIEW

In this chapter, we review some of the major problems faced by clubhouse directors and other community-building leaders. We outline the unique clubhouse management and leadership problems and discuss solutions. As we have learned, theory can aid understanding of leadership and management problems, as well as other aspects of community-building.

First, applying a systems perspective, we review the clubhouse director's responsibilities. We examine the complex meanings of management and leadership using a framework of management factors: *authority, responsibility,* and *resources.* Second, we examine some alternative theories of management and their implications for clubhouse adherence to goals and objectives. Finally, we discuss the variety of special challenges to clubhouse communities that are anchored in the nature of the staff-member relationship, the history of the model, and its place in the service system for adults with mental illness.

CLUBHOUSE DIRECTOR

Overall responsibility for the clubhouse belongs to the director. The director must comprehend the whole clubhouse community within its setting in the larger community, as well as know the individual staff and members and their clubhouse roles. The director has primary responsibility for importing and successfully replicating the clubhouse model in the local context and for maintaining the Cycle of Strengths (see Chapter 5). To insure the appropriate clubhouse balance, the director must see that the clubhouse has appropriate resources (input) and that it attains its goals and objectives (proposed output).

Concepts of *authority, responsibility,* and *resources* serve as aids to the examination of the director's role. They are complimentary—one cannot stand alone in organizations or communities except in relation to the others. For example, anyone can be assigned or assume responsibilities, but without adequate resources and authority to match those responsibilities, successful outcomes will be compromised.

Authority

A clubhouse leader needs both authority and power. These are related but not identical concepts. It is useful for us to differentiate between them. Power refers to the ability to "make things happen." It is derived from personal qualities (already possessed) and the beliefs of others (characteristics attributed). Authority is the formal permission to influence, direct, or exercise power, granted through delegation or some other kind of "authorization" by superiors as well as subordinates. Authorization is generally associated with carrying out policies or laws. All formal organizations have personnel who are "authorized" to do certain things.

A clubhouse director must also have and use skills and attributes of leadership. A leader is one who influences and enables groups of people to succeed at shared tasks. The work of a leader may be brief or long-term, depending on the work to be done. The leader helps people succeed at their work through inspiring and motivating, as well as exerting control and direction. Capable clubhouse directors and their staff are competent leaders not just managers, advisors, or consultants, although they may behave in these other roles at times.

Within groups considering the development of clubhouse model communities, there is often considerable misunderstanding about power and empowerment of members. Clubhouse communities are generally initiated by the efforts of professionals not members. Clubhouses do not simply give power to members. They do, however, genuinely invite and encourage member participation in all aspects of the work of the clubhouse and in so doing establish conditions for members to empower themselves—to see, feel, and experience their own strength and competency. Members can and do become leaders. They demonstrate their skills and abilities to such an extent that they often are asked to serve on boards of directors, are hired for staff positions, and come to occupy various positions of authority within the clubhouse and clubhouse movement.

Responsibility

Responsibility has two major aspects to consider with regard to clubhouse management and leadership. People working in organizations have:

1. Responsibility *for* certain things.
2. Responsibility *to* certain groups and individuals.

The first meaning can be thought of as an explicit or implicit job description. The second refers to the accountability required of all directors, indeed all staff and member leaders.

Resources

The clubhouse director has responsibility for insuring adequate funding and resources. Resources are those things—money, materials, supplies, personnel, training programs, consultation, vehicles, and computers—needed to carry out assigned responsibilities. In many social welfare programs, including clubhouse communities, maintaining adequate and appropriate resources is an ongoing problem. Therefore, fund-raising is a major component of the director's responsibilities. There are some formidable obstacles to be overcome. If at all possible, funding must come from a diverse variety of sources, public and private. Diversification of clubhouse funding contributes to financial security. It also helps sustain a diversity of performance obligations (accountability) so that one funding source cannot control the entire expenditure of funds and thereby, control program activities.

The growth of *managed care* in the last decade of the twentieth century has resulted in a variety of measures to limit costs for services to indigent clients. Funding of mental health services in many parts of the United States has been capitated, that is, limited to certain estimated numbers of adults with mental illnesses in a given service area. The exclusion of people with serious mental illness from private health insurance plans has resulted in the implementation of *parity laws*, requiring equal and adequate care for all people despite the severity or origin of their illnesses. The *capitation* or imposition of spending limits for service providers has been one recent effort to control expenditures. Certainly, costs must be controlled. Nonetheless, advocates must remain vigilant to make sure that control of costs is not at the expense of adequate services and resources.

The clubhouse model has inherent fund-raising problems and strengths. Stigma and fear often inhibit connections with the general public and certainly with potential donors. However, for those willing to look, clubhouses are open to anyone who is interested. Private donors can see activities, observe the work of members in clubhouses and transitional employment placements, and hear individual stories of recovery and rehabilitation. Members' narratives provide powerful, albeit anecdotal, evidence that the clubhouse works and deserves financial support.

In addition to locating and obtaining funds, the director needs to acquire adequate and appropriate material and supplies. The work focus of the clubhouse requires equipment for staff and members that clinical organizations often do not need or have. Cooking supplies and equipment, computers, and vans and automobiles are generally essential to effective implementation of a work-ordered day. Also, clubhouses that are program components of mental health centers sometimes find themselves having to get along with donated space and materials that may not be adequate or appropriate.

Under extraordinary pressures to control expenditures, service providers often try to "make do" with substandard equipment, less than adequately paid employees, and hand-me-downs. This is necessitated by the fact that many members are not able to pay for their own services, treatment, and support.

The director is specifically responsible for finding and maintaining a location and physical space that is or can be made attractive by staff and members. It cannot be a room in another organization or a set of activities alternating with other programs. It must have its own name and space over which clubhouse participants have control. It does not have to be expensive or modern, but it does need to be the kind of place about which members and staff can have pride and develop a sense of ownership.

CLUBHOUSE GOALS AND OBJECTIVES

Admission criteria for membership must be met to insure appropriateness for involvement in the clubhouse, as well as to meet funding requirements. The director is ultimately charged with responsibility for insuring that the clubhouse serves the people it is intended to serve. The job of determining appropriateness requires special assessment skill and sensitivity. Either the director carries out this function or delegates and oversees this function.

Some members are referred to clubhouses after legal commitment to a hospital, they may come from a jail or correctional facility, or they may be under some other kind of legal order. It is important that they understand that their participation in the clubhouse is voluntary regardless of their other obligations. Clubhouse staff and policies must remain noncoercive.

The goals and objectives that guide the work of the clubhouse director and other staff include individual and collective goals, separately and in combination. Goals are more general than objectives. They describe categories of work. Objectives are specific and measurable. Together they reflect the intent of the mission statement. These goals and objectives should be regularly discussed and reviewed within the clubhouse community. The following is an example of clubhouse goals and objectives:

> Mission statement: To provide effective and efficient rehabilitation and community support services to adults with mental illness.
> Goal #1: Provide socialization, housing, and rehabilitation services to members.
> Goal #2: Maintain a motivated and qualified workforce to run the clubhouse.
> Objective #1: Obtain and make available 10 new transitional employment slots within the coming year.
> Objective #2: Provide clubhouse training to all newly hired employees within the first year of their employment.

In relation to meeting goals and objectives, the clubhouse director has responsibility for establishing and maintaining policies that insure the stable ongoing functioning of the clubhouse. If the clubhouse is part of a mental health center, that organization's policies also apply to the clubhouse. Differences must be discussed and negotiated so that the needs of the parent agency—the agency that holds primary responsibility and authority for the clubhouse—and those of the clubhouse are reconciled. The clubhouse director must insure that the values and approaches of the clubhouse are addressed.

ACCOUNTABILITY

The clubhouse has many "stakeholders," individuals and groups who understand, use, and contribute to the clubhouse in different ways. They have legitimate but sometimes conflicting views about who and how many members the clubhouse should serve, what resources are needed, and what services are appropriately provided by the clubhouse. The director must listen, explain, and interpret the model to others. Such explanation and interpretation is not only carried on through talks and formal presentations, but also nonverbally and powerfully through role modeling behavior.

Members' interests, opportunities, and benefits are paramount. Directors must be skillful communicators with members as well as staff, board members, agency personnel, and others. They need to listen to members and often act on members' recommendations. Today, members in many clubhouses hold positions on Boards of Directors, planning groups, and committees.

Clubhouse directors are also responsible either to an individual, such as an administrative officer in a parent corporation or to a Board of Directors, formally constituted in the articles of incorporation of an independent, freestanding clubhouse. Many clubhouses that are not independent and do not have a formal governing body have an advisory board to interpret and represent clubhouse interests to parent organizations.

The community outside the clubhouse should be the concern of every clubhouse director. It is the source of needed personnel, financial and material resources, new members, and indeed everything that supports and sustains the clubhouse. The director is a primary interpreter of clubhouse life to the larger community and the primary guardian of clubhouse boundaries.

In addition to the director, any person holding a position of responsibility in the clubhouse, including the director, is responsible to someone else, individual or group, for meeting those responsibilities. Plans, methods, accomplishments, and problems must be reported and reviewed. It is important to note that accountability can and should accompany any assignment of responsibility.

It was suggested earlier (see Chapter 2) that mental illness can be viewed as a kind of psychological breach in the invisible boundaries of the self. Understood in this way, mental illness symptoms can be seen as efforts to compensate, reinstate, and protect these boundaries. Therefore, in systems terms, the task of a clubhouse manager and other clubhouse leaders is to shore up and protect the clubhouse boundaries that provide a reinforcing, protective structure of social relations and opportunities to assist members in regaining their own balance and stasis.

Clarity of purpose, financial health, adequacy of resources, security, and goal-directedness are all related to the director and his or her influence over the major functions of the clubhouse. The way in which the model is implemented, the balance of attention given to different activities in the clubhouse, and how others in the larger community view the clubhouse and its mission are all related to the director's own clarity, leadership, and ability to translate plans into action.

Courses of study and training for mental health clinicians often contribute to the knowledge of individuals for practice. However, education and training for clinical work with adults with mental illness is not, in itself, adequate training for clubhouse leadership. This is a problem especially in many parts of the United States where clubhouses are program elements of mental health centers or behavioral health organizations.

Mental health center directors may simply assign clinicians to manage the new program because of their treatment experience. Clinicians trained primarily to listen, observe, and reflect in treatment programs are often uncomfortable with job and program changes that might require them to become staff leaders. They are unprepared for the "hands-on" nature of the work and the framework of the work-ordered day, which requires their willing, active, and energetic participation.

The clubhouse is not an extension of clinical work. In fact, as suggested earlier, it often gains and maintains its community identity through its separation and differentiation from traditional psychiatric or mental health services.

STAFF AND MEMBER LEADERSHIP

The staff of clubhouses are comprised of people who are trained in a variety of disciplines: educational counseling, social work, psychology, occupational therapy, and others. Some staff in clubhouses have no college or university training. Although they function as generalists, each staff person has routine responsibilities assigned. To enhance their working understanding of the clubhouse model, directors work to insure that staff and members receive an extensive, three-week training at one of ten training sites throughout the world (see Appendix III). Such training is often invaluable in providing motivation, as well as clarifying and strengthening the collective purpose. Clubhouse training sites are located in St. Louis, MO; New York, NY; Salt Lake City, UT; Worcester, MA; Greenville, NC; Toronto, Canada; Melbourne, Australia; Seoul, South Korea; London, England; and Malmo, Sweden.

Staff also lead community-building and help members achieve their objectives. They need to have the qualities—values, skills, and knowledge—of a good generalist worker (Dougherty, 1994). As a group, they should be demographically representative of the community outside their clubhouse.

This group must be adequately trained, paid, and provided for so that they are able to develop their knowledge, skills, and aptitudes. Personnel, staff and members are the most important input elements in the clubhouse social system. A competent, well-trained, knowledgeable, and motivated staff is essential for the clubhouse to succeed.

MANAGEMENT THEORY

The clubhouse model is similar to other approaches to mental illness and social problems in general. They include religiously based L'Arche (Dunne, 1986; Sumarah, 1987), the settlement house movement (Trolander, 1975), and the eighteenth century moral treatment reforms of Pinel in Europe and Benjamin Rush in the United States. For anyone developing a clubhouse, it is useful to understand some of the antecedents in order to understand the social elements most critical to community-building and the recovery of individual members.

Traditional Organizational Structures (Hierarchical)

Bureaucracy, described by sociologist Max Weber, figures prominently in the administration of mental health and social welfare programs. Weber identified several characteristics of bureaucracy found in large-scale organizations of all kinds. They afford comparison with the clubhouse model. Bureaucracies are characterized by specialization of functions, hierarchy of function and accountability, depersonalization, routinization, and predictability. Bureaucracy is viewed as an acceptable vehicle for efficiency—a favorable ratio of costs to benefits—and control of organization resources. It has, therefore, been the favored organizational design for the provision of governmental social welfare services in the United States since the early 1900s.

This form of organization may be especially prone to goal displacement, the substitution of certain alternative goals for those established by the organization. For example, organization maintenance goals may displace individual rehabilitation goals. Bureaucracy is a structure based on primary notions of efficiency and control. It is sometimes criticized for favoring the conservation of power and wealth at the expense of the delivery of goods and services to populations in need.

In the last 30 years, alternative organization structures have been implemented. A great deal has been written about all aspects of private and public organizations. Today there is a considerable market of "how to" books for managers and business people. In fact, the greatest amount of research and publishing in this area has been from the management and business sector. Popular topics include social climate and organizational culture, managing chaos, and more.

Alternative Organizational Structures (The Collectivist-Democratic Organization)

Within this form of organization, authority is vested in all the participants. There are few rules. Social controls are based in the culture of the community. Control is based on personal or moral appeals rather than explicit stated or posted "company rules."

Collectivist-democratic organizations tend to employ staff based on "likemindedness" and other shared characteristics. They are expected to be able to carry out a variety of functions in the organization, not because of specialized training, but because they believe in the purposes and work of the organization and the values it holds. The organization is egalitarian in terms of salaries or wages. The notion of career advancement is not relevant because there is a relatively "flat" organizational structure, rewards are similar, and job differences are minimized. Staff hirings are based on compatibility or "fit" (Rothschild-Whitt, 1979).

The collectivist-democratic form of organization has an inherent appeal. Many of these democratic characteristics are found in the clubhouse model. These features of organization often contribute to strong decisions, considerable group cohesion, and the validation and legitimization of work roles for members. However, these same characteristics also can contribute to difficulty in recognizing outstanding staff or member personal achievement over those of the group. However, special projects, the chance to perform a variety of jobs, and the pleasure of sharing the benefits of "a job well done" may mediate the difficulties of collectivist-democratic organization.

A range of organizational development and management theories has gained interest and prominence among administrators and managers during the last three decades. They can help us understand the organization and community that is the clubhouse model. Douglas McGregor is the author of "Theory X" and "Theory Y" (Hersey, Blanchard, & Johnson, 1996). William Ouchi is the developer of "Theory Z" (Ouchi, 1981). Theories X, Y, and Z describe certain attitudes on the part of managers, how workers are viewed by managers, and how workers perceive their roles. Each theory, a network of attitudes, beliefs, and assumptions about human nature, pervades and directs the life of the organization where it predominates.

Theory X   This theory is anchored in the belief that people do not like work and must be pushed and controlled in order to get them to work. Accordingly, they require a rigidly managed environment. Threats of disciplinary action motivate them to resist their natural tendencies to avoid work. It is assumed by proponents that money is a primary incentive for employees to excel in work.

Theory X organization managers retain authority to make decisions. They may seek advice from others occasionally, but for the most part, they stay focused on the job to be done rather than employee interests.

Theory Y   This more optimistic view of employee-employer relations assumes that people are naturally disposed to work and give rein to creative impulses. Theory Y workers are very comfortable in a work environment that permits creativity and opportunities to become personally involved in organizational planning. Democratic and consensual approaches to decision-making characterize organizations applying these theoretical assumptions. Employees not only seek increased responsibility, but also seek increased authority (Dubrin, 1990; Lee, 1982).

Theory Z   William Ouchi's Theory Z is often referred to as the "Japanese" approach to management. However, it actually combines a strict American management style with a strict Japanese management style. Theory Z emphasizes the broadening of skills, generalization as opposed to specialization, and rotating jobs and responsibilities. It is a mirror of Japanese society. Japanese culture assumes that workers are inherently participative and capable of performing many and varied tasks. It is assumed that Theory Z workers can be trusted to do their jobs to their best ability as long as management can be trusted to support and protect them (Massie, 1992). Long-term association and employee loyalty are expected and obtained. The organization, therefore, exerts strong, indirect controls on its members.

The clubhouse model has some characteristics compatible with the principles of Theory Z. Generalization of roles and long-term mutual obligations of employees and employer are principles of Theory Z organizations and properties of the clubhouse model. In the clubhouse model and compatible with Theory Z, there is a commitment to the clubhouse that transcends the self. Members are guaranteed membership as long as they wish. Over time these factors build excellent group cohesion and the tendency to merge individual and group objectives. Such collective strength helps to protect the community and its members.

PROTECTING THE CLUBHOUSE COMMUNITY

The clubhouse must deal with all those interpersonal and environmental factors that impact or potentially impact the conditions of growth and change for members and the group. Early in this chapter we stated that the director's most important job is to insure member security and protect the framework for change. He or she shares this responsibility with the entire clubhouse leadership.

Physical safety, of course, is essential. Not only must members and staff be safe, but they must also feel safe. Nobody should have to feel that they are in danger from exploitative staff or other members, dangerous facilities, and so forth. While the dangerousness of individuals with mental illness is exploited and overblown in the media, sometimes individuals must be excluded if they are out of control or repeatedly disruptive of group activities. These situations are not the norm, but they do occur and can be quite demanding of time and attention. Matters of safety are generally inseparable from other concerns affecting members.

Confidentiality, important in clinical settings, cannot be allowed to separate clubhouse individuals and groups. The director must see that if hospital or treatment records must be obtained and stored, such records are protected from the view of others. However, meetings of all kinds must remain open to anyone and nonconfidential.

From time to time, members who should not be admitted to clubhouse membership may be. It may be necessary to exclude them if they continuously disrupt or threaten others. However, the exclusion of members from the community is a serious step. Disruptive behavior that interferes with individuals or groups in the clubhouse should always be discussed openly. Alternatives to expulsion should be explored and discussed within the community. Rarely will permanent expulsion be necessary.

Theft, violence, or threats of violence or exploitation of members in any form and from any source must be confronted. The laws of the land do apply to clubhouse staff and members. This is a customary assumption that should eliminate the need for posting special clubhouse rules. Clubhouses are committed to serving people with mental illnesses and resolving problems primarily through developing relationships.

Inadequate Financial and Other Resources

The population served by clubhouses, for the most part, is financially poor or indigent. Although they can and do pay membership fees, they do not have the resources to underwrite all the services they need. Therefore, a third-party payer, public or private, must pay for the clubhouse and other services. Service contracts must be obtained and maintained.

Lack of Policy Support and Changing Policy Environment

Managed care has not been friendly toward adults with mental illness or others with long-term illnesses of many kinds. Many clubhouses have had to change their focus, join with other providers, or stop operating. The future of funding is an ongoing worry in many clubhouses.

Competition Among Service Providers for Resources and Authority

The condition of inadequate resources tends to increase competition and challenge cooperation between service providers. Clubhouse directors and staff must be attentive to ways to reduce and control destructive competition.

Disagreement and Contention Between Individuals and Groups in the Clubhouse

Unresolved disagreements in clubhouses, as in other communities and organizations, can grow to destructive levels if unchecked. In addition, the symptoms of mental illnesses can have a disturbing and "disordering" influence in the clubhouse. Understandably, the behavior of some individual members may be disturbing or distracting. Any and all of these factors may tend to erode the foundations of community.

SUMMARY

A clubhouse director must be a competent leader and administrator. That individual, working with other staff and member leaders, has overall authority

Exporting the Model: Adult Probationers and Parolees

Many people, who have been convicted of crimes, return from court, jail, or prison without support for getting education or training, finding a job, and staying out of trouble. They return to familiar places and associations that will often have little or nothing to contribute to their successful adaptation. They are often estranged from their families and feared and stigmatized by others. The experience of incarceration has removed them from resources and opportunities they need to develop the ability to stay out.

Could their rehabilitation be aided by their engagement in the positive process of community-building in a noncoercive environment?

Could a clubhouse culture serve to support them and give them what they need to stay out of the justice system?

Why would this population need to be served in its own separate clubhouse, not within a clubhouse for adults with mental illness?

and responsibility for the clubhouse and the acquisition of adequate and appropriate resources. A systems perspective aids the overall vision of administrative responsibilities and available resources. The clubhouse must be maintained as a continuing place of help, support, and opportunity for members. Clubhouse leadership must safeguard key clubhouse characteristics so that members, despite changes in their lives or conditions of illness or wellness, can understand that they are wanted, needed, and expected.

APPLYING CONCEPTS

1. What are the most important tasks of clubhouse leaders including the director? Explain.
2. Describe a job you hold or have held in the past in terms of the authority, responsibility, and resources to perform it.
3. What organization structures and management assumptions are most compatible with the community-building framework? Explain.
4. Compare and contrast concepts of power and authority.
5. Describe some of the possible threats to the clubhouse environment. Explain why they are considered threats.

Class Projects

Do you see evidence of goal displacement in the organization or community in which you work? How serious is it? Draft a plan, including a full description of the goal displacement and what the organization might do to address it.

Demonstrate the character of and relationship between goals and objectives by drafting a set of both to plan your next semester.

GLOSSARY

Capitation   a cost control technique whereby a spending limit is imposed. A cap is a specified amount available to pay for treatment services without regard to the actual number or nature of services to be delivered.

Empowerment   actions that when taken contribute to the acquisition of power or the ability to influence people or things.

Leadership   qualities that when active enable groups of people to work together for shared purposes.

Managed care   a broad term that describes various approaches used to control the use of health and mental health care services. The focus is on service efficiency.

Parity laws   laws intended to provide the same insurance coverage for mental illnesses as for equally serious physical illnesses.

Theory Z   associated with the Japanese style of management; emphasizes generalist work and training, job rotation, and long-term mutual benefits for employer and employees.

Threats to the model   factors originating within or outside the clubhouse community that might tend to erode and destroy fundamental values of this approach.

REFERENCES

Dougherty, S. J. (1994). The generalist role in clubhouse organizations. *Psychosocial Rehabilitation Journal, 18*(1), 95–108.

Dubrin, A. J. (1990). *Essentials of management.* Cincinnati, OH: Southwestern.

Dunne, J. (1986). Sense of community in L'Arche and in the writings of Jean Vanier. *Journal of Community Psychology, 14*(January), 41–53.

Hersey, P., Blanchard, K. H., & Johnson, D. E. (1996). *Management of organizational behavior* (7th ed.). Upper Saddle River, NJ: Prentice-Hall.

Lee, J. A. (1982). *The gold and the garbage in management theories and prescriptions.* Athens, OH: Ohio University Press.

Massie, J. L. (1992). *Managing: A contemporary introduction.* Englewood Cliffs, NJ: Simon and Schuster Company.

Ouchi, W. G. (1981). *Theory Z: How American business can meet the Japanese challenge.* Reading, MA: Addison-Wesley.

Rothschild-Whitt, J. (1979). The collectivist organization: An alternative to rational bureaucratic models. *American Sociological Review, 44*(August), 509–527.

Sumarah, J. (1987). L'Arche: Philosophy and ideology. *Mental Retardation, 25*(3), 165–169.

Trolander, J. A. (1975). *Settlement houses and the Great Depression.* Detroit, MI: Wayne State University Press.

JOINING THEORY AND COMMUNITY-BUILDING PRACTICE

MAJOR TOPICS:

THEORY AND COMMUNITY-BUILDING PRACTICE ROLES

DIVERSE THEORIES AND COMPONENTS OF THEORY ILLUMINATE DIFFERENT ASPECTS OF GENERALIST STAFF INTERVENTIONS IN THE CLUBHOUSE MODEL.

PROFESSIONAL VALUES AND PRACTICE METHODS

WORK IN A CLUBHOUSE CAN SERVE TO CONNECT ONE'S THEORY, VALUES, AND PRACTICE APPROACHES.

ACHIEVING AND MAINTAINING CONGRUENCE BETWEEN CONCEPTUAL MODEL AND CLUBHOUSE REALITY

CLUBHOUSE MODEL REPLICATIONS REQUIRE STRONG LEADERSHIP AND ADEQUATE RESOURCES TO MAINTAIN CONGRUENCE WITH THE MODEL.

GENERALIST PRACTITIONERS AS COMMUNITY BUILDERS

COMMUNITY-BUILDING IS AN EMERGING STRENGTHS-BASED, PRACTICE ROLE IN SOCIAL WORK, COUNSELING, AND RELATED PROFESSIONS.

THE THEORY TOOLKIT

AN EVOLVING PRACTICE THEORY, DERIVED FROM MANY DISCIPLINES AND ANCHORED IN PERSONAL AND PROFESSIONAL VALUES, SERVES AS A THEORY TOOLKIT FOR GENERALIST PRACTICE.

Everything is based upon choice in the clubhouse. I and everyone else can choose what we want to do. It's not like that in a hospital. I've been hospitalized at least 14 times and I can tell you that you don't have a lot of choices in the hospital.

—A CLUBHOUSE MEMBER'S PERSPECTIVE

The revolution that the clubhouse model is creating is based on the simple notion that people with mental illness should be treated no differently than others.

—A STAFF MEMBER'S PERSPECTIVE

As we come to the conclusion of our examination of theory and clubhouse model practice, each student is invited to evaluate and draw relevant theory components into his or her personal *practice theory*. This collection of theory components will predictably be shaped by the requirements of practice setting and population and combined with the values and unique perspectives of the practitioner.

This chapter reviews elements of theory discussed in the text and their relation to values-based practice. It describes the unifying, integrating character of the work of staff and members in clubhouses, work that combines theory and practice and values. Here we summarize our essential observations about both theory and community-building in the clubhouse model.

THEORY AND COMMUNITY-BUILDING PRACTICE ROLES

The chart following reviews some of the major theoretical elements previously discussed and applies them to some examples of professional roles and responsibilities. It graphically shows the complex number and variety of practice roles carried out by staff working in clubhouses. Examined individually, these and similar roles are carried out in a wide variety of generalist practice settings.

The categories are not in a specified order nor are they necessarily complete. They do not prescribe certain interventions nor do they relieve the practitioner of decision-making. Nonetheless, they do suggest different ways of thinking about people and problems and what might be done to help.

PROFESSIONAL VALUES AND PRACTICE METHODS

More than 25 years ago, when I began working with adults with mental illness, I discovered a disconnection between my professional approaches and my values. It was both persistent and disturbing. The disconnection was demonstrated one day during a day treatment activity group when I took a group of clients in the mental health center van to the Seattle waterfront. It was a typically gray, gloomy winter morning. I drove the group of 10 clients to the waterfront and parked the van.

TABLE 11.1 THEORY TO PRACTICE

Theories and Components of Theory	Primary Purposes of Theory	Focus of Intervention	Types of Knowledge and Skills Needed	Examples of Professional Role(s) and Responsibilities
Medical Perspective	Analysis, understanding, and intervention	Client or patient (member) with mental illness	Know diagnosis and diagnostic categories	Monitoring symptoms of mental illness
			Know medication and how to monitor symptoms	Collaborating in the medical management of illness factors
			Know how to collaborate with medical personnel	Assisting members to acquire and use prescribed medication
Ecological Perspective	Understanding and intervention	Individual and social environment	Know larger community and its resources	Assisting and conducting community support activities (with members whenever possible), helping to find housing, financial support, training, or education programs
			Know individual member's interests, needs, and goals	
			Be skilled in helping members adapt or change environmental conditions (find a niche in clubhouse and larger community)	Engaging in clubhouse community-building activities at all levels
Systems Perspective	Analysis, understanding, and intervention	Formal organization and community as well as related advocacy groups, agencies, and services	Know how to engage in program planning and development	Bringing about organization change through unilateral action, board action, and staff group intervention
			Know budgeting	Changing relationships within and between groups in the clubhouse
			Know group management and organization	

Strengths and Empowerment Perspectives	Understanding and intervention	All levels of organization from individuals to community	Be skilled in managing task groups Be skilled in developing professional relationships with members, staff, and others Be skilled in identification of power differences Know what is necessary to change power differences Be skilled in finding members' strengths and developing social conditions that elicit them	Building effective, permeable systems boundaries at all levels Monitoring and protecting the interface of the clubhouse community with its suprasystem Creating temporary and permanent forums for members to express their opinions Identifying the presence of stigmatizing and dis-empowering factors present in members' lives and working to eliminate them
Social Constructionism	Understanding and intervention	Individuals, groups, and the clubhouse community	Be skilled in the creation of contributing member roles (organizing the elements of jobs so that all who want to can work) Know language and meanings Be skilled in use of language and jargon Be skilled at developing community roles at all levels of the clubhouse	Leading role-building meetings in the work unit Analyzing community language and its contribution to shared meanings

TABLE

11.1 **CONTINUED**

Narrative Theory	Understanding and intervention	Individuals, groups, and the clubhouse community	Know how to listen Be skilled at constructing the circumstances in which members can tell their stories and hear others	Using group leadership skills Creating conditions for "storytelling"
Maslow's Hierarchy of Human Needs	Understanding and intervention	Individual	Know the range of individual human needs Be skilled at prioritizing according to needs	Prioritizing work Assisting members in addressing their own priorities
Identity Theory	Understanding and intervention	Individual, group, clubhouse community, larger community	Know the effects of long-term disability on identity Know assessment of individuals and groups in the clubhouse context Know how to build and reinforce identity-building experiences	Developing the work-ordered day through valuing work, modeling work behaviors, and talking about work with others. Celebrating work accomplishments
Self-Efficacy Theory	Analysis, understanding, and intervention	Individual, group, clubhouse organization and community, and larger community (outside agencies, families, etc.)	Know assessment of individuals and groups in the clubhouse context Know how to change members' self-beliefs	Developing roles in which members can experience increased self-efficacy Reinforcing positive achievements
Role Theory	Analysis, understanding, and intervention	Individual, group, clubhouse organization and community, and larger community (outside agencies, families, etc.)	Know community resources for creating new roles Be skilled at building and maintaining relationships	Conducting analyses of opportunities for members to assume roles in the clubhouse

Socialization Theory	Analysis, understanding, and intervention	Individual, group, clubhouse organization and community, and larger community (outside agencies, families, etc.) Individuals and groups	Know how to lead the development of meaningful community roles Know how to model social behavior appropriate to the context and situation Know the nature of social exchange and observed exchange inequalities	Conducting analyses of opportunities for members to assume roles in the clubhouse Establishing new member roles in work units, on activities or social occasions, and anywhere a member can help Identifying role conflicts Giving value to work roles by assuming them regularly or from time to time Modeling task and setting appropriate dress, grooming, and behavior Drawing individuals into satisfying social relationships as they are able and choose Establishing the conditions for correcting exchange inequalities
Concepts of Culture	Analysis, understanding, and intervention	Individual, group, and clubhouse organization and community	Know basic relationship skills Be skilled at recognizing and/or creating customs,	Leading community meetings Greeting guests and new members appropriately

TABLE 11.1 **CONTINUED**

		myths, totems, and celebrations	Recognizing, enacting, and helping develop new customs, myths, and celebrations
		Know the components of culture	
		Be skilled in the development and maintenance of culture	
Management Theory	Analysis, understanding, and intervention	Know the needs of people with mental illnesses	Leading by example
			Protecting clubhouse values
	Individual, group, clubhouse organization and community, and larger community (outside agencies, families, etc.)	Be skilled in the identification and protection of clubhouse values	Insuring that members have contributing roles in the life of the clubhouse and that the conditions of being "wanted," needed, and expected" are maintained
	All levels of the clubhouse	Know how to manage personnel, time, and community activities	
		Be skilled at planning and budgeting	Convening and managing meetings for various purposes within the clubhouse
		Be skilled at public relations, public speaking, and fund-raising	Maintaining permeable social boundaries inside and outside the clubhouse
		Be skilled at eliciting abilities from others	Communicating with outside groups and individuals relevant to the interests of the clubhouse
		Know how to construct and maintain clear, yet permeable, group and community boundaries	
		Be skilled at the acquisition of resources	

We each purchased cups of hot clam chowder to chase the chill and dampness of the morning. Then we walked to the end of the pier where we could see ferries coming and going. We listened to the sounds of boats mixed with the cries of seagulls. The scenery was quite stunning, but there was very little conversation. Most of the group watched a lone fisherman sitting on a piling below us.

After we had finished our chowder, I turned to start back down the pier. The clients turned and began to follow behind me with a military precision until we were halfway down the pier. There I stepped to the side, about 20 feet, to deposit my empty cup in a trash barrel. Remarkably and without prompting, the entire group made the very same movement, following almost in my footprints and still not speaking. I was suddenly very uncomfortable. A number of unanswered thoughts and questions flooded my mind.

I had not required or requested the deference and compliance they demonstrated in this seemingly organized movement toward the trash barrel. Why did they follow so closely? They were not crippled or incompetent. In fact, they had gotten up in their own homes and apartments and had gotten themselves out the door and to the program by bus or car. Nobody was acutely psychotic or having other extraordinary problems that might require close staff attention. Nobody was intellectually impaired. I thought about the entire outing as an enactment, a microcosm, a symbol of the restrictive structures and patterns from which we had constructed treatment experiences and our own roles.

I realized that I had gained—without asking—immense and unnecessary authority over their lives. Without discussion or reflection, the group and I had divided our roles into leader and followers. Not surprisingly these roles mirrored the roles they had played in the hospital and our own day treatment program. Without asking I had been "elevated" to a role akin to custodian, day care parent, or scout leader. Our activity together served to confirm our roles and relations with each other. On one hand, the depth of their illnesses could explain their passivity, and my unquestioned authority and caretaking as an appropriate treatment approach for people so ill. We walked for a while then drove back to the clinic. Apparently, nobody in the group had the same thoughts, or if they did, they did not share them at the time.

This single event was completely ordinary and unremarkable. However, it became a complex symbol in my mind of the disjunction of professional values of self-determination and the program practices that held each of us captive in ritualized, limiting roles. It was true that several people on that outing were quite disturbed and struggling with the symptoms of their illnesses. However, the structure and interactions of the outing did not ask or offer them anything more than passive attendance and participation. Memory of this day and otherwise unremarkable outing came quickly to have great significance for me. It was the kind of event in my life and career that scientists refer to as an "ah ha" moment.

A short time later, other staff and I decided that the program I was direct-ing should change. A new staff member had told me about the clubhouse model. We set about transforming the program into a place that we could share with our former clients and service recipients, a clubhouse that normal-ized all our relationships and needed the skill and talents of its members, as well as the abilities of its staff. This major change held unexpected healing for me as I think it did for former clients. With the development of a clubhouse, I began to reintegrate my personal and professional values with my own knowledge and practice. I came to believe that the same kind of integration and normalization that supports me—the job for which I am needed—could also support clients, now members of the clubhouse. For the first time, I began to understand and experience a congruence of practice methods, theo-ries, and professional values in developing a place for people with mental ill-ness. I learned that developing and maintaining congruence was a challenging task simultaneously internal and personal, yet external and social.

ACHIEVING AND MAINTAINING CONGRUENCE BETWEEN CONCEPTUAL MODEL AND CLUBHOUSE REALITY

Applied to the social life of a clubhouse, the notion of *congruence* can be viewed as a condition in which clubhouse culture, customs, relationships, pro-cedures, and structures consistently contribute to the positive, ongoing social construction of the clubhouse and its primary purposes of sustaining the growth and recovery of individual members. Maintaining congruence can be a challenge when staff and members replicating the model naturally want to put their own stamp on it, make it their own. They may experience pressures to add program components found to be successful in other contexts. In any case, they adapt their clubhouse to the requirements of their larger commu-nity, funding sources, and other stakeholders. Some additions and changes simply add uniqueness and variety. Others create *incongruence* between the clubhouse and the model itself.

Some Sources of Incongruence

For example, some staff or members might want to add creative writing class-es every Monday morning to the schedule. They argue that such activity would encourage self-expression and creativity. The activity could be positive and could benefit members. It would be attractive. Many members might enjoy this activity. Such an activity would help structure their time and give them a chance to socialize with others.

However, if creative writing is established as a regular daytime activity, its presence will be in direct contradiction with the work unit activities that are established to build a strong, work-ordered day. Although a worthwhile activity, the implementation of such a change would be incongruent with the work-ordered day and with clubhouse values concerning the rehabilitative aspects of work. Such an activity must be scheduled for the conventional recreation times of evenings and weekends. After work is a normal time to schedule recreation.

Some staff might wish to include specialists or experts in the clubhouse staff mixture. They might perform certain specialized roles, it is argued, for which neither the regular staff nor members are trained—for instance, art therapy. The argument is strong but not persuasive. Specialists or experts may meet needs within the clubhouse. However, their expertise will displace and perhaps limit the talents and opportunities of existing members and staff. Rather than introduce art therapy to the clubhouse, the appropriate response, congruent with the clubhouse model, would be to teach, if necessary, members and staff the methods of art and establish opportunities for creative expression in the clubhouse after the workday is over. This approach brings art into the life of the clubhouse but normalizes the activity and does not take away from member roles.

In starting a clubhouse, the staff and members might be tempted to develop a single aspect, for instance, the work-ordered day. Development of transitional employment opportunities might be seen as too expensive, too difficult to obtain and maintain, or impossible because of funding limitations. However, if the work of the day is to have meaning for individual members, it must lead to further opportunities in the larger community. The possibility of working competitively contributes hope and meaning to the work carried out by members in their work units. If a clubhouse activity consists solely of work unit activities and recreation, the result will probably be a drop-in center. The meaning of clubhouse membership will be skewed, and attendance and involvement will gradually diminish. If, on the other hand, a clubhouse decides to concentrate on rehabilitation only and focus their efforts exclusively on transitional employment, supported employment, or education activities, they will tend to lose members who are currently unable to work competitively. They will not be able to provide the ongoing support that all members with mental illness need in order to negotiate difficult times.

Successful replication of the clubhouse model or any social program or activity for change does not require precise imitation. There is room for considerable improvisation and creativity. However, it does require fundamental congruence in all the important socially-constructed aspects. As we have discussed before, individual identity and social identity are bound together. Organizational incongruence tends to confuse members and staff. It should be identified and minimized whenever possible.

Maintenance of Congruence and Fidelity to the Model

Most clubhouses strive to replicate and maintain the key elements of the model such as a focus on member interests and opportunities, the work-ordered day, transitional employment opportunities, and the fundamental guarantees of membership. Consistent adherence to the model is important because paradoxical messages to members cause confusion. The entire character of the clubhouse community can rapidly change with any compromises of the model. To insure continuity and congruence with the model, clubhouses use peer clubhouses and training bases. This is done in several ways.

First, clubhouses send their staff and members to training at regional training bases, which are strong, well-developed clubhouses equipped with the facilities and other resources to conduct three-week training sessions (see Appendix III). During these intensive training sessions, staff and members learn how to start and maintain their own clubhouses. In training, as in all activities of the clubhouse, expertise is drawn from members and staff as roles are identified and developed. Training results not only in staff and members having a clearer understanding of their work, but also in an action plan that is followed-up with ongoing consultations by training bases. In addition, training bases offer one-week specialized training sessions in employment, housing, and leadership.

Second, clubhouses convene special meetings or use community meetings to evaluate the components of their clubhouse programming and activities and suggest changes that will bring the clubhouse community reality into greater congruence with the model. Needed changes and new activities are proposed, endorsed, and planned in such meetings.

Finally, clubhouses can apply for formal certification by the International Center for Clubhouse Development (ICCD). This certification, overseen by the ICCD and conducted by peer clubhouses, gives clubhouses applying for certification or renewal an opportunity to evaluate the extent of congruence between their clubhouse and the model. Members and staff carry out the ensuing self-evaluation and site visits. Certification helps to maintain an effective and vibrant group of clubhouses that are congruent with the model and responsive and accountable to members, clubhouse directors, and mental health authorities (Macias et al., 1999).

Despite the fact that they are crafted from the same design, clubhouses are often quite different from each other in important aspects. These aspects constitute unique identities and identifying features. Clubhouses have distinctive names, unique facilities, their own ways of greeting visitors, special celebrations, and customs. In each of these respects, they strive to be unique and different from each other.

Aspiration and Accomplishment: Addressing an International Seminar

Robert had come to the clubhouse from a sheltered workshop in his community that had gone out of business. He liked being around people and liked a regular routine in his life. In that respect, he enjoyed the daily life of the clubhouse, especially showing visitors around. Because he had trained and practiced to conduct tours, members and staff saw him as one of the best tour guides in the clubhouse. He knew everything about the clubhouse—its activities, hours of operation, special programs, annual events like the talent show, and the names of most, if not all, members and staff.

Everyone liked Robert. He was particularly engaging because he inspired everyone when he spoke about his personal struggles to overcome disabling mental illness and stigma in the larger community. He described with great vividness and emotion what the clubhouse meant to him and all the friends that he had made at the clubhouse. He was often asked to tell his story at special community meetings and holidays.

When the possibility of being a speaker at the international seminar in Sweden came up, everyone was excited. Of course, many staff and members wanted to go, but the clubhouse could afford to send just two people and the selection committee knew that Robert would represent the clubhouse and himself very well. One staff member and Robert were chosen. They were to be on an international panel of other staff and members discussing the problems of developing transitional employment programs. He was ecstatic and his excitement was infectious.

GENERALIST PRACTITIONERS AS COMMUNITY BUILDERS

The clubhouse movement implemented empowering methods and a strengths perspective before these terms were widely known or discussed. The clubhouse model was not the first attempt to empower people who have mental illness nor did the emergence of the model represent the first effort to enable people with mental illness to work. However, the model and the "movement," as it is now called, has sought from its beginnings at Fountain House more than 50 years ago to act on the assumption that people with mental illness can learn, adapt, and contribute to others. This kind of shift in thinking about mental illness certainly qualifies as revolutionary. It has been translated into truly extraordinary changes in the way that people with mental illness are treated.

I saw this demonstrated at the Moscow Clubhouse in Russia a few years ago. There, members, family members, and a few interested young psychiatrists gathered around the same table to share a meal of black bread and tea, making plans together for building the clubhouse and expanding clubhouse membership. Their shared work and the collegial meeting at the table seemed an important sign that their lives were being quietly, but fundamentally, changed through combined action. Everyone at the table was discussing the new clubhouse being remodeled and made ready for occupancy through their efforts. They all spoke with pride of "their" clubhouse and its importance for them. Their plans and actions could only be seen as positive and empowering.

The clubhouse model may have far-reaching implications, not as a set of methods, but as a values-driven plan for constructing egalitarian communities and a new kind of professionalism based upon community-building practice roles. This change in thought and behavior, as it relates to the clubhouse community, has been referred to as a fundamental "paradigm shift" (Mandiberg, 1997). The knowledge of the model and theoretical knowledge is not locked away. The theory toolkit is built from many of the theoretical tools discussed throughout this book. The theoretical tools and the clubhouse model are open to the examination and discussion of anyone interested.

Community-building roles are being assumed by the type of professional described by McKnight when he writes of "community guides" (McKnight, 1995). These professionals keep their credentials in a drawer and gain their sense of achievement and self-worth through constructing community well-being together with community members. Although they see themselves as performing important work, most clubhouse staff and members do not think of themselves as revolutionaries. They go about their business without the noise and planned disruption ordinarily associated with revolutions. However, their work fits Freire's definition of cultural revolution (Freire, 1994). It is the displacement of disempowering cultural meanings with new and enabling meanings combined with real opportunities.

As we have seen through the examination of the clubhouse model and various components of theory, the work of a clubhouse community builder unifies thought (theory), belief (values), and action (behavior) in natural forms of helping. It facilitates personal and professional congruence between these elements. It addresses social and psychological isolation through the shared creation of communities.

Rudyard Propst (see Appendix I) uses the phrase "mining clubhouse values," a rich metaphor that suggests a continuing exploration of the possibilities of community-building. If the model is anchored in universal human characteristics and strivings, can the model have much wider application? Evidence of the appeal of the model suggests that the answer is affirmative (Jackson et al., 1996). The lessons of the clubhouse model may have relevance anywhere that groups are stigmatized and socially excluded, social connections have been frayed or broken, and specialized helping processes have broken the natural connections between contributing work and community.

THE THEORY TOOLKIT

To assist the student in imagining theory applications in practice, we have introduced the clubhouse model, a generalist practice model that is simple in its design but extraordinarily complex with regard to the range of roles and skills it requires of staff. This complexity and richness has given us the opportunity to illuminate various aspects of theory. A primary goal has been and remains a richly complex, maturing, and evolving *practice theory*—a kind of toolkit containing the frameworks, perspectives, models, theories, and concepts needed to work in a community-building practice setting. Such a toolkit, thoughtfully developed and evaluated, should be relevant to practice as well as consistent and congruent with the worker's personal and professional values.

One of the greatest challenges the new professional faces is the integration of practice with his or her values and professional ethics. People are naturally inclined to help others. Most help to others is natural helping, provided because a need is observed and someone wants to help. Such help, understood as an expression of personal values and concern, is often spontaneous and unreflective. Help is offered and provided because it is the natural thing to do, "the right thing to do." The best professional help is an expression of personal and professional values combined with knowledge and critical thinking.

Students, as emerging professionals, must find ways to combine and synthesize theoretical knowledge and their own personal and professional values in practice. Professional integrity is quite literally based on the joining of values and theoretical elements and their behavioral applications.

> *You can't heal mental illness by dry disciplines alone; you have to touch a person's heart in the process.*
>
> —A CLUBHOUSE MEMBER'S PERSPECTIVE

APPLYING CONCEPTS

1. What is in your theory toolkit at this time? Discuss.
2. What is the relation between your practice theory and your values?
3. Discuss how community-building is becoming a new practice role for practitioners.

4. How can community builders avoid the assumption of community roles that could be done by others? How would you engage others in contributing roles?

Class Projects

Select one theory or theoretical perspective that seems especially useful and compatible with your values and style of professional work. Investigate it thoroughly and report on it to your class.

Develop a plan for community-building with another marginalized or excluded group in society. What steps would you take and what role would you play in developing leadership and creating and maintaining community?

GLOSSARY

Certification or recertification   a clubhouse status granted by the International Center for Clubhouse Development (ICCD) for successful completion of the site visit and evaluation.

Congruence   in this community-building application, refers to the comparatively positive relationship between the Clubhouse Model and the clubhouse reality.

Incongruence   in social application, a comparatively poor or inadequate relationship between the Clubhouse Model and the clubhouse reality; in personal terms, an inadequate integration of theory, practice, and values.

Practice theory   a toolkit comprised of frameworks, perspectives, models, theories, and concepts.

Site visit and evaluation   a formal review that compares clubhouse realities with Clubhouse Standards; clubhouse members and staff for other clubhouses routinely conduct such reviews.

REFERENCES

Freire, P. (1994). *Pedagogy of the oppressed* (3rd ed.). New York: Continuum Publishing Co.
Jackson, R. L., Purnell, D., Anderson, S., & Sheafor, B. W. (1996). The Clubhouse Model of community support for adults with mental illness: An emerging opportunity for social work education. *Journal of Social Work Education, 32*(2), 173–180.

Macias, C., Harding, C., Alden, M., Geertsen, D., & Barreira, P. (1999). The value of program certification for performance contracting. *Administration and Policy in Mental Health, 26*(5), 345–360.

Mandiberg, J. (1997, July). *Our future: Who we are and where we are going. The future is bright.* Paper presented at the ICCD 9th International Seminar of the Clubhouse Model, Goteborg, Sweden.

McKnight, J. (1995). *The careless society: Community and its counterfeits.* New York: Basic Books.

Fountain House, the Clubhouse Model: How It Evolved and Is Spreading around the World

RUDYARD N. PROPST

I have the honor of being asked by Robert L. Jackson to contribute to this exciting and very timely book. He said that he did so because I coauthored the first major attempt to set out the basic elements of the Clubhouse Model and I have been privileged to be at the heart of every evolutionary development in the model since 1981, as well as being instrumental in its diffusion around the world. Bob also pointed out that since I retired at the end of July 1997, this offer might be an inducement to put down on paper all that I am in a unique position to say about the Clubhouse Model, its evolution, and replication internationally. I was induced.

First, it will be my purpose to describe the seminal decisions that I was most closely involved in, initially undertaken by Fountain House itself and then disseminated everywhere in the clubhouse community to more nearly realize all of the implications inherent in our way of working. Next, I will describe the approaches we have taken to assist in the international diffusion of our way of working. I will follow with a description of the steps the clubhouse community has taken to ensure the quality and fidelity of all clubhouses to the model through the creation of a new organization, the International Center for Clubhouse Development.

Prologue

> The Fountain House model is a social invention in community rehabilitation of the severely disabled psychiatric patient. Fountain House itself is an intentional community designed to create the restorative environment within which individuals who have been socially and vocationally disabled can be helped to achieve or regain the confidence and skills necessary to lead vocationally productive and socially satisfying lives. (Beard et al., 1982, p. 172)

Over the years, the clubhouse community has come to realize that one central theme underlies, pervades, and directs every step, action taken, and structural change over the past sixteen years. It can be stated by combining three passages from Beard's 1982 article.

> Fountain House has always been and is still acutely conscious that it has not fully realized all of the implications of the concepts that underlie its efforts. . . . What Fountain House is now struggling with is a major increase in members' involvement

in program delivery . . . a bright and promising goal for the future of Fountain House is the fully realized utilization of members at maximum levels of involvement in the delivery of clubhouse activities.

The effort to fully realize this goal, that is, members as full participants and contributors to every aspect, facet, and function of the clubhouse, doing so as side-by-side, shoulder-to-shoulder peers and partners with staff, has in my view continued to be the central, unswerving driving force behind every evolutionary development in the Clubhouse Model, first at Fountain House itself and then in every other clubhouse in the world. Let us look first at some of the crucial steps that Fountain House itself took in pursuit of this goal beginning in 1981.

Fountain House Moves to More Completely Actualize Its Vision of the Clubhouse Community

For its first thirty-three years, whenever Fountain House was asked to present its work, it did so by sending only staff as speakers. By 1981, it had become obvious that doing so was a violent contradiction of the core premise. Thus, in 1981, Fountain House practice was amended to ensure that all presentations by Fountain House on the Clubhouse Model, in whatever forum, be carried out by a member-staff team.

This change created considerable unease and debate among some Fountain House staff. What happens if a member gets sick on the trip or on the stage? Are we asking too much of the members—the strain of travel, the tension that every presenter feels, being away from home? Will members decompensate? Fortunately, members did not agree. After repeated successes it was generally recognized that members are far more compelling and persuasive than staff in conveying the reality of the clubhouse, and the objections rapidly died down.

Since it had taken Fountain House 33 years to realize its error, it should be no surprise that for years after we introduced the concept of member-staff, rather than staff only, presenters at conferences and workshops in mental health, there were varying degrees of resistance by conference planners and delegates to the inclusion of members. It was expressed in a number of ways, such as the inability to find accommodations for the member or allot time on the panel for the member. Members' names were left off the program and identifying sign outside the workshop door, or no chair on the dais was provided for the member. It is, however, important to note that by 1989, these reactions had virtually disappeared. For some years now, the first thing a clubhouse is asked is "What members are coming with you?"

Fountain House Members Are Included as Part of Every Colleague Training Team and the National Training Program at Fountain House Is Amended to Require Member Participation in Every Three-Week Training Set

In 1977, Fountain House was awarded a multiyear grant to establish a national training program in the Clubhouse Model. The original design called for staff-only colleagues in the group coming for training and a staff-only training team at Fountain House. In 1978, Fountain House received a grant to institute a national member training program in the Clubhouse Model that called for two-week training sets, with the training team including Fountain House members. By 1981, it had become apparent that the member training program was a failure and at least one of the major reasons was that Fountain House had inadvertently set up a segregated and, therefore, stigmatizing design and subverted its core premise that in clubhouse *we do everything together*. As a result, when the member training grant ended Fountain House made no attempt to extend it. The three-week training program, on the other hand, was renewed at decreasing levels of funding over nine years. The ultimate learning was that Fountain House needed to integrate members into all three-week training sets and incorporate Fountain House members into all training teams.

These decisions profoundly affected both Fountain House itself and every new or existing clubhouse coming for training. For Fountain House, since training is a valued function throughout the clubhouse, drawing members into every colleague training group strikingly altered their perceived roles throughout the clubhouse. Initially, there were objections from some Fountain House staff regarding members having the stamina to sustain the intense involvement inherent in the three-week experience or staff colleagues feeling uncomfortable in expressing their real feelings with members present. Staff wondered where members were going to stay, not realizing that the answer was with them. We were told that programs could not afford to send a member, and anyhow, no members would benefit from training. Again, dying down over many years, such attitudes have totally disappeared, at least overtly. It is by now abundantly clear that had Fountain House not taken these steps, it and the entire clubhouse community would never have squeezed out stigma and achieved the extent of equality of opportunity for members all over the world that has in fact become the reality and the norm.

For clubhouses in training, the very act of coming, being, and working with a member of the house immediately had a tremendous impact on the staff who came with a member, the member who came, Fountain House, and the clubhouse back home.

In the early days of this role inclusion, new clubhouses were often far more traditional in their approach to members than they are now. Member colleagues found relationships at Fountain House to be more equal and more respectful than relationships in their home clubhouses. They often reported that when they returned to their home clubhouses they were not asked to comment on their experiences in training, let alone suggest clubhouse program inprovements. This may have contributed to member colleagues being hospitalized shortly after returning home, not in large but in alarming numbers. As I write this, I realize that it has been years since this phenomenon was widespread. It still occurs but much less frequently.

1984–1985: Invitations to the Third International Seminar on the Clubhouse Model Included the Expectations That Members and Staff Would Participate in Roughly Equal Numbers and That Members Would Be Asked to Present at the Seminar in Equal Proportion to Staff

One of the many watersheds in the consciousness-raising work carried out by Fountain House in the course of its own efforts to fully realize the promise to members inherent in the model was in these expectations. The initial reaction from the clubhouse community was disbelief that members could be away from home for a week and be active participants and presenters. Consequently, the first wave of registrations were entirely for staff. In response, a second letter went out to the clubhouse community reminding them of the initial criteria and indicating that if members could not be found to participate, no one at all should come. The outcome was that members did come, did present, but were seriously outnumbered by staff. The impact of the 1985 seminar on clubhouses everywhere was that by 1987, we found that clubhouses were proposing to send either all members and no staff or a lopsided majority of members to staff. We had to point out that the goal was a balanced number of members and staff, that in clubhouse *we do everything together.* Since 1987, every biennial seminar has superbly expressed the fully realized goal, that is, essentially a 50-50 representation of members and staff both in numbers and presenters. It is noteworthy that to this day, the clubhouse international seminars are the only mental health gatherings in the world in which at least one-half of the participant body are consumers of mental health services.

The Clubhouse Spreads Around the World

Fountain House opened in New York City in 1948. For nearly thirty years (1948–1977), it was alone in its way of working. Almost one-third of a century is a very long time to be alone, unreplicated, especially when this same way of working, over the past twenty years (1977–1997), has been one of the most successfully replicated programs in community mental health in the United States and only one of a very few to be widely successfully replicated internationally. In the 1997 Directory of Clubhouse Model Programs there were 336 clubhouses worldwide, 244 in the United States in 43 states and the District of Columbia and 92 in 20 countries and five continents, with 25–30 new clubhouses opening every year.

Numerous factors played a role in this long-delayed but now explosive growth in the clubhouse community. The most influential factors were these.

From 1948 to at least 1984 the prevailing wisdom in the mental health establishment, albeit in a descending curve over time, was that it was either hopelessly naïve or purely cruel to in any way expect individuals suffering from severe and persistent mental illness to ever reenter the open work market in any capacity. Today we still hear from members who have just been told by their therapists that they will never work again, even part-time, and ought never try to do so. On the other hand, from the day that it opened in 1948, Fountain House has taken the view that "work is a deeply generative and regenerative force in all human life" (Beard et al., 1982) and that, therefore, access to work both inside and outside the clubhouse is a right of membership.

From 1948 until the present, the dominant framework for relationships between mental health professionals and individuals recovering from serious mental illness has been that of professional-patient (more recently, professional-client) with all of its attendant features, for example, therapist remoteness, no use of the person in the relationship, and no possibility of any need of the patient (except as a source of research data and income). On the other hand, Fountain House, from the beginning, built its relationships on a peer-partner model with a strong, conscious intent to create an environment in which the staff constantly needs members to contribute their services and talents to the running of the clubhouse. Throughout this period, the professional mental health establishment utilized a symptom-pathology-deficit model to build its reports, expectations, and programs, whereas Fountain House based its entire approach to its members on seeking out and supporting all of their abilities, skills, and positive personal attributes, focusing not at all on symptoms, deficiency, and pathology.

From 1948 until the rise of family and consumer advocate groups in the mid-1980s, the professional mental health community, precisely because of the attitudes and assumptions previously described, found it wrongheaded at worst and unprofessionally awkward at best to attempt to assert or support the efforts of mental health consumers to retake control of their lives, to "empower" themselves. Fountain House, on the other hand, was creating a self-empowering community, one of peers and partners working together in every aspect of the clubhouse, learning to do it better and better over time from its very onset.

For the entire period from 1948 to the present, with virtually no deviation, the mental health establishment based its thinking about program design on the skills and competencies of the various professionals constituting the "team" to address the "patient's" need for symptom reduction, pathology repair, and deficit offset, inevitably resulting in compartmentalizing both the patient and the resulting program.

In very dramatic contrast, first Fountain House itself and subsequently every additional clubhouse has worked to create real communities (as opposed to artificial ones, for example, "therapeutic communities") in which, as in all effective communities, members and staff take care of each other, support each other, work together to keep the community going, have a method of governance acceptable to all, create a safe and respectful place to be and to do, have open and clear access to the wider community, both vocationally via transitional and independent employment and socially, and serve as a permanent place to return to for help, renewal, new opportunities, celebration, and for a lifetime.

It easily follows that Fountain House from the beginning based its hiring practice on whether:

- The candidate liked, felt drawn to, and was comfortable in the egalitarian society of the clubhouse.
- The candidate would be able to trust the members.
- Members would be able to trust the candidate.
- He or she had a high level of focused energy.
- He or she would be able to and clearly liked working as a generalist, for example, helping to set up for breakfast in the early morning, going out later on a transitional employment placement with a member, being in the clerical unit in the afternoon, and not tying his or her professional identity to a professional title, for example, social worker, occupational therapist, or rehabilitation counselor.

In the clubhouse staff work together with members to keep the community going. The focus is on ensuring that the community is alive and well, not at all on the professional or other titled background from which the staff come.

We began these efforts in community, first intuitively and then consciously, for two reasons. First, there was the realization, true in 1948 and equally true today, that our members, like everyone else, need a primary social group to belong to which provides a respected social space within which members can find their way back to self-confidence, self-respect, and with the foothold of the clubhouse, reentry into society at large. Second, we needed to create such communities for our members because preexisting primary social groups, no more successful in 2000 than in 1948, were not embracing our people, that there were no natural communities to belong to and, therefore, either we built them for people recovering from mental illness or our people would go on forever in the hopelessness of the "revolving door."

In other words in the language of a friend and colleague, Fountain House was terrifically "out of paradigm," that is, marching to a different drummer (Mandiberg, 1997, p. 1254) for virtually the entire period and melodramatically so in the early years. What has changed? Why the interest in the Clubhouse Model? Because in James Mandiberg's formulation, the clubhouse is rapidly becoming "in paradigm" in many but not all ways and not only in the United States but around the world. Everywhere in the United States at federal, state, and local levels the goal of helping individuals recovering from mental illness to return to the world of work has become the highest priority for funding support. Work has been discovered to have powerful therapeutic value, indeed to be a crucial element in recovery.

In Europe, Scandinavia, and Australia, long held prejudices against work as a potential goal for the mentally ill have been reversed in much the same way as they have in the United States. For example, the Danish government has very recently announced that it is placing its highest priority for funding for programs that demonstrate a successful ability to return people to work in commerce and industry. Clearly, the Clubhouse Model has been "ahead of the curve" for years and is seen now as a very attractive funding option.

Second, endeavoring to keep up with the curve, the mental health establishment has "discovered" consumer empowerment, indeed has begun to call for consumer-run programs, consumers on mental health program boards of directors, and consumers as podium presenters at mental health conferences. Looking for ways of working with which they are comfortable and are uniquely successful in creating communities fostering the self-improvement of those they serve, mental health funding sources, as well as families and consumers themselves, have discovered that clubhouse is that community and once again, the model becomes a very attractive funding option.

Third, although much slower to change, there has begun, at least among psychosocial rehabilitation programs in the larger mental health provider world, to arise a voice calling for a wellness approach, as opposed to a symptom-deficit-pathology approach to working with our people. Aside from the fact that Clubhouse Model programs have profoundly contributed to the ascendancy of the "wellness" perspective, the recognition that Fountain House and all other clubhouses have from the beginning grounded their work on this central value and have achieved the most completely realized culture expressing it serves to still further enhance the attractiveness of clubhouses to potential funding sources.

Finally, in the always mysterious and fickle flow of fashion in the mental health priority setting, the creation of community, the absolute centrality of the idea of community as the hitherto hidden, magic ingredient in the recovery process, has sprung to life it would seem everywhere at once. Community-building dominates conferences, seminars, new course offerings, articles, and as the organizing principle of entire volumes. Since Fountain House has founded its entire culture on the creation of living communities specifically designed to maximize the ability of members to refind their footing in the world creating the conditions for having a life and has been learning how best to do that for almost fifty years, it is no wonder that funders around the world are drawn to the clubhouse as a highly attractive option to support.

Another factor that cannot be ignored, especially in the early days when community mental health agencies as well as state central offices of mental health were dubiously committing themselves to the Clubhouse Model, is the low cost of such programs. Today, in New York state it costs an average of $21,000 per year to house and support individuals at Fountain House as opposed to $120,000 annual hospitalization costs. Clubhouse members show a marked decrease in the need for repeated short-term hospitalizations (Wilkinson, 1992). Without housing, it costs $35 per day to support a member at Fountain House as opposed to $100 per day in medical model day treatment programs. Looking at the clubhouse community as a whole, in the United States the annual cost per member to provide clubhouse rehabilitation is $3,333 (Macias et al., 1999). Fifty percent of the clubhouses have per capita costs between $2,600 and $5,000 per year. Internationally, clubhouses outside the United States provide service to their members for an average of $3,667 U.S. dollars per year (Macias et al., 1999).

The Fountain Clubhouse Model Begins to Migrate Throughout the United States

The First Stage in Replication: The National Training Program

I have spoken of some of the steps taken by Fountain House in the course of "mining our value system" that served to materially influence the thinking and practice of clubhouse, especially those taken in the period 1981–1987. I turn now to the methods we chose as we began to see what needed to be the case if our way of working was to migrate, that is, if we were to move from an N of one to anything larger than that.

John Beard was convinced and so was I that what he and the members and staff of Fountain House had created over the years was a culture expressed in a living community. This culture transcended national, ethnic, and cultural boundaries, was based on the universal human condition, and was at the core enormously simple. In its culturally transcendent humanity, we believed it should be able to be introduced successfully anywhere in the United States and indeed anywhere in the world. What follows is an account of four distinct periods, each stemming from a set of learnings from the previous one, that have resulted in our current reality—257 clubhouses in 18 countries and counting.

By the middle of the 1970s, Fountain House was receiving hundreds of visitors per year. Nonetheless, despite often intense excitement in many of these visitors the N of clubhouses remained 1. In 1977, the General Accounting Office of the United States government released an audit of the Kennedy-inspired Community Mental Health Center (CMHC) initiative, funded nationally on a front-loaded, gradually diminishing level of federal support. One section of this report caused uproar—the finding that, though mandated to do so, not one CMHC was doing anything in support of the severely mentally ill in the community. One very positive reaction came from the Special and Experimental Training Branch of the National Institute of Mental Health (NIMH). Senior staff at NIMH decided that one of the reasons for the dramatic noncompliance around this population might be that the CMHCs had no idea what to do for such people. Therefore, if NIMH could help them learn a way of working that was already successful, such an effort might lead to a dramatic rise in compliance. A request for proposal (RFP) was fielded in 1976. Fountain House applied and was awarded a multiyear grant to establish a national training program in the Clubhouse Model, which with subsequent renewal finally ended in 1985.

In two central offices of mental health I had watched training efforts repeatedly fail to result in any change in practice, and I thought I knew why. Staff were typically chosen for training to enrich their resumes, as a "perk," as recognition for outstanding service, and because they were friends. Rarely did the training office expect the staff sent for training to do anything with it when they got home. External training almost never resulted in anything new in programs. Staff coming back from training wanting to initiate a new idea soon realized that there was no energy, let alone urgency to do so, with the result that a frequent outcome of such often very expensive external training efforts was the demoralization of the staff sent for the training.

John Beard knew I had thought a lot about what would make external training effective. When the site review team said that Fountain House would not be funded unless it produced a very clear training design, he called me and I quickly drew up the design that has been the template of our training at all training bases ever since.

As I saw it, all other training centers were totally passive in their requirements of those coming for training. I proposed that we become very proactive and demanding in our criteria, specifically that we require the following of programs seeking to send a group for training:

1. That a sufficient start-up budget to operate the clubhouse be in place.
2. That the site or space for the clubhouse has been found or is to be by the end of training, is adequate to support at least 35 members per day, and is near public transportation and employment opportunities.
3. That the director, a second principal staff, and (after 1982) a member have been identified, that they will come to Fountain House (or later, any certified training base) for a three-week, in-residence training set, and that a person with major oversight responsibility come during the third week of training.
4. That the colleagues in training be able to return on a Friday and open their clubhouse the following Monday morning.

From the beginning, we conceived the entire experience to be an immersion apprenticeship. We quickly discovered that the greatest, most attitude-altering learning came from staff working with members in the units and later in the colleague group itself. The centerpiece change was a drastic, often life-altering shift in staff expectations concerning the potential in all members to pick themselves up becoming contributors to their own lives and to the life of the clubhouse community.

Fountain House began its training program in 1977. By 1987, there were 220 clubhouses in the United States in every region of the country and in cities and towns of every size. The Special and Experimental Training Branch of NIMH later said that, in terms of replication, ours was the most successful training program they had ever funded.

The Second Stage in Replication: The National Clubhouse Expansion Program

We learned a great deal during the NIMH era. We learned that the Clubhouse Model would replicate probably anywhere. By 1987, there were clubhouses in Pakistan, Sweden, Denmark, Germany, Holland, Canada, and South Africa. We learned a lot of other things, too.

1. It was not enough for a program to *come* to training. There had to be the capacity for on-site, peer-support consultation once the clubhouse was underway.
2. We needed to develop *standards of practice* for our way of working.
3. We needed additional training bases to keep up with the demand for training.
4. We needed to strengthen transitional employment programs everywhere.
5. We should be able to introduce the clubhouse into states currently lacking them.

At that same juncture in 1987, the Robert Wood Johnson Foundation announced a major thrust to increase and improve the capacity of the community to successfully support the hundreds of people coming out of psychiatric hospitals who were in need of an adequate response to their continuing needs. Fountain House responded by submitting a proposal to do everything I have just outlined. We were awarded a grant, originally for three years and ultimately for four years, to undertake the National Clubhouse Expansion Program (NCEP). We learned that this grant, the intent of which was to expand the Clubhouse Model nationally, was virtually unprecedented in that almost never did an influential foundation support the diffusion of a single way of working as the Robert Wood Johnson Foundation had here. We obtained major additional support for our very ambitious design from the Public Welfare Foundation and the Pew Charitable Trusts.

The Creation of the Standards for Clubhouse Programs

It is very clear to me now that I began to see the need and advocate for developing a set of standards for Clubhouse Model programs long before anyone else. As Director of Colleague Training at Fountain House, I had the privilege of seeing every program before they came for training, working with colleagues during training, and most important of all, visiting hundreds of programs that after training had become clubhouses. The result was that I could, at any time, draw on dozens of images in addition to Fountain House to help in responding to colleague questions. I had begun to accumulate experiences that led to an overwhelming conviction that every strong clubhouse is very much like every other strong clubhouse and every weak clubhouse is weak in predictable ways and for predictable reasons. I must admit that I had also grown tired of the standard Fountain House answer to the question "what is a clubhouse?" The standard answer of, "Oh, it can't really be described. You just have to experience it. It is all a matter of feeling. It is a way of life," was true, but to the intent of the questioner, not helpful. By 1987, I was absolutely certain that we were creating clubhouse communities with enough internal consistency to warrant codification into standards of practice.

Our method was:

1. To ask 12 well-established and highly realized clubhouses to take on the charge of asking their clubhouses the question, "If we were drawing up standards for our way of working, our community, what would they look like?" All 12 responded.

2. With these suggestions in hand, we convened a group drawn from Fountain House members and staff and from a number of additional strong clubhouses for a long weekend. By the end of the weekend, we had reached consensus on a set of draft standards.

3. Having set them in consistent, active voice form, we included a copy in the programs of all 600 member and staff participants in the Fifth International Seminar on the Clubhouse Model held in St. Louis, MO in 1989. Then, by randomizing the participants into a large number of small groups with facilitators drawn from the Faculty for Clubhouse Development, we were able, with remarkable speed, to arrive at consensus on a set of 35 standards, which were then revised to meet participants' recommendations, principally for clarity, and sent out to every clubhouse in the directory for comment and hopefully concurrence. The ensuing agreement was virtually universal with the result that we promulgated the final document at the end of 1989. This effort, I believe, marked the first and perhaps only time that *consumers* had ever been asked to participate as peers and partners in the process of creating standards governing practice for the program in which they were participants. It may also well be that our standards are among the very few that have been created and adopted through an international effort.

The Invention of the Faculty for Clubhouse Development

By the 1980s, it had become apparent that we had made at least one grave mistake in our 1977 NIMH proposal to set up a training base in the Clubhouse Model. We had failed to provide for posttraining, on-site peer support consultation for clubhouses after initial training. For a long time, we had hundreds of calls per year seeking help on one or another element of the model that we rarely had any way to respond to except by telephone. We had also learned that anything short of on-site consultation was bound to be significantly ineffectual because self-report is absolutely never accurate, not wittingly, but usually because the clubhouse is too close to the situation to see it clearly. Almost always, the clubhouse does not recognize and, therefore, cannot report on factors that, when on-site, become obvious as playing a role in the problem with which the clubhouse is struggling.

Our solution was to propose, in classic clubhouse fashion, identifying members and staff from powerfully realized clubhouses who deeply understood and could transmit, without offense, actions that would rectify the problems seen in the house. As members of the Faculty for Clubhouse Development, they would work in teams of two, one member and one staff, and spend three days on site at the end of which a verbal findings report would be made to the clubhouse, followed by a written report. I feel that it is imperative, at this junction, to point out that the only exception that the Robert Wood Johnson project staff took to our design was our intention to involve members on the Faculty. Were it not for the intervention of Dr. Leonard Stein, the Project Officer for the grants in our cycle of funding, this utterly crucial element would have been rejected by the foundation with the inevitable result that we would have withdrawn our proposal from consideration. At the end of the first year of the grant, the project staff had concluded that the inclusion of members was both congruent and effective.

I have often been asked why we dubbed the members and staff on our consulting teams a Faculty. The answer is that, in 1988, as now, there is no way to learn clubhouse philosophy and practice in colleges and universities. There are very few internship opportunities. Therefore, it was and is necessary for us by means of the growing network of training bases and the work of the consulting teams to create what has become an international "university without walls."

The first Faculty began its work in late fall of 1988, a year before the Standards for Clubhouse Programs were promulgated. It will be readily imagined that once the Standards were available, the work of the Faculty was greatly strengthened, and it was far easier to help a clubhouse understand the rationale behind consultants' recommendations.

By the third year of the NCEP, we were fielding a Faculty of more than 50 members and staff, and it had become evident that the consulting program was working. Our approach to the training of new Faculty, virtually none of whom had any prior experience as consultants, was to team an incoming consultant with an already experienced consultant, that is, an in situ apprenticeship. Because we screened potential faculty carefully, they were coming with a rich understanding from strong clubhouses, and they presented themselves as peers coming in support rather than as hatchets from an "Inspector General's Office," our reception by fellow clubhouses was, for the most part, very welcoming and positive from the start. Word of mouth, over time, was also a factor in reducing prearrival anxiety.

There were bumps, and there were problems. Early on, we encountered several instances in which a consulting team, in its zeal to assist the clubhouse to be the very best that it could be, presented their verbal findings with such intensity that members and staff felt overwhelmed and reacted with a mixture of hurt, anger, and denial. More often, the problem was the reverse, that is, in the effort not to offend, turn off, or lose willing attention, the team would so soften its recommendations as to render them nearly inaudible. Similarly, written reports tended to be less than forthcoming, even when what needed attention was a major problem in the clubhouse. (See the ICCD section following).

By far the most powerful innovation introduced in the consultation process, our conscious effort to assist the clubhouse to be as proactive in the experience as possible, was that of asking the house, months before the team arrived, to conduct its own self-study. As in every other work we have undertaken intended to enhance the clubhouse community, this request was met with enthusiasm and ready acceptance, but learning to do a self-study took several years and was greatly facilitated when we were able to send a sample self-study to act as a guide. (See the ICCD section following).

By 1997, clubhouses were regularly submitting self-studies so complete in the portrayal of their program, with recommendations for improvements and how to achieve them, that often the faculty would be in the delightful position of primarily reaffirming their proposals.

One of the expressed intentions in developing standards and creating the Faculty was to ensure that every clubhouse in the directory was, in fact, a clubhouse. At the outset, we knew that a significant number of the clubhouses listed in our directory (the criteria for inclusion being that they had been for training and had set up a clubhouse after training) were probably no longer clubhouses, despite their saying they were during our annual telephone poll. By 1988, we listed 220 clubhouses in our directory, all of whom had come into being since 1977.

By the end of the Robert Wood Johnson grant in 1992, we had taken 125 listings out of the directory, over 50 percent. The exciting news is that all of those taken out, with one exception, were without rancor because, between the standards and the offered consultations, it was clear to each program that they were not, at least any longer, a clubhouse as defined by the standards. The major reasons given for no longer functioning as a clubhouse were: (1) that a new administration had come in and rejected the clubhouse concept, (2) the original director had left before the clubhouse was securely in place, and (3) the auspice agency replaced a departing director with someone who did not intend to uphold the practice of clubhouse.

By the end of the NCEP, we had carried out 140 consultations in the United States, and there was no doubt that clubhouses across the country had embraced the process. Clubhouses had, as a result, immeasurably improved their realization of the model. Removing 57 percent of the listings in our Directory of Clubhouse Programs would have constituted a very serious threat to continuing funding support were it not for the fact that new clubhouses were opening at the rate of 25 per year.

The NCEP came to a funding end in the fall of 1992. We had succeeded in meeting every one of our goals: (1) we had created two very powerful new tools (the Faculty and the Clubhouse Standards), (2) we had identified three additional training bases, (3) we had introduced clubhouses in twelve new states, and (4) we had strengthened TE by developing a TE Track in our three-week training sets, introducing a one-week concentrated TE training curriculum for already existing clubhouses, and conducting on-site peer-support consultations, all of which took TE development as a priority. We had a far greater unity of purpose and practice throughout the clubhouse community than when we began. But, once again, we had uncovered a whole new set of challenges. Paramount among them were:

1. The need to create a method and a process for consultants to use in recommending a *formal certification status* to accompany the written report to the clubhouse.
2. The need to internationalize the consulting process.
3. The need to *diversify* and *internationalize* the *governance* of the clubhouse community.
4. The need to create a *new, formal organization* to act as the headquarters of the worldwide clubhouse federation.

Each of these was momentous in its own way and taken together constitutes the fourth major chapter in the story of "how the clubhouse spread around the world." Each one requires specific attention.

Certification Yes, Certification No: The Great Debate

I must confess that as far back as the first meeting of the Faculty in Pawling, NY in November of 1988, I had intimations that we should already have "dropped the other shoe" in our NCEP proposal, that is, designed in a formal certification status as an integral part of the written report. We had not, I was not sure enough to push it, and we had run four years without it by 1992. However, by then I had become absolutely convinced that were we not to introduce certification soon, the fine consultation process we had been honing for four years would begin to sputter to a halt. Why?

First, because in the absence of a certification status for a *specific period of time,* there would be no guaranteed reentry to a clubhouse after the first consultation. In other words, there would be no requirement for a clubhouse to seek recertification. I knew that if we did not move now to adopt certification that in less than ten years we would be right back where we were in 1988, with many clubhouses listed in our directory that were no longer even adequate expressions of clubhouse. We already could see it happening. Clubhouses having had a consultation in early 1989 were not seeking another, even late in 1992. By the end of the debate it was 1994, and Fountain House itself, having had its first consultation in 1991, had made no move to have another.

Second, as many of us were aware, all of health care was moving swiftly to require determinations of program quality and fidelity, with formal certification being by far the preferred option.

Thirdly, by 1992, our very conscious mission as a faculty had become to help every clubhouse be the very best that it could be. Our learning had made it obvious that only periodic revisits could possibly ensure this outcome.

During the NCEP era, I had come to see that the Faculty, coming together every fall, served a second major function, that is, a fine, powerful representative think tank. I put certification on the agenda of the 1992 Faculty Meeting, and at once, lines began to be drawn. There were the "how do I presume" voices, that is, who are we to certify our peers? There were "oil and water" voices, that is, the same people cannot be consultants and certify. There were the "someone else should do it" voices, that is, that yes, certification, but by an already existing certifying body, like Commission on Accreditation of Rehabilitation Facilities (CARF). There were the "yes certification and we should and can do it" voices among whom I was fervent. I believed that we had to move forward; that we dared not stall.

I need to speak to the oil and water voice. I knew the theory that it simply is not desirable or really possible to combine help with judgment, and I respected the concerns that it raised. (During 1989–1990, Barry Carson, Mental Health Director of CARF, proposed that CARF adopt our newly minted standards to use when certifying clubhouses. For "oil and water" reasons, I was willing to pursue it. The upper management of CARF, however, flatly rejected the idea, and I have since been deeply grateful that they did. The idea of *clubhouse members* on the Faculty was totally foreign to them. They thought we were far too prescriptive. Besides, I really believed that we should do our own certifying.

By 1997, we had completed 120 consultations ending in a certification status. (See the ICCD section following). Reentry was working. There were those who postponed the second consultation/certification visit. There were those who argued that certification should be "once and for all time." There were those who argued that the distinction between a one-year and a three-year certification stigmatized the one-year clubhouse and, therefore, was counterproductive. At the same time, however, there were no voices urging the rescinding of certification or of turning it over to another certification body. The value of certification was clearly perceived both in terms of quality assurance and in the rising importance of accreditation for funders. In the fall of 1998, the major agenda of the annual faculty meeting was to review our combined experiences. After extensive and highly detailed discussion, the faculty unanimously supported continuing the consultation/certification process unchanged.

Combining consultation and certification in one process appeared to be working for the clubhouse community. For me, there are two major contributing factors to our success. Unlike the two other principal accreditation bodies in the United States, CARF and Joint Commission on Accreditation of Healthcare Organizations (JCAHO), we are certifying *good practice.* In turn, it is clearly defined in our Clubhouse Standards, whereas the others are principally focused on administration and infrastructure, for example, safety, health, personnel, record-keeping, and other policies. Lacking standards, their practice requirements are profoundly less prescriptive than ours and indeed are vague and generalized. Ultimately, clubhouses accept our faculty's recommendation of a certification status because they know it is based on standards compliance, and the vast majority have embraced the standards as their own.

To strengthen the directory as a registry of programs following the Standards for Clubhouse Model Programs, the 1998 Directory of Clubhouse Programs listed only those clubhouses that belonged to the International Center for Clubhouse Development (ICCD) and who had been or were planning to be certified. As was true when we took 125 listings out of the directory in the four years of the NCEP, this decision resulted in a tremendous drop in the total number of clubhouses in the directory, from 342 in 1997 to 203 in 1998. At the annual Faculty Meeting in 1997, there was prolonged discussion concerning whether this action should be taken. Once again, our commitment to continuous quality improvement won the day.

Secondly, our design calls for the consulting team to *propose* a certification status. It holds if only three ICCD personnel concur after reading the written report that the recommended certification status is clearly derivable from the report. We have, in other words, a second, clearly objective review before the ICCD director formally confirms the status in a letter accompanying the written report.

By the fall of 1993, the work of the Faculty had greatly diminished (we were in a funding trough). I considered not holding a Faculty Meeting but decided to do so because I wanted to again put certification on the table, together with the concept of a new organization, the International Center for Clubhouse Development. (See the ICCD section following.)

We held the Faculty Meeting in Worcester, MA, immediately after the Seventh International Seminar on the Clubhouse Model. Everyone who was there agreed that it was a profoundly harrowing meeting. Counting the house, I was confident that a large plurality favored certification, but I also knew that the minority was fiercely opposed, highly vocal, and politically canny. I also, sadly but fortunately, knew that the majority would fall mute in a hot debate, and they did. It became a matter of holding on while the opposition went through all of its arguments over and over again. When it came to a yes or no vote, the yes was overwhelming. The violence of the opposition tended to conceal the fact that it was essentially comprised of four people out of fifty.

The Creation of the International Center for Clubhouse Development

The next two challenges, to internationalize the consultation/certification process and to diversify the governance of the clubhouse community, are so interwoven with a third, the creation of a new organization, the International Center for Clubhouse Development (ICCD), that clarity urges that I take up the ICCD first.

The idea of a distinct organization, created to act as the headquarters for the entire clubhouse community to enable, support, protect, defend, and represent the interests of clubhouses everywhere, surfaced as early as 1987, in Seattle, WA at the Fourth International Seminar on the Clubhouse Model when a straw poll resulted in a vividly clear "yes" mandate. From that time on, there were those of us who never stopped pondering the idea. It was nudged along when drafting our proposal to the Robert Wood Johnson Foundation for the National Clubhouse Expansion Program in 1988. We found that we were required to answer the question, "what happens when the money runs out?" We said we did not know, but our intent would be to work out the answer during the grant cycle. We were convinced that it would take the form of a new, permanent organization.

Three years later, after working closely with the Faculty, with the clubhouse community by telephone and during the Sixth International Seminar on the Clubhouse Model in Greenville, SC, and with Kenn Dudek (now Executive Director of Fountain House, then working with me in the NCEP), the following conclusions have been reached:

1. The new organization would be called the International Center for Clubhouse Development (ICCD).
2. The ICCD would be conceived as a freestanding, nonprofit 501(c)(3) entity with its own Board of Directors.
3. In order to take advantage of the enormous cachet of Fountain House itself and because it had become obvious that if it were to remain alive and current it would have to be located in a clubhouse, we concluded that we should launch the ICCD as a subsidiary corporation of Fountain House.
4. Once created, the ICCD would, among other things, take responsibility for ensuring the integrity and evolution of the Standards for Clubhouse Programs, ensure the quality and effectiveness of the Faculty for Clubhouse Development and internationalize its work, ensure the quality and equivalency of existing and newly identified Training Bases, encourage and engage in advocacy on behalf of the community, support and conduct research on the fidelity and effectiveness of the model, coordinate the biennial international seminars, and act as a major resource and information center.

Once it was concluded that the ICCD should be a corporation under the Fountain House umbrella, it became an issue of crucial importance to bring Fountain House itself on board. As it turned out, I had a ready vehicle for this purpose in the form of the Fountain House Council on Education, Research, and Training, a committee of the board of Fountain House, the chairman of which had to be a member of the board. The Council, unlike the board, focused entirely on program issues. I had been the staff representative for training for years. As a result, the Council was far ahead of most of the board on the reality of the ever-expanding clubhouse community and could, therefore, readily see the advantages of the proposed center. Since the Council was now on the agenda of every board meeting (because it was talking about the ICCD), the Council quickly became the advocacy group for the ICCD with the board, and understandably, more and more board members began coming to the Council meetings. Soon, I was invited to directly present my thinking about the ICCD at meetings of the board of Fountain House.

In May 1993, at a Council retreat, John Ingram, the newly elected President of the Fountain House board, essentially ended the discussion by saying that he saw no reason not to move at once to incorporate the ICCD, overriding lingering worries of some board members concerning the fiscal viability of the ICCD concept. At the opening plenary sessions of the Seventh International Seminar on the Clubhouse Model in Worcester, MA, in August 1993, he formally and enthusiastically announced that the ICCD was officially incorporated. At the previously mentioned Faculty Meeting after the seminar, it was proposed to set up an interim Steering Committee to oversee the creation of a detailed structure for the ICCD and to act as the Nominating Committee for the first board of directors. I asked Joel Corcoran, now Executive Director of the ICCD, to chair the Steering Committee comprised of members, staff, and board members from the clubhouse community, including board members from Fountain House who had been most closely involved in the evolution of the ICCD concept.

In March 1994, I sent out a mailing to the entire clubhouse community worldwide detailing the ICCD structure and functions as the Steering Committee was seeing them and asked for comments and suggestions. The response was highly positive. On June 2, 1994, the newly elected board of the ICCD met for the first time and appointed me as Executive Director.

From the beginning, we had envisioned the ICCD as a membership organization. With the help of the Faculty, we had already achieved consensus that an equitable method of calculating dues would be one-quarter of 1 percent of the total clubhouse budget. From dues and major support from the Public Welfare Foundation and the van Ameringen Foundation, the ICCD was able to spring to life.

By November 1994, the Faculty was again in operation with certification as an outcome of all consultations. We had achieved consensus not only to certify clubhouses, but also to do so in three categories: (1) *one year* for programs clearly striving to abide by Clubhouse Standards but needing to make improvements in one or more categories of the Standards, (2) *three years* for clubhouses found to be at a high level of realization in all seven categories, and (3) *deferred* for those programs that, though currently in the Directory of Clubhouse Programs, are seriously out of compliance, have no plan to achieve compliance at the time of the consultation, but wish help in working to become a clubhouse.

The Internationalization of the Consultation/Certification Process

It will be remembered that throughout the NCEP it was impossible, by grant stipulation, to do any work outside the United States. Thus, from the formation of the Faculty in fall 1988 until the ICCD was officially established in June 1994, we were unable to internationalize its work despite a steadily rising demand, especially in Scandinavia and the United Kingdom.

The highest priority of the ICCD staff, therefore, was to internationalize the faculty, now carrying the charge to recommend certification status in their written reports. We did so in November 1994. Using our existing apprenticeship method, we built a team of eight, four experienced faculty members from the United States and four to-be faculty drawn from the United Kingdom and Scandinavia.

All eight met first in Malmo, Sweden, for an all-day briefing on all aspects of an on-site consultation. We then broke into two teams of four, two members and two staff and two new and two existing faculty. One team stayed in Malmo, and one team left for Copenhagen, Denmark, with no one going to his or her own country.

Over the first weekend, we all gathered in Copenhagen to debrief each other, a great cross-learning experience. Then one team left for Dartford, England, and the other team traveled to Helsingborg, Sweden. At the end of the second week, we all met together in Helsingborg both to attend and present at the Second Swedish Clubhouse Conference and for our final debriefing. It was a tremendous, taxing, and rewarding experience for all of us.

I had hoped that these two weeks together would be sufficient to engender enough self-confidence in the new faculty members that they would be willing to take the lead in the second venture, and after some hesitancy, they were. In early spring 1995, a second team of eight, four experienced and four new faculty all from the United Kingdom and Scandinavia, followed the same scenario, one team of four going to Alborg, Denmark and Stockholm, Sweden and the other team traveling to two clubhouses in Ipswich and Stowmarket in England. The consulting process was thus firmly established in Scandinavia and the United Kingdom.

In fall 1997, the ICCD staff brought the consultation/certification process to Australia, following this same plan. We had already brought the Faculty to Canada.

Formal Faculty Training

The process just described, although effective for the United Kingdom, Scandinavia, and Australia, was also very expensive. Additionally, since early 1995, current faculty members had been advocating for a formal faculty training design that all new faculty would be required to experience. By early 1996, ICCD staff and members had formulated a five-day training design to be held in strong clubhouses, together with a manual detailing every step leading up to, during, and after a consultation/certification visit.

In August 1996, we convened the first group of eight new faculty members and five experienced faculty members, including ICCD staff, hosted at Fountain House. The plan called for going through the manual first, then breaking up into four teams, each with a member and staff, each spending a full day visiting different units focusing on two crucial elements of the Clubhouse Model, the work-ordered day and member-staff relationships. Later different neighboring clubhouses were used when we held training at smaller clubhouses.

At the end of this day, the whole group came together to focus on the findings meeting, that is, the oral report made to the clubhouse at the end of the visit. The third day consisted of hearing the findings reports from all four teams and critiquing them. Finally, the ICCD staff discussed the expectations of the written reports. That evening, each team wrote their reports and on the fourth day presented them to the whole group for their comments. The fifth day focused on transitional employment and an evaluation of the training experience.

In the beginning, we had expected that existing faculty would be grandfathered. However, it was immediately obvious at the final session that we were all passionate that all faculty should go through this training.

Formal faculty training has proved to be a powerful tool in ensuring interconsultant reliability, a high level of consistency in the on-site experience, and congruence between the report itself and the faculty recommended certification status. By January 2000, 66 of the now 78 faculty members have been through training.

The ICCD and Diversification of Governance

Among the many benefits accruing from the creation of the ICCD was one of overwhelming importance, that is, it provided us with the perfect vehicle for diversifying and internationalizing governance in the clubhouse community. The need to do both of these things was undoubtedly clearer to me than to anyone else. As the lead figure in Clubhouse Standards creation, training base development and the introduction of our consultation process (1988), and the certification process (1984), I was intent on and successful in drawing as many voices as possible into the work. It remained true that there existed no formal way to ensure and demonstrate that, for example, initiating work to develop standards was not simply an idea of mine and we had no way at all to diversify and internationalize governance in our community since the only way that it could be done was through the creation of an international organization.

The only current venue for expression of concern about governance was the Faculty for Clubhouse Development which met as a whole only once each year and, to some extent, in settings like the Second European Clubhouse Conference in Amsterdam in 1992. Even in the latter case, it was I who purposely raised the understandable concern with governance issues that were bound to be a growing factor in thinking about the rise of clubhouse in Scandinavia, the United Kingdom, and northern Europe. I also announced the intention to establish the ICCD from the outset with mandated international representation on every working body, from the board of directors through the faculty, the training bases, and the clubhouse research group. I also purposely forecast the near certain reality that, once established, the ICCD would more than likely find it essential to fashion regional bodies of the ICCD in areas of strong clubhouse activities, for example, Scandinavia, the United Kingdom, Canada, and Australia.

In 1997, it had become apparent that the most parsimonious way of responding to this need was to set up a Clubhouse Coalitions Working Group as a formal body of the ICCD, thereby assuring a representative group drawn from on-the-ground autonomous organizations, a direct and regular dialogue with those that have become the strongest local and regional focus for advocacy and quality assurance. The Clubhouse Coalitions Working Group began functioning in 1998.

With the completion of the Ninth International Seminar on the Clubhouse Model in Goteborg, Sweden in summer 1997, we have at last literally internationalized the venue of the seminar itself, and the Tenth International Seminar was held in Ottawa, Canada in October 1999.

Clubhouse Research

There is one last piece of this intricate puzzle that must be put in place. For decades Fountain House and, by association, clubhouses everywhere were assailed by their critics for the total failure to mount serious research studies of the Clubhouse Model way of working. Other models, for example, PACT, had begun to study its efficacy, long-term outcomes, and cost effectiveness, among other things, from their beginning, and thus, was held in high regard by the mental health research community, state and federal departments of mental health, and the Alliance for the Mentally Ill (AMI). Our seeming indifference to studying our own model lent credence to those who charged Fountain House with being too rigid, indeed cultlike, more a religion than a well-researched, well-documented rehabilitation program.

Our work during the NCEP was directed toward clarifying and codifying our practice, ensuring fidelity to the Clubhouse Model, and strengthening our program delivery, all in the service of insuring efficacy. By 1990, in our discussions leading to the concept of the ICCD, we had concluded that we must create a focused high priority research capability to study the Clubhouse Model. In 1992, we put out a first effort to create a group portrait of the clubhouse community in the form of a questionnaire sent out to every clubhouse in the Directory of Clubhouse Programs.

In the fall of 1993, Cathaleene Macias, Ph.D., became the Director of Research at Fountain House with the understanding that she would also serve as Research Director of the ICCD when it came into being. With her arrival, the sun came up on research in the clubhouse community. She immediately redesigned our clubhouse survey and, once the ICCD was in place, began a series of interrelated studies. The fruits of her work have been sweeping. She has already been successful in reversing the long-held image of the clubhouse community as indifferent to research, gaining the respect of the metal health community both at the program and research levels.

In 1999 alone she put out a comparison study of ICCD-certified clubhouses and non-certified clubhouse programs substantiating that ICCD certification is a valid indication of quality performance and fidelity to the Standards for Clubhouse Programs (Macias, Boyd, & Fleming, 1999), a benchmarks paper allowing clubhouses to compare their performance with other comparable clubhouses (Macias & Boyd, 1999), and a third report confirming the value of model-based (here ICCD) certification in performance contracting (Macias, Harding, Alden, Geertsen, & Barreira, 1999).

In fall 2000, Dr. Macias will send the benchmarks paper to all state departments of mental health for use in performance contracting. She has also completed a rich five-year research agenda. The last piece of the puzzle is in place.

How rich and freeing it all is! By now there are over 200 members, staff, and board members volunteering their services in one of the bodies of the ICCD and several hundred more volunteering in coalitions and associations. Every year sees us all growing closer and more trusting of each other in this extended international family, and every year it becomes more apparent that clubhouse is by far the most successful transcultural model in community mental health.

REFERENCES

Beard, J., Propst, R. n., & Malamud, T. J. (1982). The Fountain House model of psychiatric rehabilitation. *Psychosocial Rehabilitation Journal, 5*(1), 47–53.

Macias, C., & Boyd, J. (1999). *Benchmarks of clubhouse excellence: A guide for evaluating clubhouse organizational performance.* New York: International Center for Clubhouse Development.

Macias, C., Boyd, J., & Fleming, C. (1999). *A report on the 1998 ICCD clubhouse survey: Comparison of ICCD certified and non-certified clubhouse programs.* New York: International Center for Clubhouse Development.

Macias, C., Harding, C., Alden, M., Geertsen, D., & Barreira, P. (1999). The value of program certification for performance contracting. *Administration and Policy in Mental Health, 28*(5), 345–360.

Macias, C., Jackson, R., et al. (1999). "What is a Clubhouse? Report on the ICCD 1996 survey of USA clubhouses." *Community Mental Health Journal* 35(2), 181–190.

Mandiberg, J. (1997, July). *Our future: Who we are and where we are going. The future is bright.* Paper presented at the ICCD Ninth International Seminar of the Clubhouse Model, Goteborg, Sweden.

Wilkinson, W. H. (1992). New Day, Inc., of Spartenberg: Hospitalization Study. *Psychosocial Rehabilitation Journal, 16*(2), 163–168.

Standards for Clubhouse Programs

The International Standards for Clubhouse Programs, consensually agreed upon by the worldwide clubhouse community, define the Clubhouse Model of rehabilitation. The principles expressed in these standards are at the heart of the clubhouse community's success in helping people with mental illness stay out of hospitals while achieving social, financial, and vocational goals. The standards also serve as a "bill of rights" for members and a code of ethics for staff, board, and administrators. The standards insist that a clubhouse is a place that offers respect and opportunity to its members.

The standards provide the basis for assessing clubhouse quality through the International Center for Clubhouse Development (ICCD) certification process. Every two years the worldwide clubhouse community reviews these standards and amends them as deemed necessary. The process is coordinated by the ICCD Standards Review Committee, made up of members and staff of ICCD-certified clubhouses from around the world.

Membership

1. Membership is voluntary and without time limit.
2. The clubhouse has control over its acceptance of new members. Membership is open to anyone with a history of mental illness, unless that person poses a significant and current threat to the general safety of the clubhouse community.
3. Members choose the way they utilize the clubhouse and the staff with whom they work. There are no agreements, contracts, schedules, or rules intended to enforce participation of members.
4. All members have equal access to every clubhouse opportunity with no differentiation based on diagnosis or level of functioning.
5. Members, at their choice, are involved in the writing of all records reflecting their participation in the clubhouse. All such records are to be signed by both member and staff.
6. Members have a right to immediate reentry into the clubhouse community after any length of absence, unless their return poses a threat to the community.

Relationships

7. All clubhouse meetings are open to both members and staff. There are no formal member only meetings or formal staff only meetings where program decisions and member issues are discussed.

8. Clubhouse staff are sufficient to engage the membership, yet small enough in number to make carrying out their responsibilities impossible without member involvement.
9. Clubhouse staff have generalist roles. All program staff share employment, housing, evening, weekend, and unit responsibilities. Clubhouse staff do not divide their time between clubhouse and other major work responsibilities.
10. Responsibility for the operation of the clubhouse lies with the members and staff and ultimately with the clubhouse director. Central to this responsibility is the engagement of members and staff in all aspects of clubhouse operation.

Space

11. The clubhouse has its own identity including its own name, mailing address, and telephone number.
12. The clubhouse is located in its own physical space. It is separate from the mental health center or institutional settings and is impermeable to other programs. The clubhouse is designed to facilitate the work-ordered day and at the same time be attractive, adequate in size, and convey a sense of respect and dignity.
13. All clubhouse space is member and staff accessible. There are no staff or member only spaces.

Work-Ordered Day

14. The work-ordered day engages members and staff together, side-by-side in the running of the clubhouse. The clubhouse focuses on strengths, talents, and abilities. Therefore, the work-ordered day is inconsistent with medication clinics, day treatment, or therapy programs within the clubhouse.
15. The work done in the clubhouse is exclusively the work generated by the clubhouse in the operation and enhancement of the clubhouse community. No work for outside individuals or agencies, whether for pay or not, is acceptable work in the clubhouse. Members are not paid for any clubhouse work nor are there any artificial reward systems.
16. The clubhouse is open at least five days per week. The work-ordered day parallels normal working hours.
17. All work in the clubhouse is designed to help members regain self-worth, purpose, and confidence. It is not intended to be job-specific training.
18. Members have the opportunity to participate in all the work of the clubhouse, including administration, research, intake and orientation, reach out, hiring, training, and evaluation of staff, public relations, advocacy, and evaluation of clubhouse effectiveness.

Employment

19. The clubhouse enables i\ts members to return to paid work though Transitional Employment and Independent Employment. Therefore, the clubhouse does not provide employment to members through in-house businesses, segregated clubhouse enterprises, or sheltered workshops.

Transitional Employment

20. The clubhouse offers its own transitional employment program that provides, as a right of membership, opportunities for members to work on job placements in business and industry. As a defining characteristic of a clubhouse transitional employment program, the clubhouse guarantees coverage on all placements during member absences. In addition, the Transitional Employment program meets the following basic criteria:

    a. The desire to work is the single most important factor determining placement opportunity.
    b. Placement opportunities will continue to be available regardless of success or failure in previous placements.
    c. Members work at the employer's place of business.
    d. Members are paid the prevailing wage rate but at least minimum wage, directly by the employer.
    e. Transitional employment placements are drawn from a wide variety of job opportunities.
    f. Transitional employment placements are part-time and time-limited, generally 15 to 20 hours per week and from six to nine months in duration.
    g. Selection and training of members for transitional employment is the responsibility of the clubhouse not the employer.
    h. Clubhouse members and staff prepare reports on transitional employment for all appropriate agencies dealing with members' benefits.
    i. Transitional Employment Placements are managed by clubhouse staff and members and not by transitional employment specialists.
    j. There are no Transitional Employment Placements within the clubhouse. TEP at an auspice agency must be off-site from the clubhouse and meet all the preceding criteria.

Independent Employment

21. The clubhouse assists and supports members to secure, sustain, and upgrade independent employment.
22. Members working full-time continue to have available all clubhouse supports and opportunities including advocacy for entitlement and assistance with housing, clinical, legal, financial, and personal issues, as well as participation in evening and weekend programs.

Functions of the House

23. The clubhouse is located in an area where access to local transportation can be assured, both in terms of getting to and from the program and accessing transitional employment opportunities. The clubhouse provides or arranges for effective alternatives whenever access to the public transportation is limited.
24. Community support services are provided by members and staff of the clubhouse. Community support activities are centered in the work unit structure of the clubhouse and include helping with housing and advocacy, as well as assistance in finding quality medical, psychological, pharmacological, and substance abuse services in the community.
25. The clubhouse is committed to securing a range of choices of safe, decent, and affordable housing for all members. The clubhouse has access to housing

opportunities that meet these criteria or if unavailable, the clubhouse develops its own housing program. In clubhouse housing:

a. Members and staff manage the program together.
b. Members who live there do so by choice.
c. Members choose the location of their housing and their roommates.
d. Policies and procedures are developed in a manner congruent with the rest of the clubhouse culture.
e. The level of support increases or decreases in response to the changing needs of the member.
f. Members and staff actively reach out to help members keep their housing, especially during periods of hospitalization.

26. The clubhouse provides members education, which focuses both on basic tools such as literacy and computer skills as well as more advanced educational opportunities. As a significant dimension of the work-ordered day, members serve as major resources for tutoring and teaching in the member education program.

27. The clubhouse assists members to take advantage of the adult education system in the community in support of their vocational and personal aspirations.

28. The clubhouse has a method and takes responsibility for objectively evaluating its own effectiveness.

29. The clubhouse director, staff, and other appropriate persons participate in a three-week training program in the Clubhouse Model at a certified training base. Consultations by the Faculty for Clubhouse Development are provided to all programs seeking to implement the Clubhouse Model.

30. The clubhouse has recreational and social programs during evenings and weekends. Holidays are celebrated on the actual day they are observed.

31. The clubhouse provides an effective reach-out system to members who are not attending, becoming isolated in the community, or rehospitalized.

Funding, Governance, and Administrative

32. The clubhouse has an independent board of directors or, if it is affiliated with a sponsoring agency, a separate Advisory Board comprised of individuals uniquely positioned to provide fiscal, legal, legislative, consumer and community support, and advocacy for the clubhouse.

33. The clubhouse develops and maintains its own budget, approved by the board or advisory board prior to the beginning of the fiscal year and monitored routinely during the fiscal year.

34. Staff salaries are competitive with comparable positions in the mental health field.

35. The clubhouse has the support of appropriate mental health authorities and has the required licenses and certifications. The clubhouse seeks and maintains effective relationships with family, consumer, and professional organizations.

36. The clubhouse holds open forums and has procedures that enable members and staff to actively participate in decision making regarding governance, policy making, and the future direction and development of the clubhouse.

Revised 1998

International Center for Clubhouse Development
425 West 47th Street
New York, NY 10036-2304
Telephone: 212-582-0343
Facsimile: 212-397-1649
e-mail: iccdnyc@compuserve.com
Located at Fountain House, Inc.

General ICCD e-mail: iccdnyc@compuserve.com

The Executive Director of the ICCD is Joel Corcoran
    e-mail: jdcorcoran@compuserve.com

Send mail to ICCD Webmasters Team with questions or comments about this website.

Last modified: February 6, 1999

Clubhouse Model Training Bases

International Center for Clubhouse Development (ICCD)
425 West 47th Street
New York, NY 10036-2304
Joel Corcoran, Executive Director
Internet web page: www.iccd.org
For information e-mail iccdnyc@compuserve.com
Telephone 212-582-0343

Genesis Club, Inc.
274 Lincoln Street
Worcester, MA 01605
Telephone: 508-831-0100
Fax: 508-753-1286
e-mail: genclub@ix.netcom.com
Website: genesisclub.org/
Director: Kevin Bradley
Training Coordinator: Mark Warren

Progress Place
576 Church Street
Toronto, Ontario
Canada M4Y 2E3
Telephone: 416-323-0223
Fax: 416-323-9843
e-mail: ppclub@idirect.com
Website: idirect.com/~progress
Director: Brenda Singer
Training Coordinator: Robyn Evans

Gateway House
P.O Box 4241 Rutherford Road
Greenville, SC 29608
Telephone: 864-242-9193
Fax: 864-242-3861
e-mail: Gwhouse@aol.com
Website: members.aol.com/gwhouse/
Director: Phil Emory
Training Coordinator: Sally Bissada

Fountain House
425 West 47th Street
New York, NY 10036-2304
Telephone: 212-582-0340
Fax: 212-582-6971
e-mail: infotech@fountainhouse.org
Website: fountainhouse.org
Director: Kenneth Dudek
Training Coordinator: Kathleen Rhoads

West Pine House
Independence Center
4380 West Pine Boulevard
St. Louis, MO 63108
Telephone: 314-533-6511
Fax: 314-531-7372
e-mail: trainingic@aol.com
Executive Director: Robert Harvey
Director: Cathy Commack

Alliance House
1724 South Main Street
Salt Lake City, UT 84115
Telephone: 801-486-5012
Fax: 801-466-5077
e-mail: ah@vmh.com
Director: Jon Paulding
Training Coordinator: Margaret Currin

Bromham Place
10 Bromham Place
Richmond 3121, Victoria
Melbourne, Australia
Telephone: 61-39-427-7377
Fax: 61-39-427-9308
e-mail: bromham@vicnet.net.au
Director: Kim Kerr

Taiwha Fountain House
#620-1, Ahyon-Dong
Mapo-Ku
Seoul 121-101
South Korea
Telephone: 82-2-392-1155
Fax: 82-2-364-5468
Director: Bong Weon Lee

Fountain House/Malmo
Engelbrektsgatan 14
S-211 33 Malmo
Sweden
Telephone: 46-40-120-013
Fax: 46-40-305-386
e-mail: fontanhuset@swipenet.se
Director: Bengt Jarl
Assistant Director: Marie Hagstrom

Mosaic Clubhouse
126 Atkins Road
Balham, London SW1 0AN
England
Telephone: 44-181-674-2349
Fax: 44-181-671-7835
e-mail: mosaicuk@compuserve.com
Director: Nigel Allen

Index